Schooling at the Speegnt

Schooling at the Speed of Thought

A blueprint for making schooling more effective

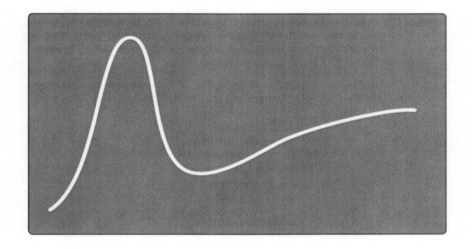

Mike Lloyd

Spiderwize

Schooling at the Speed of Thought

Spiderwize
Office 404, 4th Floor
Albany House
324/326 Regent Street
London
W1B 3HH
UK

www.spiderwize.com

ISBN: 978-1-907294-91-4

The views represented in this book are those of the author and do not represent the views of the Microsoft Corporation.

CONTENTS

FOREWORD

What a remarkable century for Learning this is already turning out to be. After a 20th century which unambitiously finessed its model of learning, tinkering with class sizes, coursework and leadership, while tackling problems along the way like the European post war baby boom, we now find ourselves unequivocally in a very new century where merely finessing won't begin to do. A century where the outcomes of research are often counter intuitive, where children—given the right opportunities—are showing just how simply stellar they can be and where nations are increasingly committing resources and imagination to their most precious natural resource of all—their children.

We seem to have progressed from great teaching as an art form—with captivating lessons lovingly crafted over the decades, to great teaching as an applied science, with careful observations, complex outcomes and reflective practice all propelling learners forward at a remarkable rate. We are indubitably in a Learning Age. Even on our televisions the multiple choice world of "Who Wants to be a Millionaire" has given way to the compelling reality TV processes of everyone from dancers to cooks learning their art in front of a gripped audience. And whatever else learning is, we are all in agreement that, at its best, it is complex, challenging, seductive and engaging. As the children who have only ever inhabited this century become ever more ambitious for themselves, propelled forwards by a combination of tech-savvy confidence and social-networked collegiality, we start to realise just how depressingly under ambitious we had been for them in the past. Of course, it has been new technologies in our learning spaces and institutions that have challenged us to think afresh, and of course the pace of technological change has only really just started its acceleration.

At this point we might all shudder with nervousness—not for the headlong rush into a world of learning that is producing ingenious, gregarious, collaborative, tech-rich, engaged, committed young learners, but for the schools, regions and nations who are left behind, still finessing and tinkering, but not remotely aware that the express train has left the station and the best they might do is join a later slow and stopping one. If we are going to move forward to a world of equity and peace, then we will have to address the rapidly widening gap between these remarkable 3rd millennium learners and the dullard education systems of the last century.

To do that, we will need more and better science. We will need everyone from learners and their teachers, to parents and grandparents, to be actively engaged in the reflective practice of great learning. Helpfully, this excellent book is one more significant component in that applied science of learning, one more useful provocation from which to begin that reflective and critical examination of what we have done and what we might do. The book is built on the sound foundations of Mike's careful observations and reflections, underpinned by his vast experience from a career centred right at the heart of change.

It is timely, wise and needed.

Professor Stephen Heppell
www.heppell.net

INTRODUCTION

The fact that you can read this sentence is attributable to your schooling. That you have chosen to read a book that deals with immensely complex and important issues means you are amongst an elite of highly educated people. Wouldn't it be fantastic if everyone on the planet was as highly educated?

But imagine how much more you *could* have learned, if only your schooling had been more effective. Could you have acquired another language perhaps; or mastered deeper levels of Mathematics; or acquired a wider appreciation of the arts? How much of what you learned was due to excellent teachers who managed to rise above a system that left their creativity boxed-in and under-rewarded them for their excellent work? How much of your learning came from your own personal determination to understand and master something, perhaps in spite of some poor teachers and badly behaved students in your classes? How much did your parents help? How much did you learn outside school, and how much of what you learned in school helps you now? Is your education really what was left behind after you forgot what you were taught?

So schooling taught *you* a lot—but at what cost? Globally $2.4trn is spent on education every year. Yet according to the World Bank (Abadzi, 2003) the efficiency of education systems may be as low as 7% in some countries. Whilst the sheer scale of the amount of money being wasted every day on out-dated schooling systems is hard to imagine, let alone quantify accurately, the bottom line is that schooling needs to change.

It's often said, "If you think education is expensive, try ignorance!" But education *is* expensive, and we should be getting much better value for money from it. With 1.2bn learners, 55m teachers, and 4.3m institutions, schooling represents one of the biggest single areas of public expenditure on the planet, and access to it is virtually universal and compulsory in most countries. Whilst, according to the OECD, it's clear that expenditure on schooling results in increases in GDP, the process of schooling itself is massively inefficient and out-dated. The industrial approach to schooling reached its limits a very long time ago.

Our future is increasingly a race between education and catastrophe. More learning needs to happen, at a higher quality and much faster than before to combat the very serious issues the planet faces. Increasing population and corresponding demand for ever more teachers puts schooling on a collision course with the slow, inefficient, out-dated production-line approach which has defined it since the industrial revolution.

What happens in schooling today profoundly influences the lives of individuals and the health of whole communities for decades to come. Yet, schooling decision-making is mostly about dealing with pressing immediate issues or seeking more efficient ways of maintaining established practice, rather than shaping the future. Unless we are prepared to believe that the schooling systems we have are the best we could have, we have to believe that the breakthroughs are out there outside of the boxes that have constrained our thinking for so long.

The road to realising our highest hopes for our schools is not an easy one. But with breakthroughs occurring every day in understanding how children learn and how they build intellectual capacity, there is a great opportunity to make strides in the years ahead, provided we do so with an understanding of the root causes of why schools have struggled so much. If we embark upon the journey laid out in this book, we can make schooling more motivating for all involved, and help build better economies, societies and communities.

Organisations behave in the way they are designed to. The woes in our schools evidenced by metal detectors; strikes; absenteeism; poor learning performance; bullying; disruption to learning; violence, etc., are therefore attributable to the design of the schooling organisation. As one colleague recently quipped—"I'm surprised that children are as patient with us as they are!" Some would blame society, but if we accept that the role of schools is—in part at least—to shape society, schooling systems are only reaping what they have sewn.

A key question addressed in this book is why everything in society over the last 200 years has evolved apart from schooling. Innovative change tends to happen in individual schools where you have a charismatic, driven, principal hell-bent on making change happen. Thankfully, there are many of these people to learn from. Unfortunately, however, there are way too few to be impactful at scale.

So the key question then is how do we scale innovation in schooling? Part of the answer, I believe, can be found by unravelling the mind-boggling complexities of schooling, then disassembling and re-assembling schooling architecture. Easy!

So Why Write Another Book on Transforming Schooling?

Book upon book, article upon article have been written on the subject of schooling transformation. An industry has grown up around schooling change management with speech upon speech, consultation upon consultation; declaration upon declaration. This new industry even has two feature films espousing the importance and urgency of change—"We Are the People We've Been Waiting For" from the UK, and "Waiting for Superman" from the US.

Terabytes of advice, examples, case studies, sound-bites, pamphlets, clever thinking, technologies, all offer pieces of the jigsaw puzzle—but to date, there has been very little by way of prescriptive architectures linked to phased implementation. At government level, there seems little resistance to the notion that transformational change is necessary—witness the annual pilgrimage by governments from across the world to BETT in London every year to soak up the latest ideas for how technology can transform schooling. However, even the most well-resourced ministries around the world struggle when it comes to the practicalities of modernising schooling. The problem is that there is no straightforward, actionable blueprint that can act as a model.

The challenge that all those involved in schooling face is how to run the system and change it at the same time—a bit like rebuilding a ship whilst it is sailing at sea. My belief is that there's a need for something that is sufficiently abstracted to be digestible at high levels in schooling organisations, but of sufficient detail to provide workable models that decision makers at all levels can use.

Schooling at the Speed of Thought was written originally as a series of workshops to help fill this gap. The content was derived from interaction with the full spectrum of stakeholders in the schooling system. The book was written for schooling leaders in national and local governments; policy makers;

superintendents; private school owners; entrepreneurs; administrators and school boards. It also has relevance to academics; school leadership/management and teacher training; schooling community stakeholders—interested parents, local employers.

Schooling at the Speed of Thought has a simple but bold mission—to set out a standard for a holistic architecture for schooling. This involves explaining how schooling can be modernised to enable more learning to take place, faster, to a higher quality and at lower costs. It explains how the rules of high performance, once restricted only to the private sector, are now being applied to schooling. The book includes first-hand accounts from leading organizations that are running the gauntlet of conservative thinking and daring to risk criticism and worse in order to serve better the needs of students and stakeholders. It is designed to inject pace, structure and methodology into an area that is as complex as it is contentious.

I wrote this book in a personal capacity. The views within it do not represent those of the Microsoft Corporation for whom I am privileged to work.

The overall goal of the book is to arrive at a Schooling Enterprise Architecture. Each chapter takes you through explicit steps which hopefully will become your blueprint for driving change.

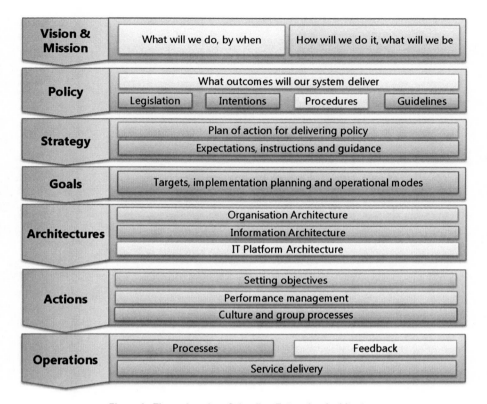

Figure 1. The end goal—a Schooling Enterprise Architecture

To implement the methodology set out in *Schooling at the Speed of Thought* in a practical way, workshops, seminars and courses are available in a variety of formats. Contact the author at mikestevelloyd@msn.com for more details.

ACKNOWLEDGEMENTS

I acknowledge with gratitude the help and contributions that have made this book possible. In writing this I stand on the shoulders of giants—Stephen Heppell, who inspired me to "go deep" on ICT when I was teaching, and has continued to inspire me to this day; Hedley Beare, who sadly died recently, but was responsible for the foundations on which this book was built; Lewis J Perelman, who challenged the establishment with the provocative *Schools Out*; Bill Gates, whose book *Business at the Speed of Thought* so clearly articulated the value of technology in the modern world; Tom Peters, who's passion for change influenced my attitude; Richard DeLorenzo—one of the few people on the planet who has truly implemented the ideas contained in this book; Clayton Christensen and Michael Horn, whose *Disrupting Class* gives clarity to the forces of change facing schooling systems.

Other influences come from: Tom Bentley (Demos, Learning Beyond the Classroom); Mark Treadwell (School 2.0); Michael Fullan (education change management guru); Paul Kelley (pioneering headteacher); Malcolm Gladwell (Tipping Point, Outliers); Seymour Papert (constructivist pioneer); Ricardo Sembler (pioneering industrialist and key enabler for the Instituto Lumiar); Dr John Kotter, who contributes important principles through his book *Leading Change*. I also gratefully acknowledge the OECD, UNESCO, and the World Bank, whose contributions provide quantification behind some of the core principles— thanks, in particular, to Andreas Schleicher, Tarek Shawki, Helen Abadzi, and to Michael Trucano for his excellent blog. FutureLab in Bristol and the now defunct BECTA were also important sources of thinking.

At Microsoft, my boss, mentor and colleague of 12 years, Mark East, who made this project possible. My friend and colleague, Edgar Ferrer Gil, who provided valuable initial feedback on the book and guided me in Latin America where I learned so much. Joey Fitts and Bruno Aziza who's *Driving Business Performance* was both an influence and a catalyst for this project. Kati Tuurala and Marsjanne Damen, who provided encouragement and feedback. Mike Chase, Matt Cocks, Dee Bradshaw and David Langridge for encouragement and insights. Brad Tipp for his incredible technical insights. Walid Mohammed; Manou Marzban; Janine Rogan; Neil Ross; Larry Nelson; Anthony Salcito; Dolores Puxbaumer and all my colleagues in the Worldwide Education Group.

I'm grateful to all my colleagues in Microsoft subsidiaries across the world who have trusted me to work with their Ministry of Education customers—especially Igor Balandin and Anton Shulzhenko in Russia; Lina Dzene in the Baltics, and Sandis Kolomenskis in Central and Eastern Europe. Dr Mamdouh and Najla Al-Kebsi in Saudi Arabia; Zeid Shubailat in the Middle East and Africa; Jason Trump and Neil Jackson in Asia Pacific; Donna Magauran, Lisa Faia, Sean Tierney, Jane Mackarell and all my Microsoft colleagues in Australia; Emilio Munaro and Silvia Fernandez in Brazil; Julieta Zuázaga Gutiérrez in Argentina; Rocio Milan Yarez and all my Mexican colleagues; Elsa Poirier and Thierry De Vulpillieres in France; Angela Schaerer who helped me begin to understand schooling in African countries; Reza Bardien in South Africa; Rich Seidner, Rob Curtin, Bob Pfeiff and Rich Langford who's work on analytics in the United States, and *School of One* in New York has been an inspiration.

Outside Microsoft, I have been inspired by many innovative companies and their leaders. Long-time colleague and true expert Chris Poole of lookred, and his colleague Matthew Woodruff; Jim Wynn at Promethean; Mehool Sanghrajka and Sarah Armstrong at LP Plus; Moacyr Galo of Gestar; Herve Borredon at ITOP; Aidan McCarthy at Apple; Curt Allen of Agilix. I'd like to thank Randall Fielding and Clare Friedrich of Fielding Nair International Architects for their vision, generous help and insights. Thanks also to Heather Chirtea at Tool Factory for much enjoyable sparring.

The way that Australia approaches schooling is inspirational and I gratefully acknowledge Melbourne University—Jack Keating, and Patrick Griffin. David Warner of Eltham College, Victoria; Richard Eden and his team in Queensland; Clayton Carnes and the children of Hermit Park School, Townsville; and the staff and students of the Presbyterian Ladies College and Scotch College in Perth.

I am grateful to my friend Carmen Nigro who contributed many great ideas and provided encouragement, support and feedback; my friends at Education Impact, Paris—Philippe Mero, Monika Kavanova and Fred Fulton; Education Impact Fellows, from whom I have learned so much—especially Dan Buckley, Bruce

Dixon, Owen Lynch, Neil Butcher and Gavin Dykes. A special mention goes to my good friend Kelvyn Hicks for teaching me the importance of combining professionalism with fun and humour.

Finally, my biggest acknowledgement and thanks go to my family—Elizabeth, Rhys and Roslyn Lloyd, and all in Wales, who have supported me so fully in all that I do.

1. SCHOOLING AT AN INFLECTION POINT

'It is not the strongest that survive, nor the most intelligent, but those that are most adaptable to change.'

Charles Darwin

The purpose of this chapter is to give you an understanding of the following:

- How schooling originated and evolved over the ages
- Origins of some of the key characteristics of today's schools
- How the industrial paradigm came to dominate the organisation of schooling
- The challenges and difficulties that schooling systems are currently experiencing in the face of radical social, economic and technological change
- How technology has become a disruptive force in schooling
- Different options, new metaphors and change scenarios for schooling systems.

The key points made in this chapter are:

- An array of issues are applying forces for change
- Young people are making extensive use of digital technologies which is changing their expectations of schooling
- Technology is a disruptive force that has significantly changed most spheres of human life—apart from schooling
- Formal schooling needs to evolve and modernise for it to remain relevant
- Increasing expenditure is not going to yield correspondingly increased results unless the paradigm changes
- Schooling systems are eco-systems
- There is no single right model for effective schooling but technology and modern management methods can be used to drive success.

A Brief History of Schooling

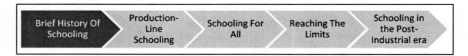

The Origin of Schools

In 385 BC: The Greek philosopher Plato founded a philosophical school at the Akademia in Athens, later known as the Academy. The heads of the school, called "scholarchs", taught many of the brilliant minds of the day, including the famous Greek philosopher Aristotle. The next notable development in schooling was the development of Gurukuls in ancient India. This was teaching centred around a teacher's house—a model echoed later in the widespread development of the single schoolhouse in the United States.

From 425 to 1453 AD the Byzantine Empire had a schooling system that began with primary education. This was necessitated by the large government of the Byzantine Empire which needed an educated workforce and citizens. The medieval Islamic world made major contributions to education, including the first universities and systems of qualification—"Doctor of Medicine". In the Islamic world, the emphasis was on a publically accessible way of spreading knowledge which resulted in purpose built structures—the Madrassa.

By contrast, in Europe during the Middle Ages formal education was a privilege for the few. It was openly elite, privately funded and dealt with intellectual pursuits such as literature, languages, history, the arts, philosophy and theology. This kind of education was called "liberal" because it freed the mind and intellect. There was a very strong emphasis on learning Latin—hence the proliferation of "Grammar Schools" in the English speaking countries. Our public schools also conform to principles laid down in the Middle Ages—for example, schools get long summer vacations because students used to be expected to spend their summers tending animals and harvesting crops.

As schooling developed during The Middle Ages, their organising principles were based on the monastery. In a monastery the superior is called a Principal and the learners are "novices". There are uniforms (habits) and discipline is monastic with obedience, conformity and punishment for deviation. The academic gowns derived from the monastic habits are still worn by some teachers and principals. Early schools also borrowed from feudal armies— school shields, crests with Latin mottos, school hymns, sporting contests, house systems, class captains and prefects. Today, scholastic ceremonies and assemblies preserve the idea of service to King, Country, God and Church. Buildings in top private schools in the English speaking world still often resemble the manor houses of the rich.

Production-Line Schooling

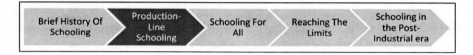

The Industrial Origins of Today's Schooling Systems

Since the 17th Century, industrialization came to dominate, not only the economies of Europe and North America, but the social lives in those countries as well. The assembly line—the technology for the mass production of commodities—was a huge breakthrough which transformed both work and the patterns of living in society. From the early 1800s Europe, North America and their colonies invented mass education too. Production-line education arrived. During the Industrial Revolution, educators were deeply influenced by the lessons of the assembly line, cheap mass production and scientific management methods. During the early 20th Century, economies of scale in education were achieved by creating large schools to replace the one-room schoolhouses that had sprung up, especially in the United States.

As widespread public schooling proliferated, students were seated in rows in ways that resembled the factory floor. They were given identical lessons in mechanistic sequences modelled on the assembly line (Senge, P, 2000). To be able to operate, the new industrial society required a degree of literacy and basic education in all its production workers, and hence universal elementary schooling arrived. It became a public necessity that no-one should miss out, so governments of industrialised nations made such schooling compulsory, in effect overruling any parents who might want to withhold their children's rights to a formal education. In agricultural communities children could contribute to the family's income by helping their parents on the farm. Becoming a functional citizen in an industrial economy, however, required the learning of a consistent set of knowledge and the acquisition of certain basic competencies—literacy and numeracy are still referred to as 'basic skills'.

The big factory, the big corporation which supported it, and big government that regulated it, produced a new entity—the large-scale organization, and with it a one-best-way form of management called bureaucracy. Bureaucracy and industrialization grew up together, one influencing the other. The size of the schools was generally modelled on factories. As has been the case in factories, unions have flourished in state schools. To control and administer the state schools, large-scale organizations called Education Departments were developed; both the large schools and the large departments were run along the lines of the large-scale bureaucracies that ran factory production. The same terms were used, the same analogies, the same ideas, the same control devices, the same frameworks and metaphors.

Between the two World Wars secondary education became more widely available, in schools that were funded and run by government. Vocational streams were added to secondary school curricula, apprenticeships expanded in number, technical education became an entity in its own right, and technical high schools were invented. In the developed world, after the Second World War, 'secondary education for all' became accepted. University and post-secondary education was made available on the basis of academic ability rather than on the ability to pay. There was growing emphasis in many occupations on gaining a formal qualification.

The curriculum, too, was modelled on the factory production line. Children were divided into year groups; knowledge was subdivided into subjects; teachers became specialists and credentialed (like trades people) and organised into hierarchies; the students were controlled in class groups or batches, moving in linear, time based progression through graded curricula, from easy to more complex, from lower grades to higher grades. They were 'promoted' (as workers in factories) up the steps until they graduated. They were then examined at the end of this process, issued with certificates and qualifications and let loose into the community. Even the private schools applied the factory model.

So, the model of schooling that most of us are familiar with not only grew out of the industrial era but adopted the blueprint of industry. Evidence of this runs deep in the language of schooling, for example:

- Class and grade (as though students are work-teams under a supervising foreman, the teacher)
- Departments and faculties, offices and divisions (as though these elements are parts of a bureaucracy still)
- Promotion and advancement (as though school still thinks and acts like a trade)
- Learning programmes and modules (as though the school is manufacturing component parts of something called education).

(Beare, Creating the Future School, 2001)

Principles of Mass Production Schooling

Schooling in the 19th Century embodied the characteristics that make industry successful.

- Standardisation, including standardised to mass-manufacture "facts" which made up a heavily content-based syllabus.
- Specialisation: with the work batches broken up into subjects, year groups, classes and sequencing.
- Synchronization: promotion was a year-by-year progression through primary, secondary and tertiary graded lessons, and a hierarchy of certificates—the huge, mass conveyor belt.
- Concentration: concentrating learners in one place. Workers were concentrated in factories, criminals in prisons, and children in schools.
- Maximisation: at the time, big institutions meant economies of scale and relative efficiency.
- Centralization: not only were schools and systems of schools run on bureaucratic lines, but the curriculum itself was standardised, centrally prescribed, and centrally policed—not least by centrally set and marked examinations.

Schooling for All

Universal Schooling

Nowadays some kind of compulsory education exists in most countries. Due to population growth and the proliferation of compulsory education, the pressure on schooling systems, generally, has never been greater and will inevitably grow.

For developing countries, the main driver is to provide schooling for all, to drive down illiteracy and increase the amount of time learners spend in school. Overall, great progress has been made—illiteracy and the percentage of populations without any schooling have decreased in the past several decades. However, even today, in some parts of the world, literacy rates are below 60 per cent (for example, in Afghanistan, Pakistan, Bangladesh and most of Africa), and the disparity between male and female literacy rates are a major cause for concern. Many developing countries face economic pressure from those parents who need their children to make money in the short term rather than attend school and gain longer-term benefits from education.

The key education challenges in the developing world are reflected in UNESCO's 'Education for All' (EFA) Goals

1. Expanding and improving comprehensive early childhood care and education, especially for the most vulnerable and disadvantaged children
2. Ensuring that by 2015 all children, particularly girls, children in difficult circumstances and those belonging to ethnic minorities, have access to, and complete, free and compulsory primary education of good quality
3. Ensuring that the learning needs of all young people and adults are met through equitable access to appropriate learning and life-skills programmes
4. Achieving a 50 per cent improvement in levels of adult literacy by 2015, especially for women, and equitable access to basic and continuing education for all adults

5. Eliminating gender disparities in primary and secondary education by 2005, and achieving gender equality in education by 2015, with a focus on ensuring girls' full and equal access to and achievement in basic education of good quality

6. Improving all aspects of the quality of education and ensuring excellence of all so that recognized and measurable learning outcomes are achieved by all, especially in literacy, numeracy and essential life skills.

(UNESCO)

For developed countries, much energy is being expended on making schooling more relevant and personalised, but the main driver is to improve the quality of schooling and close the gap between high and low achievers.

Uneven Distribution

There are major disparities in schooling performance between different countries. The PISA 2003 reading assessment found that 20% or more of 15-year-olds in Austria, Germany, Greece, Hungary, Italy, Luxembourg, Portugal, Spain and Turkey performed at or below the lowest proficiency level. Achievement levels are lower in developing than in developed countries. For example, in TIMSS 2003, 20% to 90% of grade 8 students in low and middle-income countries did not reach the lowest benchmark level. *(UNESCO, Education for All Global Monitoring Report, 2006).*

Spending on schooling throughout the world is very unevenly distributed. For example, according to UNESCO Institute for Statistics (UIS) the entire sub-Saharan African region spends less on education than a single country like France, Germany, Italy or the United Kingdom. North America and Western Europe account for more than one-half of the global total of public education spending. Yet, less than 10% of the world's children and young people live in these countries. East Asia and the Pacific region have the second-highest share of global public spending on education at 18%. Latin America and the Caribbean accounts for 8% to 9% of global education spending. The United States is the single greatest investor in education. Its public education budget is close to that of the Arab States, Central and Eastern Europe, Central Asia, Latin America and the Caribbean, South and West Asia, and sub-Saharan Africa combined (UNESCO Institute for Statistics, 2007). Yet, expenditure itself is a poor indicator of learning output. The United States may have one of the highest levels of expenditure on schooling, but it has one of the poorest performing schooling systems in the developed world.

The distinction between developing and developed markets is often far from clear. There are patches of very poor provision even in highly developed countries. In some developed countries, there are large sections of the schooling system that are equivalent or below the standards achieved in developing countries. According to a recent McKinsey report, "educational gaps impose on the United States the economic equivalent of a permanent national recession." (McKinsey & Company, 2009). The reverse is true also—for example, developing countries usually have within them well-resourced private schools and pockets of excellent public provision, often within metropolitan areas. In developing countries the outcomes in some subject areas are actually higher than in developed countries; for example, it is not at all uncommon for students in many developing countries to be reasonably fluent in multiple foreign languages, whereas this is much more of a rarity in developed countries where much of the population is monolingual.

Reaching the Limits of Industrial Schooling

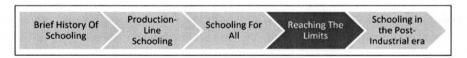

Despite everything, education in the industrial age actually worked. High school graduation rates increased many-fold in OECD nations between 1900 and 1960. However, the world has moved on and we can now see that mass production schooling was based on two assumptions that no longer apply—

1. That learning is the act of acquiring authorised knowledge which experts have generated
2. That learning is a conveyor belt which constructs knowledge by fabricating pre-existing simple components together into complex finished pieces

"There is little more learning effectiveness and productivity that can be squeezed out of traditional modes of providing schooling, so new models of schooling are needed which break from the old patterns." (Beare, *Creating the Future School*, 2001).

In recent years, there has been a considerable increase in spending levels, both in absolute terms and as a share of public budgets. For example, the total amount of public spending on educational institutions rose in all OECD countries over the last decade, on average by 19% between 2000 and 2005 alone. Yet despite this scale of sustained investment many educational systems have failed to improve significantly. (OECD, *Education at a Glance*, 2008)

Mark Treadwell in School 2.0 argues that the book-based paradigm, which has dominated the organisation of schooling for two centuries, can't really become much more efficient (Treadwell, 2008). Treadwell cites Robert Branson in *Why Schools Can't Improve*, who argues that "all possible improvements to schools under the current management model had been implemented by 1950 or 1960 at the latest" (Branson). He argues teachers are *very* good at teaching in this paradigm, but that it's just not that good a paradigm. For all the money we've spent on numeracy and literacy, over the last 60 years we have had very little effect on test results.

"…poor teaching practices, leadership and principals, lack of good parenting, inappropriate curriculum, poor discipline etc. are all blamed for why schools are not improving—but these are not the real reasons. The simple fact is that schools cannot improve within the present context of the book-based education paradigm. Educators are putting enormous amounts of effort and huge amount of time in trying to improve the system which has simply met its upper limits and cannot improve any further." (Treadwell, 2008)

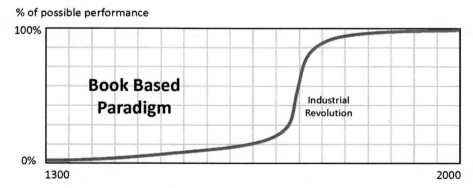

Figure 2. Reaching the limits of the book-based paradigm

There are plenty of indications of the need for a shift in paradigm—for example, poor learning performance, increasing truancy, and high absenteeism rates amongst teachers (UNESCO, 2005).

In developing countries, children are often only too glad to go to school in order to get the opportunity to learn and therefore to come out of poverty. School can also be the place where at least they get minimum levels of nutrition or security. In many developed countries, however, student disaffection has become a major issue. Schooling can and should be an intrinsically motivating experience. This too often is not the case. Student absenteeism and disaffection with school pose widespread challenges for teachers and policy makers, according the OECD, drawing on data from 42 mostly developed nations. While most 15-year-olds in these countries regularly attend classes, one in five admits to being regularly absent. (OECD, 2003)

In the UK almost one in ten 16-18 year olds are not engaged in education, employment or training (NEET), and government efforts to bring this number down have met with limited success. This is because many of these young people have had negative experiences of the education system (Demos, 2009).

Alongside increasing student absenteeism there has been a sharp rise in home schooling, particularly in the United States. The U.S. Department of Education's National Center for Education Statistics report showed that approximately 1.5 million children (2.9% of school-age children) were being home-schooled in the spring of 2007, representing a 36% relative increase since 2003 and a 74% relative increase since 1999 (U.S. Department of Education, National Center for Education Statistics, 2009). Similar increases in home schooling are occurring in other parts of the world. For example, there were 20 families home educating in the UK 20 years ago; now there are more than 30,000 (Steven Hastings, 2003).

Teaching at the Limits

In the UK, Matthew Horne (Demos, RSA) conducted in-depth research into teaching in the UK and concluded: "Schools need to become more appealing places to work, and teachers themselves must be able to drive the necessary changes." The UK is far from alone in this.

A study on Brazil (Pernanbuco State), Ghana, Morocco and Tunisia showed that teaching time losses due to teacher absenteeism ranged from twelve to forty-three days per year, or between 6% and 22% of official intended instructional time (UNESCO, *Education for All by 2015, Will we make it?*, 2008). Much absenteeism comes from dissatisfaction, and much of this comes from low level disruption to classes. With children increasingly disaffected by schooling, it's not hard to find examples where teachers are less than enthusiastic about the conditions they work in.

A recent OECD study shows that in Mexico, Italy, the Slovak Republic, Estonia and Spain, more than 70% of teachers at lower-secondary level work in schools where it was felt classroom disturbances hinder the teaching process "to some extent" or "a lot". On average, teachers spend 13% of classroom time maintaining order, but in Brazil and Malaysia the proportions rises to more than 17%. Besides classroom disturbances, other factors hindering teaching included student absenteeism (46%); students turning up late for class (39%); profanity and swearing (37%); and intimidation or verbal abuse of other students (35%). (OECD, *Teacher effectiveness hampered by lack of incentives and bad behaviour in classrooms,* 2009*)*.

Schooling in the Post-Industrial Era

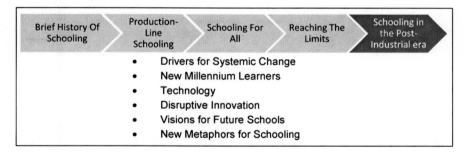

| Brief History Of Schooling | Production-Line Schooling | Schooling For All | Reaching The Limits | Schooling in the Post-Industrial era |

- Drivers for Systemic Change
- New Millennium Learners
- Technology
- Disruptive Innovation
- Visions for Future Schools
- New Metaphors for Schooling

In the developed world, fewer people are now involved in factory production; manufacturing's share of employment has fallen from near half the population about fifty years ago to around 15 or 10 per cent now. Manufacturing is still producing profits, but employment in manufacturing has been collapsing, while the new occupations and jobs have appeared in the services sector and in the professions.

So if the context in which schools operate has changed, what new metaphors should replace the production line approach? The answer to this lies in part with the drivers and challenges that are exerting pressure on schooling systems to change.

Drivers for Systemic Change

According to the OECD, the estimated long-term effect on GDP of one additional year of education is around 6%, so the incentive to expand provision and increase output is clear.

There are several pressures on provision. Firstly, in developing countries the absolute growth in population is rising, so the demand for school places rises too—but the growth of urban populations places a disproportionate burden on municipalities to deliver schooling.

Secondly, as universal access to primary education has largely been achieved, the pressure now is to provide increased access to higher levels of education. Expanding access at these levels requires enormous investments in school infrastructure and the recruitment of high numbers of qualified teachers. For example, in 2002, Paraguay, Malaysia and Jamaica would have required additional investment amounting to 2.6, 1.6 and 1.0 of their GDP just to reach current WEI (World Education Indicator) averages in upper secondary participation rates. Education systems in developed countries, on the other hand, have faced decades without population pressure. Here the need is for improved output from schooling systems to increase human capital and increase economic output (UNESCO-UIS/OECD, 2002).

The net is that most countries need to further increase participation to meet their own national standards (UNESCO, 2005), but mere participation is nowhere near enough on its own. Education systems need to be efficient at developing learning. A study by the World Bank entitled *The Economics of Classroom Time* (Abadzi, 2003) illustrates that by the time factors like absenteeism, the ineffectiveness of rote learning and non-productive time are taken into account, in some countries the actual efficiency of a schooling system could be as low as 7%.

Whilst in the world's best schooling systems one would expect to see far higher levels of efficiency, the out-dated industrial metaphor is making it increasingly difficult for schools to be as effective as they might be.

Challenges Facing Schooling Systems

Each country and their constituent schooling systems face very different challenges. Education Impact (www.educationimpact.net), an independent group of education consultants, lists the kinds of challenges that seem to be raised most frequently by their clients:

- **Relevance**—in terms of what is learned and how schooling is organised
- Ensuring **equitable access** to affordable, quality education; high levels of student learning; and learning outcomes that:
  - o provide appropriate levels of literacy, numeracy and more general life skills
  - o ensure access to higher levels of education
  - o ensure access to gainful employment
- Developing **relevant curriculum**—curriculum aligned with the needs of society, including with the world of work
- Providing education that is **efficient and effective**; that represents responsible stewardship of the funds entrusted to it
- Maintaining wider **community confidence**, understanding and trust in the education system and the measures of individual success achieved by learners
- Addressing **Maths, Science, Engineering and Technology**, given their importance to national and local economies.

At the operational level, challenges vary from country to country and in accordance with the way that education is organised. Municipalities, local authorities or school districts play a role in supporting and working with schools, while in other cases schools are largely autonomous.

Challenges can also be broken down into local, national and stakeholder issues:

Local and Institutional issues	National issues

• Addressing issues of inclusion including gender, ethnicity and disability and learner achievement
 	
• Providing appropriate curriculum and assessment
 	
• Achieving learner engagement and appropriate behaviour
 	
• Meeting required levels of attendance, achievement and quality
 	
• Establishing school leadership
 	
• Recruiting and retaining leaders and teachers. For example:
   o 30% of all Heads in English schools plan to retire by 2011…
   o …whilst fewer than 5% of teachers aspire to become a Head
   o 4.5m teachers required in Africa by 2015
 	
• Developing the role of school within the community
	• Setting the degree of autonomy for schools and provision of support appropriate to their working at that level of autonomy
	
	• Managing relationships with and between school types. These include, for example, Charter Schools in the US, Faith Schools in Australia and the UK and both public and private schools
	
	• Alignment of the sector with other elements and subsystems of the larger education system; aligning knowledge and skill outputs between levels
	
	• Sharing good, best or next practice to raise standards
	
	• Raising standards through targets and raising achievement
	
	• Building capacity within the overall system, and developing appropriate levels of institutional autonomy

Learner/parent issues	Teacher issues
• Choice and selection of subjects that might be constrained by curriculum or institution • Role and ability of parents or carers to support learners • Learning in the context of culture and society and other pressures or responsibilities that make demands on learner time • Conflicts arising from lack of match between local opportunity and educational achievement • Poor, and poorly designed learning environments	• Achieving learner engagement, standards of behaviour and attendance • Pay and conditions • Personalising learning to provide appropriate levels of support and stretch • Development of new teaching methods and changing roles of the teacher to reflect the context of the school in the wider community and national or local initiatives • Achieving success with frequently limited resources

Table 1. Challenges facing schooling systems. Education Impact, 2009.

New Millennium Learners

There is a widespread consensus among educators and policy makers that digital technologies have given rise to a new generation of students who see the world in a different way. Growing up with the internet has transformed their approach to education.

"New Millennium Learner" is a phrase coined by the OECD in 2008 to describe people for whom digital technologies already existed when they were born, and have therefore grown up with digital technologies such as computers, the Internet, mobile phones and MP3s. Other terms used for this group of people—which of course describes today's students—are "Digital Natives" and "Generation I" (Internet).

At home, these students will be capable of electronic multitasking. For example, they are likely to be simultaneously:

- Searching and using several Internet browser windows at the same computer
- Using several different applications at the same computer—usually including MSN Messenger
- Using several devices at the same time

They will use digital technologies to develop their social lives, develop and project their identities, and make sense of the world they live in. "Today's digital kids use ICT to meet, play, date, and learn; it's an integral part of their social life; it's how they acknowledge each other and form their personal identities" (John Seely-Brown, 2004).

Whilst obviously learning is in everything everywhere, now "everywhere" is increasingly represented electronically; the informal classroom for many children now spans the globe.

In the developed world, for most young people, technology is part of their daily lives. For example, by the age of 21 the average person in the UK will have spent 15,000 hours in formal education, 20,000 hours in front of the TV, and 50,000 hours in front of a computer screen. Those young people with access to digital technologies are already using these resources to tailor their informal learning to their own interests, to access information of relevance to them, to communicate with people who can support their learning, and to share ideas and expertise within informal learning communities. It is clear that for many young people their digital learning landscape already affords them a high degree of personalisation which is currently unacknowledged by their formal school experiences (Futurelab, 2005).

This lifestyle revolution is not restricted to the developed world either. According to one source 24% of urban 8-14 year-olds globally use the Internet as primary communication. 21% find the Internet the easiest way to make new friends—44% in China (Lindstrom, 2005).

It would make no sense to think of all students as a homogeneous mass of digital learners—every student has individual learning styles and unique backgrounds and dispositions. However, the notion of students generally being able to integrate technology into everyday life raises profound questions such as:

- Where and when is school?
- How can learners gain learning credits beyond the classroom?
- How does formal education react/respond to increasingly rapid change?

Technology

Information and Communication Technologies (ICT)—which refers to computers, the Internet, radio and television, and telephony—is far from new to schooling. For over forty years radio and television have been used for open and distance learning. In 1944, the Alice Springs School of the Air was established to educate children in the Outback in Australia. In 1969, "Sesame Street" was first broadcast, marking a breakthrough in the use of television to capture children's attention long enough to teach them something. Today, the Education Technology business is worth $64bn.

However, whilst ICT is an increasingly influential factor, we are a very long way from fully exploiting what technology can do in formal schooling. There are few areas outside schooling that haven't been transformed by ICT. Take medicine, for example. A Victorian surgeon would be lost in a modern-day operating theatre, but a Victorian teacher would be quite at home in the modern classroom.

Whilst technology has been used to transform business, in schooling it is little more than a veneer on top of out-dated organisational structures.

According to the OECD, we have not yet updated our schools to exploit the information revolution. The world of business uses the fruits of the information revolution to achieve efficiencies, innovate, and create new markets, products and services. Increasingly business has been exploiting technology to deliver different products for different customers as opposed to relying on mass markets where consumers want the same thing (OECD, 2006).

Saying that, technology is increasingly being used in schooling—if not yet for transformation and deep innovation, it is certainly being increasingly used to complement established education practices.

One of the earliest observations about the use of technology in schooling was increases in student motivation (Lancaster University). Teachers using computers with multimedia and project are better able to gain the attention of a media savvy generation of students than just with the traditional "chalk and talk" methods.

One of the reasons that this has been successful is that by using multimedia content teachers are able to address more learning styles—visual, auditory, and in some cases kinaesthetic too.

In addition to students having access to content in a wider range of learning styles, technology offers wider choices of content and courses of study. In some places—for example the United States and Australia—there has been a phenomenal growth in online learning. This is giving students increased choice to learn what they are interested in and in ways that suit their lifestyles. Students with Internet access no longer have to rely solely on teachers for subject matter expertise.

Technologies such as blogging, wikis, instant messenger and social networking sites are transforming the way in which students learn how to communicate and collaborate. In some cases virtual schooling is beginning to replace traditional teaching.

Access to productivity tools means that students are able to produce work of higher presentation quality, faster and in greater quantities than if they were using traditional pen and paper methods.

Technology has fantastic potential for easing the teacher workloads. For example, assessing students is a labour intensive process for teachers everywhere, but technology can play a role in helping teachers and stakeholders understand students' knowledge capabilities and skills. In a Virtual Learning Environment, for example, students can undertake learning tasks which can be assessed and reported on automatically. Another example is the use of Audience Response Systems, which allow immediate feedback tests and classroom discussions.

In administrative functions, technology saves time and money by making processes such as reporting, timetabling, student record keeping, examination, attendance, HR, and financial management faster and more efficient.

In developing countries, ICT in schooling is in its infancy. Limited infrastructure, high costs of access, lack of teachers and skills all play a part. However, there are beacons of excellence throughout the developing world—for example, Uganda is now rolling out new ICT-based learning to schools across the country. Schools throughout the developing world are making use of interactive whiteboards to meet the needs of their students. Students in countries such as the Seychelles are using tracking and monitoring technologies to understand the natural world and environmental change better. Throughout the developing world there are cases of creative use of mobile phones and shared access computing in formal and informal learning.

Disruptive Innovation

Clayton Christensen, in his book *Disrupting Class*, predicts that virtual schooling in the United States will force massive change to formal schooling systems there.

Christensen cites the steep increase in online enrolments which have risen from 45,000 in 2000 to 1 million today in the US. Online learning is gaining hold in the advanced courses that many schools are unable to offer; in small, rural, and urban schools that are unable to offer breadth; in remedial courses for students who must retake courses in order to graduate; with home-schooled students and those who can't keep up with the regular schedule of school, and for those who need tutoring.

> "Although computer-based learning is in its infancy, classes that follow this approach possess certain technological and economic advantages over the traditional school model that should allow them to grow and improve rapidly. Not only does computer-based learning provide accessibility for students who otherwise would not be able to take the course, but it also enables one to scale quality with far greater ease. In addition, as it scales, its economic costs should fall.
>
> In the United States, on average, it already costs less to educate a student online than it does in the current monolithic model. Furthermore, over time, computer-based learning can become more engaging and individualized to reach different types of learners; software developers can take full advantage of the medium to customize it by layering in different learning paths for different students.
>
> There are exciting possibilities on the horizon for education. The reason we haven't progressed down these paths doesn't have to do with the state of the technology. It has to do with how the technology has been implemented. Employing a disruptive approach presents a promising path toward at long last realising the vision of a transformed classroom." (Clayton M. Christensen and Michael B. Horn, 2008)

Christensen describes this "disruptive innovation" as the process where an innovation transforms a market where services are complicated and expensive into one characterised by simplicity, convenience and accessibility. "Disrupting Class" represents a wake-up call for those schooling systems that believe that they can resist the tide of technology driven learning innovation that is surrounding them.

Visions for Future Schools

Vast numbers of books, papers, pamphlets, lectures, videos in television programmes have been produced on the subject of schools for the future. Of these, two summaries stand out as being particularly useful.

OECD Future Schooling Scenarios

In 2001, the OECD described the following six schooling system scenarios (OECD, 2001). The future of schooling in any single country is likely to be a mix of some of these:

---

1 Bureaucratic school systems continue

- Powerful bureaucratic systems, resistant to radical change, continue to function as they have done for many years
- Schools knit together into national systems within complex administrative arrangements
- Political and media commentaries are frequently critical in tone; despite the criticisms, radical change is resisted
- No major increase in overall funding. The continual extension of schools' duties further stretches resources
- The use of ICT continues to grow without changing schools' main organisational structures
- There is a distinct teacher workforce, sometimes with civil service status; strong unions/associations but problematic professional status and rewards.

2. Schools as Focussed Learning Organisations

- Schools are revitalised around a strong knowledge rather than a social agenda, in a culture of high quality, experimentation, diversity, and innovation
- Flourishing new forms of evaluation and competence assessment
- A large majority of schools justify the label "learning organisations"—strong knowledge management and extensive links to Further and Higher Education
- Substantial investments, especially in disadvantaged communities, to develop flexible, state-of-the-art facilities
- ICT is used extensively
- Equality of opportunity is the norm
- Highly motivated teachers, favourable working conditions
- High levels of R&D, professional development, group activities, networking, and mobility in and out of teaching.

3. Schools as Core Social Centres

- Schools enjoy widespread recognition as the most effective protection against fragmentation in society and the family
- Schools are strongly defined by community tasks
- There are extensive shared responsibilities between schools and other community bodies, sources of expertise, and Further and Higher Education
- A wide range of organisational forms and settings, with strong emphasis on non-formal learning
- Generous levels of financial support—to ensure quality learning environments in all communities and high esteem for teachers and schools
- ICT is used extensively, especially for communication and networking
- A core of high-status teaching professionals, with varied arrangements and conditions, but good rewards for all—many others around the core.

4. *Extending the Market Model*

- Market features are significantly extended as governments encourage diversification and withdraw from much of their direct involvement in schooling, pushed by dissatisfaction from customers/ stakeholders/consumers
- Many new providers in the learning market, with radical reforms of funding structures, incentives and regulation. There is diversity of provision, but schools as we know them survive
- Key role of choice—of those buying educational services and of those, such as employers, giving market value to different learning routes
- Strong focus on cognitive outcomes and values
- Indicators and accreditation arrangements displace direct public monitoring and curriculum regulation
- Innovation abounds as do painful transitions and inequalities
- New learning professionals—public, private; full-time, part-time—are created in the learning markets.

5. *Learning Networks and the Learning Society*

- Dissatisfaction with schools and new possibilities for learning leads to schools being abandoned. Learner networks as part of the broader "network society"
- Networks based on diverse parental, cultural, religious and community interests—some very local in character, others using distance and cross-border networking
- Small group, home schooling and individualised arrangements become widespread. A substantial reduction of existing patterns of governance and accountability
- Exploitation of powerful, inexpensive ICT
- Specific professionals called "teachers" disappear. Demarcations—between teacher and student, parent and teacher, education and community—blur and break down
- New learning professionals emerge.

6. *Teacher Exodus and System Meltdown*

- A major crisis of teacher shortages, highly resistant to conventional policy responses
- Crisis triggered by a rapidly ageing profession, exacerbated by low teacher morale and buoyant opportunities in more attractive graduate jobs
- The large size of the teaching force means long lead times before policy measures show tangible results on overall teacher numbers
- Wide disparities in the depth of the crisis by socio-geographic, as well as subject, area
- Different possible pathways in response to "meltdown"—a vicious circle of retrenchment and conflict or emergency strategies spur radical innovation and change.

Table 2. OECD Future Schooling Scenarios

Hedley Beare's "Creating the Future School" Scenarios

Another useful perspective is provided by Hedley Beare. In his seminal book *Creating the Future School*, Beare describes the following features of a modernised schooling system:

The Borderless School	Student Management
The self-contained, standalone school located in isolation on its "island" premises is superseded. Its successor is a process orientated learning brokerage enterprise, providing programmes suited to each of its learners through a network of places, agencies and people.	Age-cohort classes have given way to the grouping of students into "learning areas" where all students have their own learning station and a set of mentor teachers to guide them in their projects and where learning activities are usually undertaken in teams. The "learning areas" and its services are open and available at all hours of the day and night.
The Computerised School	**Professionalised Teachers**
The book-and-paper school has been comprehensively computerised; its administration processes are all IT run. Every student and learning space is equipped with access to computers, and all its academic profiling and learning outcomes data are stored and made accessible to anyone in the institution for analysis.	The best teachers no longer work in the mode of a "tradesman" for the industrial bureaucracy for a set salary. They are now thoroughly professional, paid a market rate for their expertise, contracting for the professional work they do, and negotiating its performance indicators. They are comfortable with a portfolio career that at times sees them working with more than one employer and in more than one location at the same time.
The Networked Curriculum	**Teacher Cooperatives**
The old steps-and-stages, linear, age-cohorts and classes-dominated, subject-orientated curriculum has been superseded. Its successor is a "thinking curriculum", based on a search for knowledge, on developing competencies rather than content, on being information rich, multi-layered, and borderless.	Teaching unions have developed into cooperatives, helping their members to negotiate contracts, to guarantee a continuous flow of employment, to lease out their services for adequate remuneration and to manage their portfolios.

Schooling as Networks

The old organisational structures have gone—those which were based on the central control; the chain of command; supervision from above; standardised provisions; awards and regulations; and work conditions which imposed consistency and conformity. The schooling enterprise is now a network organisation which is lean, has fuzzy boundaries, is organised for interactivity, and works through strategic alliances. Its separate functions are contracted to satellite or subsidiary units, each of which has its own budget. The whole is co-ordinated by the leadership team who safeguard the enterprise's core mission of learning.

Table 3. Scenarios for the future school, Hedley Beare

According to Beare, there will be other developments too. Other education providers will emerge and deal with certain aspects of learning but do not attempt to provide the full 360 degree of services which most schools struggle to build, resource, maintain, and keep up to date.

Some schools would diversify radically, using their premises as, for example, childcare facilities as well as formal schools, or overnight residences for children whose parents are out of town. Others, driven by the idea of full-service-schools, will have strategic alliances with other community services, and will treat each of the learners holistically, with a richly documented case study approach (Beare, *Creating the Future School*, 2001).

New Metaphors for Schooling

Throughout the ages, different metaphors have been used to articulate ideas about what schooling should be, and to model their physical structure—the monastery, castle, fiefdom, teachers' house, factory and production line.

With those metaphors appropriate only for ages that are past, what metaphors should we use now to replace them? There are many new metaphors being used to describe so-called "schools of the future". Networked learning communities, virtual learning co-operations, centres for social innovation, learning studios etc., but perhaps one of the most powerful metaphors now is that of schooling as ecosystem.

A colleague articulated this idea with the following short story:

A modernising programme in one Caribbean country was attempting a full range of measures to try to improve literacy and numeracy. There were mixed results from a spectrum of activities, until one day a correlation was noticed between improving results and a routine upgrade in basic facilities.

The students' toilets had previously been in an appalling condition, but after the toilets had been refurbished and upgraded, the results improved. The reason was that when the toilets were in their poor condition students tried not to use them too frequently and so avoided drinking water throughout the day. But when the toilets were refurbished, the students were much happier using them, so drank more water during the day, which in turn helped them concentrate better in their lessons.

As in an ecosystem, everything is connected to everything else. Parents, teachers and principal know all too well how quickly rumours spread throughout a student population; how an individual disruptive student can affect entire classes; or how disputes can quickly lead to the entire system grinding to a halt. Weather, viruses, logistical, and infrastructure issues can all potentially affect the operation of a school. Likewise, stakeholders will know how positive factors—like engaging parents more deeply in the learning process—can quickly benefit entire communities.

Like an ecosystem, effective schooling systems behave like a responsive web. Touch one part, and all the elements will eventually react as one.

Case Studies

Disruptive Behaviour in UK Schools

In 2009, a survey carried out by a major teachers' union calculated how much total lesson time was being lost because of learner disruption in the UK. According to the report, more than five whole weeks of secondary school are wasted each year because of bad behaviour.

The NASUWT teachers' union surveyed its members and found "significant amounts of teaching time are lost every day as a result of disruptive or poor behaviour by learners".

Much of this disruption is low-level annoyance—such as arguments between learners, a refusal to pay attention, or being unready to start a lesson.

The survey found that on average, secondary schoolteachers lose 50 minutes each day because of learner misconduct. But for a fifth of these teachers there is an even greater problem, with 75 minutes being lost. And for a tenth of teachers, there were two hours of teaching time wasted each day because of learner disruption.

There were also problems with behaviour in primary school, with an estimated 16 full days lost each year because of misconduct. The average primary teacher reported losing 30 minutes of teaching time each day.

There was also evidence that teachers did not feel they had sufficient help, with 61% saying they did not have confidence that they would receive "swift support" with tackling disruptive learners.

(BBC, 2009)

Schooling Issues in Brazil

Whilst Brazil is developing at a very rapid pace, its schooling leaves much to be desired.   In PISA tests, Brazil is near the bottom in Maths and Science. According to *The Economist* (The Economist, 2009) 45% of the heads of poor families have less than a year's schooling.   As in India, Brazil spends a disproportionate amount on its universities rather than on teaching children to read and write.   With 50m in education, Brazil's schooling system represents one of the biggest education challenges on the planet.

The current government has implemented a number of initiatives, including supplementing local funding for teachers' pay and schools in poor districts and providing cash for poor families conditional on their children attending school. Thanks to these programmes 97% of children aged 7-14 now have access to schooling.   But the main task of improving schooling is largely the responsibility of state and municipal governments that face particularly serious problems.

In 2006, in schools run by state governments, 13% of all schooldays were lost owing to absent teachers. Teachers' absenteeism can reach 30% on some days. Brazil suffers from teacher shortages, due in part to low pay and poor conditions. Unions are strong and have been very obstructive to change and modernisation.

Another problem is that too many learners repeat entire school years over and over again.   The result is that just 42% complete high school.

There are, however, plenty of positive signs in Brazil including increased willingness to work with the private sector and an emerging network of schools (Procentro) run by professional managers rather than unsackable civil servants.

In Sao Paulo State—the largest state in Brazil—there are hopeful signs too.   In 2009 the state cut the number of teaching days lost to supposed ill-health (the biggest cause of no-shows) by 60% in a year after changing the law.   At that time, the São Paulo State Secretary of Education, Professor Maria Helena Guimarães de Castro, clearly recognised what needed to be done.   Schools in São Paulo were the first in the country to set academic goals—and to be rewarded with more money if they achieved them (Veja, 2008).

2. WHAT DO WE WANT FROM SCHOOLING?

Alice: "Would you tell me please, which way I ought to go from here?"
Cheshire Cat: "That depends a good deal on where you want to get to."
Alice: "I don't much care where…"
Cheshire Cat: "Then it doesn't matter which way you go."

Lewis Carroll, Alice in Wonderland

The purpose of this chapter is to give you an understanding of the following:

- What is schooling for?
- Who are the stakeholders, and what do they want from schooling?
- What do students need to learn?
- What is "outcomes based schooling"?
- What instruments can be used to measure success?

The key points made in this chapter are:

- The primary purpose of a schooling system should be to serve the needs of its students
- It's essential to take an outcomes-based approach to schooling if we are to make it more effective
- It isn't possible to serve all the interests of all stakeholders equally—it's essential to prioritise
- Investment in schooling should be connected to higher level economic and developmental goals
- The modern world demands far more than just academic qualifications from our students
- 21st Century Skills constitute the key for a student's success in a rapidly changing world
- Assessment and instruments of measuring success need to evolve.

B efore exploring how our schooling systems should be made more effective and relevant for the age we live in, we first need to understand what we want out of them—what exactly do we expect our schooling systems to deliver?

Developing a schooling system is a bit like rebuilding a ship whilst sailing in it. There are two key processes that have to take place in parallel. The first task is to operate the system in its current state to meet immediate needs. The second task is to change it while it's still operating to meet future needs. The hard part is balancing these two pressures.

So how do we begin to plan for the future? The first step is to work out who the stakeholders are, and broadly the kinds of needs that each of these groups has. Next, we need to build a picture of what we believe schooling is for, including what students should be learning. After that it's a matter of defining the outcomes we want from the system and understanding how we will know when we have achieved them.

Who are the Stakeholders and What do They Require?

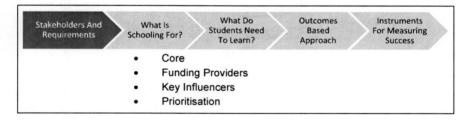

The fact that there are just so many stakeholders in the schooling system makes changing it very hard. There are few enterprises—public or private—that have such large numbers and diverse groups of people who are directly affected by what they do. It helps to start with an understanding of who the stakeholders are and to develop a view of the input that they should have into the modernisation process.

School stakeholders are not only the school board, parents, staff, and students, but also local business owners; community groups and leaders; professional organizations; potential enrolments; youth organizations; the faith community;

media, etc. Anyone who affects or is affected by the school's actions can be considered a stakeholder, and these can be categorised as follows:

Core
- Students
- Parents
- Teachers
- Principals
- Local Community

Funding Providers
- Local Education Authority/State
- National Government
- Voters/Tax Payers

Key Influencers
- Non-Government Organisations (NGOs)
- Employers
- Investors
- Higher Education
- The Media

Core

Students are clearly the biggest stakeholder in the schooling system, but so often placed at the bottom of the "food chain". From their participation in schooling, students need the skills and dispositions to live happy and productive lives, as useful members of society. These outputs are largely represented as academic and vocational qualifications, and 21st Century Skills. However, as the world gets more complex, and students will need to know and be able to do more in order to succeed, they should be able to expect much more from their schooling. Working directly with children, FutureLab, a UK based NGO, devised the following "Learner's Charter":

Choices

- To be considered as an individual with wide-reaching potential irrespective of age, gender, disability, ethnicity or socio-economic status
- To take joint responsibility for and be seen as an active agent in determining my own learning priorities
- To understand and critically engage with the choices open to me in the education process
- To understand the potential implications of these choices personally, socially and economically
- To develop the personal and social skills and attributes necessary to make these choices and to engage with the people and resources of the education process.

Skills and knowledge

- To be supported to co-design my own curriculum and learning goals
- To draw upon and make connections between the expertise and competencies I develop across all areas of my life
- To develop my expertise and understanding in knowledge domains which are of personal significance to me
- To be supported to take risks and develop understanding in unfamiliar knowledge domains
- To have access to learning that will prepare me well for when I become a member of the adult population.

Appropriate learning environments

- To have access to different teaching and learning approaches and resources which meet my needs
- To have access to people who are able to extend and develop my understanding in my chosen areas
- To have access to learning environments and resources which enable me to develop my understanding and experience in authentic and appropriate contexts.

Feedback

- To use diverse assessment tools to enable me to reflect upon and develop my own learning at times and in sites appropriate for me and in ways which inform decisions about my future learning
- To have access to a diverse range of assessment mechanisms and media that are appropriate to the activity I am participating in
- To achieve recognition for learning irrespective of the context of my learning (in home, in school, in workplace, in community)
- To achieve recognition for learning that enables me to progress within the wider community
- To participate in assessment activities that provide feedback to the education system and are used to improve the learning environments in which I learn.

(Green, 2006)

Engaged parents can make a massive difference to the educational success of their children but are frequently overlooked as potential partners in the schooling process. When parents and schools share the same values and goals, high achievement becomes a lot easier. Getting parents on-side means less resource wasted dealing with complaints. The kinds of outputs that parents can expect from schooling systems include their children gaining useful qualifications; safe and secure child-minding; and extracurricular activities for broadening their children's' development. They need their children to be well looked after during the school day, information about their children's' progress, and content and guidance to support learning at home.

Because of their central position and range of responsibilities in schooling, teachers are viewed in many different ways—for example, employees; subject matter experts; child-minders; subordinates; shop-floor workers; trades people; caring professionals, just to name a few. Teachers, as a category of stakeholder, can be broken down into the following sub categories:

- Primary, Secondary
- Specialists
- Senior Teachers
- Head of Department
- Head of Year
- Classroom Assistants

Teachers can expect to be well-managed; respected; recognised and rewarded fairly; well supported; and appropriately resourced and trained.

In a centralised system, principals largely carry out bureaucratic functions. In some places they are considered curriculum leaders, and are there to oversee the routine operations of schools. In devolved systems, however, principals take on the role of school CEO with people and financial management responsibilities, and have extensive sets of accountabilities. A large part of a principal's role is to ensure legislative compliance. Principals are invariably expected to raise achievement, and need the autonomy, support and resources to make decisions that positively affect outcomes.

Schools largely exist to serve local communities and it is very much in the interest of local communities to have thriving schools. Schools have a role in social cohesion as well as local economic development. Local communities can expect schools to help children acquire the skills and knowledge to integrate into society, and make positive contributions. Likewise communities have roles in supporting thriving schooling systems, and schools need communities to value education, provide expertise and participate in relevant activities.

Funding Providers

As funding providers for schooling, the organisational units above individual schools naturally hold a stake in the outcomes from schools. They provide funding to schooling systems to drive social and economic development—in fact some local authorities and states now consider investing in schools as investments in future tax revenues. LEAs (Local Education Authorities, or School Districts) and states therefore need schools to develop human capacity linked to their economic development plans, through students successfully exploiting further or higher education, productively entering the workplace, and making positive contributions to their communities. At LEA and state levels, the success of schooling systems have knock-on financial effects on other public services run by those organisations, such as policing, health and social services. For example, in the United States it would be less expensive to send students to private school than to foot the bill for the imprisonments that inevitably follow schooling in some areas.

As with LEAs and state bodies, national governments contribute funding to schooling, but at this level it is largely about economic competitiveness, social cohesion and democratic participation. Successful outcomes from schooling systems expected at national levels include: improved positions in international league tables; increased skills for improved productivity; higher overall numbers of graduates; results in priority areas such as Maths, Science and Engineering; and value for tax payer's money. Ultimately, national governments are interested in outcomes that improve their perception with voters.

In most, if not all democratic countries, education is a major policy issue for respective governments. The attitude of voters towards education matters a great deal to politicians, and the will of voters ultimately have a strong influence on schooling. Voters are also taxpayers, so tangible value for money is a key requirement for this group. School discipline, the curriculum, taxation levels, safety, results, strikes, youth crime, how religion and sex education are handled, can all affect how voters feel about schooling.

Key Influencers

The number of NGOs involved in education around the world is huge. Religious groups; campaigns; trade unions; research institutes; public interest groups; commercial organisations; lobbies; associations; think tanks, etc.—all contest with one another for different kinds of influence over different parts of the schooling system. Often these groups actively invest in aspects of schooling, so their influence becomes magnified. There is a need for schooling systems to organise themselves in ways that don't leave them exposed to requiring funding from organizations that have interests that are in conflict with the mission of the organisation. For example, it would be unacceptable if schooling systems became reliant on advertising money linked to promoting products which were not in students' best interests.

The productivity of an organisation's workforce ultimately traces back to the quality of schooling received by their workers. The cost of poor schooling to employers can be great—for example, rectifying low levels of literacy and numeracy in the workplace is far more expensive than dealing with it in schools. Employers are particularly important stakeholders because the business and organisations they represent are ultimately the source of the tax revenues used to pay for schooling systems. Employers need workers who are well educated—evidenced by academic and vocational qualifications; possess 21st Century Skills; and are motivated and adaptable.

The private sector invests billions of dollars in schooling every year. Everything from independent schooling operations to school buildings, insurance, furniture, content, contracted services and ICT all require private sector investment from which investors expect a return.

As with employers, Higher Education organisations benefit from effective schooling systems. Examinations systems—which drive so much of schooling—were originally put in place as a set of filters for entry into university, and still serve a similar purpose today. Higher Education is therefore a major influencer on the goals and purpose of schooling. Their needs are for students who have good basic skills; interest and good levels of knowledge in the subjects they offer—evidenced by academic qualifications; the ability to learn independently; and the characteristics of perseverance and determination.

The media too can be considered stakeholders. All too often the media will sensationalise or narrow the schooling debate by focusing on topics such as "how much harder examinations were in bygone ages", or lack of discipline in the classroom. The media plays a significant role in influencing public opinion about schooling and can be considered stakeholders because they affect and influence it externally. Schooling systems need to focus the media on the positive aspects of modernisation, and understand how not to be manipulated.

Prioritisation

It's simply not possible to satisfy all stakeholders equally, all of the time. It's essential therefore to be able to prioritise stakeholders and map where the more important relationships are, and understand just who is at the centre of the service.

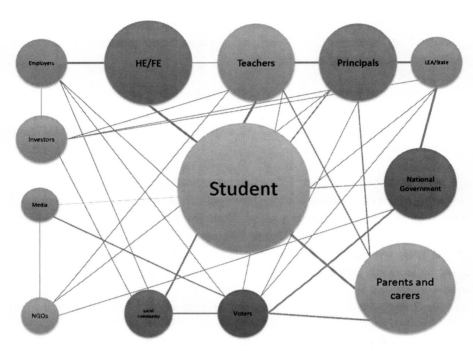

Figure 3. Who is at the centre of the service and what are the key relationships?

When you have prioritised your stakeholders, you can then prioritise their requirements—for example:

Stakeholder	Need
Student	Academic and Vocational Qualifications
	21st Century Skills
	Increased learning choice and opportunity
Parents	Children well looked after
	Information about their child's progress
	Content to support learning at home
Teachers	Higher pay, more professional status
	Reduced administration
	Higher quality work environment
Principals	Raising achievement
	Ensure legislative compliance

	Autonomy to make key decisions
LEA/State	Outputs linked to economic development plans
	Increase transparency and accountability
	High quality of workforce
National Government	Develop competiveness and economy
	Effective, open and well regarded workforce
	Improved position in international comparisons
	Population with at least upper secondary education
	High performance in priority subjects – e.g. Science, Technology, Engineering and Maths (STEM)
	Full employment
Local Community	Curriculum aligned to local needs
	Socially integrated children
	Access to schooling assets
Employers	Workforce with 21st Century Skills
	Vocational and academic qualifications
Higher Education	Students with academic qualifications
Voters/Tax Payers	Value for money

Table 4. Example stakeholder requirements map

What is Schooling For?

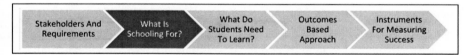

We have high hopes for our schooling systems. Foremost is the hope that they will nurture the spiritual, moral, social, cultural, physical and mental development of our children. There is hope that schooling will provide equality of opportunity for all, a healthy and just democracy, a productive economy, and sustainable development. Schools are places where values are developed, including valuing ourselves, our families and other relationships, the wider groups to which we belong, the diversity in our society and the environment in which we live. Schooling should also nurture the virtues of truth, justice, honesty, trust and a sense of duty.

According to Beare, there are three broad categories of purposes for schooling:

- Induction of young people into society
- Preparation for the world of work
- Personal formation

In order to participate fully in society, there are some essential skills and knowledge that all people need to acquire. Social conventions such as honesty; fairness; respect for alternative viewpoint; concern for well-being of others; political structures and government operations; acceptable and unacceptable behaviour; taboos to be respected and laws to be observed. Schooling has a role in facilitating a vibrant, participative democracy in which we have an informed electorate that is capable of making objective decisions. The State approves the curriculum that helps deliver these teachings and pays for schools to deliver those aspects of education that are deemed to be "in the public interest".

Schooling is also preparation for the world of work, and it is assumed that every member of a society will acquire the skills to use his or her time productively for the good of society. Because education for employment is so crucial to the economic well-being of the society, national governments pay schools to deliver that part of education which contributes to the country's wealth creation and economic performance.

Schooling is also the means whereby an individual cultivates his or her own unique set of skills, temperament, potentialities and physical attributes which in time develop into his or her "best self". Personal formation includes an individual's self-image; system of beliefs; developing a world view; behaviours; physical fitness and competencies; social relationships; and intellectual, emotional and spiritual well-being. Governments are likely to fund an individual's personal formation to the extent to which it is seen as an investment in human capital. Parents often supplement this by paying for outside school activities (Beare, *Creating the Future School*, 2001).

Another perspective comes from the UK's Qualification and Curriculum Authority—

> "People leaving our schooling systems, more now than ever, will need to be able to respond positively to the opportunities and challenges of

the rapidly changing world in which we live and work. In particular, they need to be prepared to engage as individuals, parents, workers and citizens with environmental, economic, social and cultural change, including dealing with the effects of global warming and the continued globalisation of the economy and society, with new work and leisure patterns and with the rapid expansion of communication technologies."

(Qualifications and Curriculum Authority)

This is a comprehensive set of requirements, but too often progress towards these goals is measured in crude academic terms—test scores and examination results. As we move schooling into its next phase of development, we will need to develop sophisticated ways of planning, delivering and measuring outcomes—the most significant of which is learning.

What do Students Need to Learn?

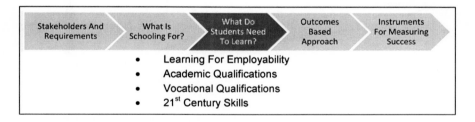

- Learning For Employability
- Academic Qualifications
- Vocational Qualifications
- 21st Century Skills

"A human being should be able to change a diaper, plan an invasion, butcher a hog, conn a ship, design a building, write a sonnet, balance accounts, build a wall, set a bone, comfort the dying, take orders, give orders, cooperate, act alone, solve equations, analyse a new problem, pitch manure, programme a computer, cook a tasty meal, fight efficiently, die gallantly. Specialization is for insects."

Robert A. Heinlein, Enough Time for Love

What students need to learn will differ considerably across the world, but with the march of globalisation it's worth looking at how employment patterns are changing.

Learning for Employability

Levy and Murnane show how the composition of the US work force has changed (Murnane, 2004).   What they show is that, between 1970 and 2000, work involving routine manual input, the jobs of the typical factory worker, was down significantly.   Non-routine manual work, things we do with our hands, but in ways that are not so easily put into formal algorithms, was down too, albeit with much less change over recent years—and that is easy to understand because you cannot easily computerise the bus driver or outsource your hairdresser.

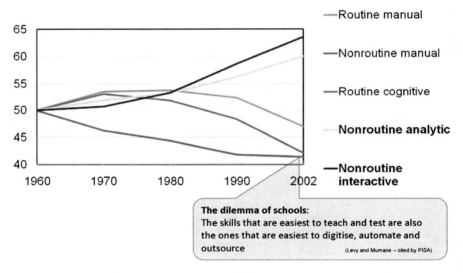

Figure 4. Dilemma for schools—easiest subjects to teach are of lowest value

Citing this study, Prof. Andres Schleicher from OECD makes an excellent point when he talks about the importance of preparing children for work that delivers higher levels of value than computers do.

> "Among the skill categories represented here, routine cognitive input— that is cognitive work that you can easily put into the form of algorithms and scripts—saw the sharpest decline in demand over the last couple of decades, with a decline by almost 8% in the share of jobs.   So those middle class white collar jobs that involve the application of routine knowledge are most at threat today.   And that is where schools still put a

lot of their focus and what we value in multiple choice accountability systems." (Schleicher, 2009)

If we focus schooling on teaching skills and knowledge that can be tested easily, we are positioning students to compete with computers. This is because the skills that are easiest to teach and test are also the skills that are easiest to digitise, automate and offshore. Manipulating non-complex knowledge is something that computers can do better than humans. In a global economy, the drive for cost effectiveness will ensure that all work that *can* be digitised, automated or outsourced, *will* be digitised, automated or outsourced. So, we need to ask ourselves what key competencies education systems need to provide for young people to succeed, and how can schooling better align with these needs?

The winners in a globalised economy are those who can engage in expert thinking (up 8%) and complex communication (up almost 14%). A strong foundation of subject specific knowledge will always have significant value, but it is no longer enough—other skills are increasing in importance. These include:

Versatility	*Editing and Communicating*
Being able to apply depth of skill to wide scopes of situations, gaining new competencies, building relationships, and assuming new roles. Schools need to nurture individuals who cannot only apply subject matter knowledge, but have the ability and motivation to expand their horizons, and transfer and apply skills and knowledge in new settings.	With the explosion in the amount of information available through the internet, people who can meaningfully sort and filter information and explain specialised content will become increasingly important. Again, this needs to be reflected in modern assessments.
Creativity and Synthesis	*Collaboration and Orchestration*
Creativity and innovation enabled through strong communication and collaboration skills are what will give individuals and nations the competitive edge. In today's workplace, value is created by synthesising unrelated pieces of data and information. Many roles now require people to have expertise in several fields, then create and exploit new knowledge by synthesising information from each field. E.g.—combining financial, scientific and political skills and knowledge in the new field of environmental consulting. We need to reflect the skill of creative synthesis in modern assessments.	With exponentially increasing complexity in the global marketplace, the more organisations need more sophisticated co-ordination and management. Valuable skills and attributes are interpersonal skills, teamwork and leadership. The problem is that in the vast majority of schools, students learn individually and at the end of the school year their individual achievement is certified. In the interdependent world of work, collaboration is a core skill. In assessments at school, collaboration is usually considered cheating.

Table 5. Key skills required in the modern workplace, Schleicher 2009

If these are the skills that we need to develop, we need to base modern assessments of learning outcomes at school on key competencies, rather than solely assessing the efficiency with which students have remembered what they have been taught.

To summarise Schleicher's points:

- The skills and knowledge that are easiest to teach and test are also easy to digitise, automate and offshore—and therefore have low value.
- Creativity, synthesising, communication and collaboration, orchestration skills and versatility have higher value.
- Schooling needs to nurture the ability to expand horizons and apply knowledge and skills in novel settings.

(Schleicher, 2009)

Academic Qualifications

Whilst it's clear to see that a modern curriculum needs to go beyond its grounding in academic discipline, the reality for most schools is that they are judged by last year's final examination performance or their academic test scores. According to Sir Ken Robinson, a leading thinker on the role of schools, "our education system is predicated on the idea of academic ability which has really come to dominate our view of intelligence" (Sir Ken Robinson, 2006).

So where does academia's dominance over the education system come from?

Academia has its roots in the subjects of the ancient "Trivium" and "Quadrivium", which provided the curricular models for the first universities in medieval Europe. The "Trivium" comprised the three subjects taught first: Grammar, Logic, and Rhetoric. This prepared students for the Quadrivium which consisted of Arithmetic, Geometry, Music, and Astronomy. In turn, the Quadrivium was considered preparation for the study of Philosophy and Theology. Over the centuries, the universities designed the education system in their image. Most academic institutions today—be they schools, colleges or universities—still reflect the divide of disciplines and are divided internally into departments or programmes in various fields of study. There are still schools called "Grammar Schools" in some parts of the world.

As Ken Robinson puts it, "if you think of it, the whole system of public education around the world is a protracted process of university entrance"… "if you were to visit education, as an alien, and say 'What's public education for?' I think you'd have to conclude that the whole purpose of public education throughout the world is to produce university professors"… "The consequence [of academia dominating schooling] is that many highly talented, brilliant, creative people think they're not, because the thing they were good at in school wasn't valued, or was actually stigmatized."

Let's be clear though—academia has played a massive role in human achievement.   The scientific, technological, medical, financial and social revolutions that have led us to the prosperity that so many of us enjoy today owe a huge debt to "academic" thinking, research, discipline and rigour.   For increasing numbers of students, a university education is a natural choice. On the other hand, for many students a university degree has no relevance or appeal. It's quite possible for people to make valuable contributions to society without needing formal academic thinking skills or qualifications, so the question is—"to what extent is academia relevant to schooling *today*?"

Most involved in education would argue that there continues to be a strong role for academia, but increasingly people are realising that it's not the *only* focus that a schooling system should have. Yes, of course, there is knowledge, skills and understanding based on academic principles that are critical for successful induction into society, preparation for the world of work, and personal formation—but academic principles aren't the *only* principles on which these capacities are built.

It's time to re-think academia as *the* blueprint for schooling, and the assumption that the dominant criteria for judging schools are academic results.

So what other outcomes, besides academic achievement, do we want from schooling?

Vocational Qualifications

Incorporating vocational qualifications into the schooling system is far from new but gaining significance. Vocational qualifications prepare learners for manual or practical activities—jobs that have no or low academic demands. Vocational education traditionally focused on "trades" such as cooking, nursing, building, welding or car mechanics, but has now diversified across a vast spectrum of industries.

In UK secondary schools it is possible to gain work-related qualifications during the last two years of compulsory schooling. Students who choose to study for a vocational "Diploma" can do it instead of the General Certificate of Secondary Education examinations—the "standard" exit examinations from UK schools.

Students choosing the vocational path at 13-14 years of age, can also re-join the academic path later on, if they so wish by taking Advanced Diplomas that will enable them to enter university.

Diploma subjects include:

Business, Administration and Finance	Construction and the Built Environment
Creative and Media	Engineering
Environmental and Land-based Studies	Hair and Beauty Studies
Hospitality	Information Technology (IT)
Manufacturing and Product Design	Public Services
Retail Business	Society, Health and Development
Sport and Active Leisure	Travel and Tourism

Table 6. Diploma subjects in English schools

Some students can also do work-related courses called Young Apprenticeships, which cover a range of vocational courses similar to the Diploma.

These programmes give students a 'real taste of work' while still in school. Young Apprentices spend the equivalent of two days a week working on their apprenticeship. For the rest of the time they study the normal school curriculum and work towards GCSEs and other qualifications. There is a mix of classroom learning and practical hands-on experience in various settings—for example, college, training centre or workplace. Assessment is via a mix of examinations, assessment of a portfolio of evidence and observation by an assessor.

21ˢᵗ Century Skills

"I must study politics and war that my sons may have liberty to study Mathematics and Philosophy. My sons ought to study Mathematics and Philosophy, Geography, Natural History, Naval Architecture, Navigation, Commerce and Agriculture in order to give their children the right to study Painting, Poetry, Music, Architecture, Statuary, Tapestry and Porcelain."

John Adams, U.S. President

Every era has its own learning requirements, and the world has changed a lot since the foundation of academia in Greek times and the medieval universities in Europe.

The combined effects of demographics, ecology, technology, and consumer demands are radically changing the nature of work, prosperity and life chances for the 2.2bn under 18-year-olds on the planet.

For example, Tom Peters, management guru and author of *In Search of Excellence* claims that:

- Lifetime employment is over
- Stable employment at large corporations is gone
- The average career will most likely encompass two or three "occupations" and a half-dozen or more employers
- Most of us will spend sustained periods of our career in some form of self-employment.

"Stability is dead; 'education' must therefore 'educate' for an unknowable, ambiguous, changing future."

(Tom Peters)

The knowledge, skills, values and attitudes that students will need in order to lead full and socially integrated lives are quickly becoming much more sophisticated than can be addressed purely within an academic framework.

New standards for what students should be able to do must replace—or at least build on—the basic skills and knowledge expectations of the past. To meet this challenge schools must enable students to acquire the sophisticated thinking, flexible problem solving, collaboration and communication skills they will need to be successful in work and life.

Below are selected highlights from the 21st Century Skills Assessment work being done by University of Melbourne, Cisco, Intel and Microsoft (ATC21s.Org, 2010):

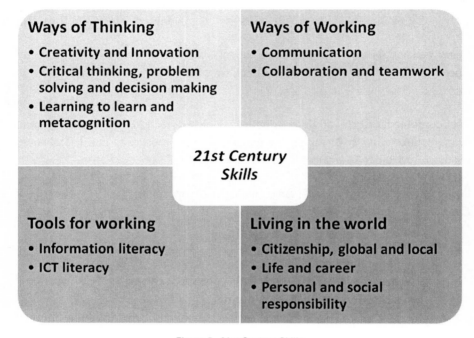

Figure 5. 21st Century Skills

Ways of thinking

These skills emphasize the upper end of thinking skills, and incorporate more straightforward skills such as recall, and drawing inferences. A major characteristic of these skills is that they require greater focus and reflection.

Creativity and Innovation

- Know a wide range of idea creation techniques (such as brainstorming)
- Know the real world limits to adopting new ideas and how to present them in more acceptable forms

- Be able to elaborate, refine, analyse and evaluate one's own ideas in order to improve and maximize creative efforts
- Be open and responsive to new and diverse perspectives; incorporate group input and feedback into group work
- View failure as an opportunity to learn; understand that creativity and innovation is a long-term, cyclical process of small successes and frequent mistakes.

Critical thinking, problem solving and decision making

- Understand the importance of evidence in belief formation and re-evaluate beliefs when presented with conflicting evidence
- Identify gaps in knowledge and ask significant questions that clarify various points of view and lead to better solutions
- Clearly articulate the results of one's inquiry
- Analyse how parts of a whole interact with each other to produce overall outcomes in complex systems
- Be trustful of reason; inquisitive and concerned to be well informed; open and fair minded; flexible and honest.

Learning to learn and metacognition

- Understand one's preferred learning methods, the strengths and weaknesses of one's skills and qualifications
- Effective self-management of learning and careers in general: ability to dedicate time to learning, autonomy, discipline, long periods of concentration, perseverance and information management in the learning process
- Ability to reflect critically on the object and purpose of learning
- Ability to communicate as part of the learning process by using appropriate means (intonation, gesture, mimicry)
- Positive appreciation of learning as a life-enriching activity and a sense of initiative to learn.

Ways of working

In business we are witnessing a rapid shift in the way people work. Outsourcing services across national and continental borders is just one example. Another is having team members telecommute while working on the same project. For instance, a small software consulting team has members located on three continents. They work on developing prototypes using teleconferences, text messaging, with the occasional "sprint" sessions where they gather in a single location. To support these types of work scenarios, excellent communication and collaboration skills are essential. Communication must be rapid, concise and cognizant of cultural differences.

Communication

- The ability to listen to and understand various spoken messages in a variety of communicative situations and to speak concisely and clearly
- Ability to read and understand different texts, adopting strategies appropriate to various reading purposes (reading for information, for study or for pleasure) and to various text types
- Ability to write different types of texts for various purposes. To monitor the writing process (from drafting to editing and proofreading)
- Ability to formulate one's arguments, in speaking or writing, in a convincing manner and take full account of other viewpoints, whether expressed in written or oral form
- Skills needed to use aids (such as notes, schemes, maps) to produce, present or understand complex texts in written or oral form (speeches, conversations, instructions, interviews, debates).

Collaboration and teamwork

- Know and recognize the individual roles of a successful team and know own strengths and weaknesses recognizing and accepting them in others
- Know how to plan, set and meet goals and to monitor and re-plan in the light of unforeseen developments
- Use interpersonal and problem-solving skills to influence and guide others toward a goal
- Respond open-mindedly to different ideas and values
- Act responsibly with the interests of the larger community in mind.

Tools for working

"Tools for working" are about information and ICT literacy and skills—critical skills given that work is increasingly represented electronically. Just to paint a picture of how important it is to be truly literate in the use of ICT, consider that it is estimated that a week's worth of the *New York Times* contains more information than a person was likely to come across in a lifetime in the 18th century. In one year more unique information will be generated this year than in the previous 5,000 years. In light of this information explosion the coming generations must have the skills to access and evaluate new information efficiently so that they can effectively utilize all that is available and relevant to their tasks at hand. One of the ways they will capitalise on this information explosion is through skilled use of ICT.

Information literacy

- Ability to search, collect and process (create, organise, distinguish relevant from irrelevant, subjective from objective, real from virtual) electronic information, data and concepts and to use them in a systematic way
- Positive attitude and sensitivity to safe and responsible use of the Internet, including privacy issues and cultural differences
- Interest in using information to broaden horizons by taking part in communities and networks for cultural, social and professional purposes
- Use digital technologies (computers, PDAs, media players, GPS, etc.), communication/networking tools and social networks appropriately to access, manage, integrate, evaluate and create information to successfully function in a knowledge economy
- Ability to use information to support critical thinking, creativity and innovation in different contexts at home, leisure and work.

ICT literacy

- Employ knowledge and skills in the application of ICT and media to communicate, interrogate, present and model
- Understand and know how to utilize the most appropriate media creation tools, characteristics and conventions

- Use technology as a tool to research, organise, evaluate and communicate information
- Awareness of the opportunities given by the use of Internet and communication via electronic media (e-mail, videoconferencing, other network tools)
- Apply a fundamental understanding of the ethical/legal issues surrounding the access and use of information technologies.

Living in the world

Essentially people must learn to live not only in their town or country but also in the world in its entirety. As more and more people individually move in the 21st Century to connect and collaborate, it is even more important that they understand all the aspects of citizenship. It is not enough to assume that what goes on in your own country is how it is or should be all over the globe.

Citizenship, global and local

- Knowledge of civil rights and the constitution of the home country, the scope of its government
- Understand concepts such as democracy, citizenship and the international declarations expressing them
- Knowledge of the main events, trends and agents of change in national, and world history
- Participation in community/neighbourhood activities as well as in decision-making at national and international levels; voting in elections
- Acceptance of the concept of human rights and equality; acceptance of equality between men and women
- Appreciation and understanding of differences between value systems of different religious or ethnic groups.

Life and career

- Be prepared to adapt to varied responsibilities, schedules and contexts, recognize and accept the strengths of others
- See opportunity in ambiguity and changing priorities
- Incorporate feedback and deal effectively with praise, setbacks and criticism

- Demonstrate commitment to learning as a lifelong process
- Demonstrate ability to: work positively and ethically; manage time and projects; effectively; collaborate and cooperate effectively with teams; be accountable for results.

Personal and social responsibility

- Knowledge of how to maintain good health, hygiene and nutrition for oneself and one's family
- Ability to express one's frustration in a constructive way (control of aggression and violence or self-destructive patterns of behaviour)
- Ability to negotiate
- Showing interest in and respect for others
- Compromise, integrity and appropriate assertiveness.

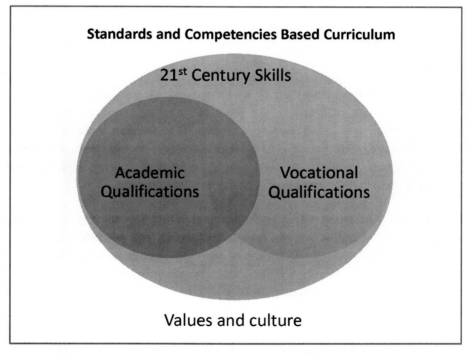

Figure 6. Students need to acquire skills and qualifications within a competencies based curriculum and framework of values and culture

Taking an Outcomes Based Approach

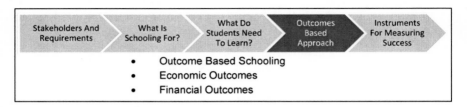

A key step towards building more efficient and effective schooling systems is to shift the focus away from managing by inputs to managing by outcomes.

All too often schooling systems will describe their progress in terms of inputs as opposed to outcomes. In response to questions such as "How do you think you are progressing with technology in your schools?" the answer is frequently framed around the number of interactive whiteboards available, or the student to computer ratio. You often hear people talking about capacity development in terms of the amount of training delivered as opposed to implementation of that training in everyday practice.

Whilst inputs are a necessary condition for success, on their own they do not guarantee outcomes. Ultimately, the point of investing resources and human energy in schooling is to get learning outcomes. The problem is that it is much easier to manage inputs than it is to manage outcomes. For example, it's much easier to acquire computers or send people on training courses, than it is to ensure that these investments result in higher quality outcomes.

The problem with dealing with schooling outputs is that they are very hard to get consensus on. Schooling systems are national assets, and practically everyone has a stake in their success. There are as many different demands on schooling systems as there are parents, children, teachers, administrators, policy makers, employers, and religious groups—literally billions of different demands adding up to a complex cauldron of influences and pressures.

To move forward, however, we simply have to get a firm grip on what outcomes we want from our schooling systems. As the Cheshire Cat in *Alice In Wonderland* clearly understood, progressing is about knowing where you want to get to, and in schooling terms that means what outcomes you want the system to achieve.   Whether we move forward at all, or take a particular direction, simply doesn't matter without agreement on what outcomes we want.

Outcome Based Schooling

Outcomes Based Schooling (OBS) is a student-centred approach that requires students to demonstrate that they have learned skills and content.

For many decades, schooling was managed according to inputs: how many teachers? How much seniority did each teacher have? How many hours of in-service training? How many hours should students spend in a given class? These were the criteria used to allocate resources and adjust rewards. Now, as in other industries like healthcare, the attention is shifting from inputs to outputs.   In healthcare we hear of "outcomes research"; in education, we hear of academic standards and accountability (OECD, 2006).

While it is important to know how what inputs are required to run a schooling system, policy makers recognize that it is equally important to know what students are learning in the classroom: What kind of knowledge, skills and attitudes does the education system develop?   How do assessed learning outcomes reflect the stated goals and objectives of national education systems? What factors are associated with student achievement? Do particular sub-groups in the population perform poorly?   How well are students being prepared to succeed in an increasingly knowledge-based economy? (World Bank).

The key measure of a whether a schooling system is succeeding or not is whether it is producing expected levels of learning outcomes. A learning outcome goes beyond simple academic attainment.   It is the particular knowledge, skill or behaviour that a student is expected to exhibit after a period of study. Measuring learning outcomes provides information on what particular knowledge, skill or behaviour students have gained.

Generally, outcomes are expected to be measurable—e.g. "Student can..." rather than "Student enjoys..." A complete system of outcomes for a subject area normally includes everything from recitation of fact ("Students will name three tragedies written by Shakespeare") to complex analysis and interpretation ("Student will analyse the social context of a Shakespearean tragedy in an essay").

Key features of an OBS Model include:

- Standards based curriculum framework that outlines specific, measurable outcomes
- A commitment to *require* learning outcomes for advancement to the next level
- Standards-based assessments, which can take many different forms
- A commitment that all students will reach the same minimum standards, but most will exceed these.

Economic Outcomes

It's pretty clear that in the globalised knowledge economy that human capital--i.e. what people can and will do—is a key determinant of economic growth. According to UNESCO (UNESCO Institute of Statistics, 2002) the evidence shows that better-educated people are more likely to be in work, and therefore contributing to the economy. In all WEI (World Education Indicators) countries, labour force participation rates and wage levels increase with the level of education attained.   There is evidence too that indicates that economic growth is also associated with a wide range of other benefits such as better health and well-being. Growth in economic output not only provides the resources for tackling poverty, social exclusion and poor health but also expands the range of human choice.

Hanushek et al (Hanushek, 2008) found that when the average number of years of schooling in a country was higher, the economy grew at a higher annual rate over subsequent decades.   Specifically, they found that, across the 50 countries they studied, each additional year of average schooling in a country increased the average 40-year growth rate in GDP by about 0.37 percentage points.   That may not seem like much, but since World War II, the world economic growth rate has been around 2 to 3% of GDP annually.   Lifting it by 0.37 percentage points is a boost to annual GDP growth rates of more than 10%.   The OECD average annual spend on education (all-up) was 6% of GDP in 2005 (OECD, *Education at a Glance*, 2008), so it's clear to see that expenditure on education more than pays for itself. According to Schleicher (Schleicher, 2009), in 1989 the USA declared its intention to close the education gap on the top performing countries. If it had done so, it would have paid for *the entire education system* after 15 years.

Financial Outcomes

Any organisation in receipt of public funding is obligated to ensure that expenditure is within agreed limits and that it has maximum impact. Key financial outcomes are:

- **Value for Money.** High levels of value added by the organisation, which is managed within budget
- **Efficiency.** Efficient and effective use of resources including staff, physical infrastructure, materials and content
- **Stability and Sustainability.** Even levels of cashflows, allowing continuity and progress. The ability to maintain and grow levels of provision
- **Transparency.** Openness to scrutiny from stakeholders to challenge expenditure and to identify possible savings and alternative use of resources
- **Accountability.** Expenditure is challenged in terms of its effectiveness against strategic goals. Purchasing on a fair and open basis.
- **Planning and Controls.** Ensuring economy and accountability, and that development plans are fully and realistically costed. The organisation has proper financial administration, procedures, including competitive tendering, for significant expenditure
- **Maximisation.** The organisation receives all the funding to which it is entitled, and is entrepreneurial in obtaining other sources of funding
- **Strategic Focus.** Investment is targeted at making significant differences and the organisation isn't doing anything that could be better provided by someone else, and with the strategic use of resources and getting best value for expenditure.

What Instruments can be used to Measure Success?

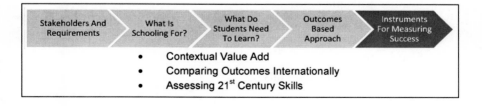

- Contextual Value Add
- Comparing Outcomes Internationally
- Assessing 21st Century Skills

Contextual Value Added

One of the problems with measuring the impact of a schooling system is the variance between the students each school has to work with. Again, using inappropriate factory analogies, this is often referred to as the "raw material". In a factory, if the raw material is of a low grade, more work is required to bring it up to the required standard than in a factory where the raw material is of a high grade.

Schools argue—quite rightly—that if they are situated in areas where there is high social depravation, and/or there is a low value placed in education in their communities, they are at a disadvantage to those schools whose students, parents and communities value education and play an active role in it.

In general, it's relatively easy to get good exit examination results from schools in affluent areas, so judging how good a school is purely on examination or test results give a distorted view.

To get around this problem, and to get a fair and accurate picture of where schooling is successful, the UK Government uses a system of "Contextual Value Added" (CVA).

CVA shows the *progress* children have made whilst attending a particular school. Unlike examination performance, CVA factors in the circumstances of children attending the school that are beyond the control of the school.

CVA works by comparing a child's learning performance with that of children with a similar prior performance in similar circumstances. It takes into account nine factors that are known to affect the performance of children, but outside of the schools control:

- Learner prior attainment
- Gender
- Special Educational Needs
- First language
- Measures of learner mobility
- Age
- An "In care" indicator

- Ethnicity
- Free School Meals
- Income Deprivation Affecting Children Index
- Average and range of prior attainment within the school.

Whilst CVA is not without its critics, it does seem a much better way to evaluate the relative effectiveness of schools than raw test score or examination data.

Comparing Outcomes Internationally

PISA

Programme for International Student Assessment (PISA) is a comprehensive international assessment of the quality of schooling. It is a three-yearly global assessment to examine the performance of 15-year-olds in key subject areas as well as a wider range of educational outcomes including students' attitudes to learning and their learning behaviour. PISA collects contextual data from students, parents, schools and systems in order to identify policy levers shaping learning outcomes.

PISA tests roughly half a million of children in OECD countries in key competencies. Representative samples of between 3,500 and 50,000 15-year-old students are drawn in each country. Most federal countries also draw state-level samples. The programme checks not only whether students have learned what they were recently taught, but also to what extent students can extrapolate from what they have learned and apply their knowledge and skills in novel settings.

In a growing number of countries PISA is embedded in national assessment strategies and used for monitoring performance within countries *e.g.* Australia, Belgium, Canada, Germany, Italy, Mexico, Spain, Switzerland and the United Kingdom.

The International Association for the Evaluation of Educational Achievement (IEA)

The IEA is an independent association education focussed research agency. Founded in 1958, IEA is based in Amsterdam. IEA studies student performance in key subjects such as Maths, Science, and Reading and evaluates whether certain policies in a particular educational system cause positive or negative effects on learning.

Key IEA programmes include:

- Trends in International Mathematics and Science Study (TIMSS)
- Progress in International Reading Literacy Study (PIRLS)
- TIMSS-R Video Study of Classroom Practices
- International Civic and Citizenship Education Study (ICCS)
- Information Technology in Education Study (SITES)
- Pre-primary Education Study (PPP)

Of these, TIMSS is one of the best known.

Trends in International Mathematics and Science Study (TIMSS)

The Trends in International Mathematics and Science Study (TIMSS) is an international assessment of the Mathematics and Science knowledge of fourth- and eighth-grade students around the world. TIMSS consists of an assessment of Mathematics and Science, and surveys student, teacher, and schools.

TIMSS allows participating nations to compare students' educational achievement across borders. In 2007, 48 countries participated in TIMSS.

UNESCO

UNESCO is also involved in comparing education outcomes internationally, and conducts extensive research in support of two key policy areas, Education for All and Millennium Development Goals.

The UNESCO Institute of Statistics (UIS) collects education data from about 200 countries and territories through two annual surveys. Both are based on similar definitions and concepts which ensure the international comparability of the data. The most recent surveys cover:

- Pre-primary, primary, secondary and post-secondary non-tertiary education
- Educational finance and expenditure
- National education programmes

International Standard Classification of Education—ISCED

The world's education systems vary widely in terms of structure and curricular content. UIS addresses the need for internationally agreed definitions, making it possible for policymakers to compare their own education systems with those of other countries. The current version, known as The International Standard Classification of Education (ISCED 97), contains two components:

- A statistical framework for the complete description of national education and learning systems
- A methodology that translates national educational programmes into an internationally comparable set of categories for the levels of education

Assessing 21st Century Skills

Assessing academic and vocational attainment can be complex enough, but addressing the newer 21st Century Skills will pose a different set of challenges. For example:

- One characteristic of 21st Century Skills demands is the being able to adapt to evolving circumstances and to make decisions and take action in unfamiliar situations. Judging someone's ability to deal with uncertainty represents a new challenge for curriculum and assessment.
- Standards and assessments will need to be largely performance-based. Students claiming to possess 21st Century Skills will need to demonstrate that they can integrate, synthesize and creatively apply content knowledge in novel situations. 21st Century Skills Assessments must therefore ask students to apply content knowledge to critical thinking, problem solving, and analytical tasks throughout their education.
- Successful learning is as much about the process as it is about facts and figures, so another aim of assessing 21st Century Skills is to make students' thinking visible. The assessments should provide insights into students' understandings and the conceptual strategies a student uses to solve a problem.

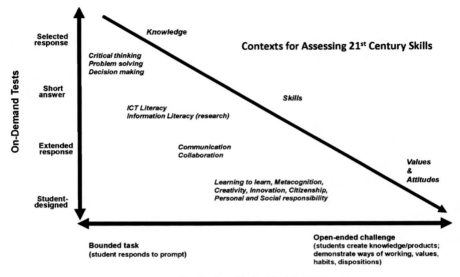

Figure 7. Assessing 21st Century Skills

In Figure 7, as one moves from knowledge towards demonstrations of skills, attitudes, values, the need for more open-ended and extended opportunities to demonstrate abilities increases. The most complex demonstrations of competencies—e.g. unstructured inquiry, problem solving, learning to learn, creativity, communication, collaboration, citizenship, and personal and social responsibility—must be examined in contexts that allow tackling larger-scale tasks over a longer period of time with more performance-based demonstrations.

Conclusion

We, the stakeholders in schooling, are a demanding lot! We want our schooling systems to deliver social cohesion and economic growth. We'd like the curriculum to be several times bigger than there are hours in the day to accommodate. We want our children to be well looked after, in secure and safe environments, and for them to become happy, healthy, prosperous, socially and environmentally responsible adults, capable of looking after us in our old age. We want them to evolve and become more relevant to the age that we live in whilst remaining fully operational. All of this at the lowest possible price, with evidence of performance, financial responsibility and regulatory conformity. Little wonder that our schooling systems struggle so much to meet these demands.

Case Studies

Lessons from Finland and Sweden

Finland and Sweden share a border, but apart from the fact that neither country practices selection, the organisation of their education systems couldn't be more different.

The Economist published an article comparing Sweden and Finland's schooling systems (*The Economist*, 2008) and highlighted the following points:

Finland

Finland routinely comes top, or occasionally second, in PISA tests of 15-year-olds' abilities in Reading, Mathematics and Science. This success has been put down to the following factors:

- Keeping the status of teachers high—in terms of pay, training and quality of management
- Finnish teachers are highly regarded and the very best young people compete for this coveted job
- Teachers study for at least five years and are given excellent teacher training
- Students take the PISA tests seriously, leaving very few questions blank
- Finnish children are good at tests because they get them in school all the time, to help them understand how they are doing
- In a country with harsh weather it is understood one has to work hard, so Finnish students pay attention and apply themselves to their learning
- Finnish children start formal schooling late and gently
- The Finnish education system doesn't have school inspections
- Ubiquity of print: "Almost every family has a newspaper delivered to the home," "and foreign language programmes are subtitled, not dubbed"

- Finns trust teachers and schools—"what Finnish schools do is genuinely effective"
- Finland invests heavily in special needs and does well by its weakest students.

There is no doubt that across a range of measures, the Finnish Schooling system has to rank amongst the top worldwide. The big question is how replicable the Finnish system is. Can a system based on "teacher knows best"; no choice; no school inspectors; practically unsackable teachers; and no published exam results work in other countries?

It's also important to ask whether success in PISA is a true measure of whether a schooling system is successful or not. The PISA organisation itself acknowledges that the skills that matter are changing so evaluation and assessment need to change as well (Schleicher, 2009).

Countries looking to replicate the Finnish model will need to invest very heavily in the teacher workforce and make teaching a highly desirable career choice. Many would have additional investments to make in developing positive cultural attitudes to hard work and learning.

Sweden

The Swedish model, on the other hand, represents a more market lead approach. In the 1990s it introduced private competition into its state-education system. This allowed new privately funded schools to receive the same amount for each learner as the state would have spent on that child. Independent schools are funded by the state through a "voucher" scheme. For each learner an independent school teaches, it receives what the local government would have spent educating the learner in one of its own schools. Independent schools cannot charge anything extra, and must accept all students who apply. Crucially, providing they follow Sweden's national curriculum, they can innovate freely.

Sweden's market-driven system has enabled schooling enterprises such as Kunskapsskolan to evolve. Kunskapsskolan is Sweden's biggest chain of independent schools (21 secondaries and 9 gymnasiums). It operates internationally too, and has recently been awarded a contract to open two "academies"—independent state schools—in the UK.

At Kunskapsskolan, the entire curriculum is posted on a website. Each week students agree on their goals for the next week, and the timetable of classes and lectures they will attend, individually, with a tutor. They do most of the work on their own. The following week their progress will be reviewed.

In Sweden, Education is considered a service industry and like all service industries, it has customers. According to Per Ledin, their CEO, for an independent schooling organisation like Kunskapsskolan to make a profit, they need to be popular, in the same way as it works for a hotel, which only makes money if it has guests in most rooms most nights.

The key point to this comparison is that a system should evolve according to the outcomes you want—what characteristics a country's schooling should be developing in its young people. Sweden aims to produce socially conscious generalists. The Finnish system, by contrast, drives at academic success.

3. LEVERS FOR IMPROVING SCHOOLING

"Give me a place to stand, and I shall move the earth"—Archimedes

The purpose of this chapter is to give you an understanding of the following:

- What are the levers that policy makers can pull to increase the effectiveness of a schooling system?
- Where resources should be prioritised to get maximum effect
- How time can be used to much better effect
- What relevant tools and methods can be borrowed from business
- The importance of accountability and transparency
- How the learning process can be accelerated.

The key points made in this chapter are:

- Increasing funding is not in itself sufficient to increase effectiveness
- The quality of the workforce is a critical factor in improving the effectiveness of schooling
- Managing performance is crucial for driving change and improving outcomes
- The status of teachers needs to be raised, but teaching also needs to become much more like a profession and less like a trade
- A standards-based curriculum is an essential foundation for schooling
- New understandings of learning and how to speed it up should be exploited
- The role of content, and who produces it, should be re-thought
- Personalising the learning experience is an essential component of increasing effectiveness
- Involving parents and the wider community in student's learning is an effective way to improve outcomes.

C hapter 2 will have given us a clearer idea about what we want from our schooling system, so let us now turn to the question of how we make schooling more effective. A big problem that we have is that most of the studies in this area have been based on the system as it currently is.

For example, in 2007 McKinsey published a report on 'How the world's best-performing school systems come out on top' (Barber, 2007). The report identifies three factors that they suggest are common to the high-performing school systems:

- Getting the right people to become teachers
- Developing them into effective instructors
- Ensuring the system is able to deliver the best possible instruction for every child.

It also concluded that:

- Equality of an education system cannot exceed the quality of these teachers
- The only way to improve the outcome is to improve instruction.

This is a bit like saying, to get the best performance from a ship, you need only to get the best possible crew and ensure that they excel in handling the rigging. However, faster, better ships came from fitting them with modern engines and changing the materials used in their construction. Of course, the performance of a ship at sea is a function of the quality of its crew—but that is not the *only* factor.

Whilst teaching obviously plays a key part in learning, it's far from the full story. Learning is in everything everywhere. Students are only in formal learning for about 15% of any one year, and that for the remaining time they are mostly still learning. Learning is about intrinsic curiosity; finding things out for yourself; collaborating with others; play and experimentation; re-applying knowledge in new contexts; face to face interaction; collaboration and group interaction. Increasingly, formal learning is now available beyond the school gates. The idea that learning is *just* a function of teaching, and at that learning can only come from teachers is nonsense.

So instead of looking at current generation high-performing schools, we need to take a much wider view, and look at those factors that affect the effectiveness of schooling from both outside and within.

Resourcing

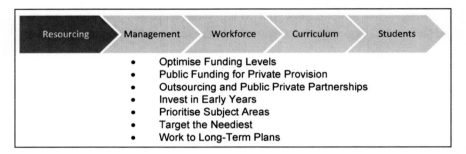

One of the most common objections to doing anything new in schooling is "we don't have enough money". Demands on schooling systems are growing—driven by the move towards knowledge-based economies. At the same time demands for schooling opportunities are also growing, driven by individuals wanting to prepare themselves for a globally competitive world. But the plain truth is that there will never be enough money in the public purse to fund everything that everyone wants schooling to do.

So the choices are clear—achieve more with the same or less, or find new ways to bring money into the system.

Optimise Funding Levels

The overall amount of investment in education varies greatly between countries. Even among countries with similar levels of GDP per capita there can be substantial differences. For example, Greece and Portugal have roughly similar levels of GDP but Portugal devotes a share to education that is one third greater. In most OECD countries, the share of investment falls in the range of 4.5 to 6.5 % of GDP, regardless of the level of GDP per capita (OECD UNESCO, 2002).

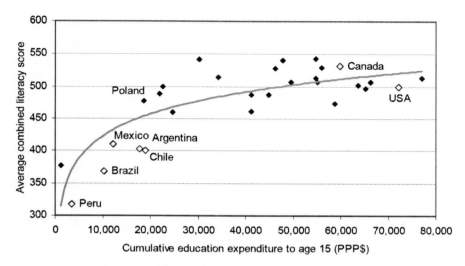

**Figure 8. PISA combined literacy performance and expenditure to age 15,
Source, OECD/UNESCO-UIS, 2003.**

Whilst the amount of money that is spent on schooling is not in itself a determinant of outcome, levels of investment in schooling matter. For example, Figure 8 shows a clear correlation between expenditure and literacy rates.

However, education services are provided at very different costs in different parts of the world—clearly, teachers' salaries and other costs vary greatly between countries. And there are also significant differences between the costs per student at different phase of education. For example, the average cost per student for secondary education in OECD countries is $5,501 which goes up to $11,109 (50%) per student for tertiary education (UNESCO, 2006). But for Brazil it leaps to 1200% whilst their neighbours, Uruguay, see a 75% increase. This is significant for policy makers who have to choose whether to provide tertiary education for one more Brazilian student or to expand access to 12 students at the secondary level (OECD UNESCO, 2002).

The foundation for education expenditure is universal primary schooling, but once this is accomplished, the way in which additional money is spent makes a huge difference to effectiveness.

Take the US for example. Figure 8 shows that whilst the US invests much more than average in schooling, literacy levels aren't significantly higher than Poland who spend roughly ¼ of what the US does. McKinsey & Company go further: "The United States spends more than any other country per point on PISA Mathematics test"... "Yet in 2006 the United States ranked 25th of 30 nations in Math" (McKinsey & Company, 2009). This shows that whilst overall levels of expenditure are important, *how* that money is spent really matters.

Whilst few would dispute that investment in schooling leads to multiple benefits—the World Bank calls it the "single most important key to development and poverty alleviation"—there is also constant downward pressure on public expenditure, so it's crucial to direct spending at the areas that have the biggest and most relevant impact. Worldwide finance-driven reforms seek to reduce the amount of money spent on education whilst improving outcomes. In schooling, this is about leading financial, human and technological resources to achieve ever improving outcomes.

Public Funding for Private Provision

The key question that governments face is how you provide compulsory, free schooling for the widest possible population, at the highest possible quality, with the highest levels of consistency and within a finite public sector budget. At times of rapid growth of the school age population, this can be a particular challenge but, even through periods of relative demographic and economic stability, no government can afford to disregard the private sector.

In one sense private sector involvement in schooling is virtually unavoidable. Students and families pay considerable amounts towards education even if their children don't attend private schools. Books, computers, pens, paper, trips, uniforms, private tuition, etc., all add up to significant private sector economic activity and subsidy to publically funded schooling systems. How the state regulates the role of the private sector in schooling has significant implications for the delivery and quality of educational services and, especially, for the equitable distribution of access to learning opportunities.

According to the OECD and UNESCO, private schools can represent between 3 and 57% of the upper secondary sectors in WEI countries. Most countries use public funds to support independent and private schooling in order to improve the equitable distribution of schooling opportunities and to drive efficiencies through competition for resources. The overall balance between public and private funding varies widely by level of education and type of school, and also varies considerably between countries. For example, the proportion of public expenditure used to subsidize private education amounts to 4% in the United States, and almost 12% in France (OECD UNESCO, 2002).

There are several different models for channelling public funds into independent schooling systems, for example:

- Direct funding to independent schools
- Vouchers
- Grants and Cash Transfers
- Conditional Cash Transfers

Many countries provide public funding directly to independent and private schools. One well known independent schooling system financed through the public funding is the Charter School movement in the United States. Primary and secondary Charter Schools are free from some of the rules, regulations, and statutes that apply to other public schools in exchange for a degree of accountability. However, it's far from clear whether they are more successful than other types of schools in the United States.

On the other hand, New Zealand—which has one of the highest PISA ranked schooling systems in the world—seems to have successfully integrated independent schools into its state funded schooling system.

Since 1980, the education system in Chile has provided financial resources to public and government-dependent private schools through a voucher system. Voucher payments are based on the number of students attending school; the time students spend at school, the geographic area in which the school is located and the level of education. Since 1994, both public and private schools have been allowed to generate revenues on their own initiative. Both can charge for tuition while receiving a subsidy, but the amount of the subsidy will depend on the average fees charged to students (OECD UNESCO, 2002).

Several WEI countries make grants for schooling directly available to students and their families to receive schooling. In 1999, the OECD average of just over 10% of public education expenditure was spent on grants.

Community Grants are grants given to a group of students and linked to attendance in a community-created institution. The amount of money is typically based on the number of students. Targeted Bursaries are funds that are transferred direct to schools, municipalities or provinces for specific purposes such as improving the curriculum or increasing school access for minority, indigenous or poor children. Grants can be made to private schools to pay for or subsidise bursaries which in turn help the families pay school fees; or indeed, grants for the same purpose can be made directly to the families themselves.

In the Philippines, Fund for Assistance to Private Education (FAPE) enabled secondary students in overcrowded public schools to enrol in private schools. The state paid tuition fees to the private institution at a rate not exceeding the cost per student in public schools. More than 200,000 secondary students were supported by this scheme in 1998/99.

Conditional Cash Transfer (CCT) programmes are a popular tool for improving the education outcomes of poor children in developing countries such as Brazil, Honduras, Nicaragua, Turkey and Mozambique. Many of these programmes are modelled on the Mexican PROGRESA. In a typical CCT, mothers from poor backgrounds receive cash conditional on school. According to the Institute of Fiscal Studies, this has "substantially increased the school attendance of 12- to 17-year-olds in Columbia (Orazio Attanasio, 2005).

Outsourcing and Public Private Partnerships

The core business of schooling is to educate children, so outsourcing those functions that are not core to this mission makes a lot of sense. For example, it would be ridiculous to expect a school to generate its own electricity or make its own furniture. Whilst both may be within the realms of the school's possibility, it would be wholly inefficient for the school to focus on these activities.

In the corporate world, outsourcing is normal practice. The primary benefit is cost saving, which is achieved through using customised services which are delivered through standardised processes at scale. For example, if a set of IT services used by two separate organisations have a significant number of common elements (e.g. HR processes), it makes sense for the two organisations to buy a tailored version of the service from a third party, which effectively pools the costs of the common elements. Other benefits include being able to have a Service Level Agreement enforced by contract; transfer of risk; access to knowledge, expertise, and talent.

The introduction of ICT into schools accelerated discussions about outsourcing. Computing is increasingly becoming as ubiquitous as running water or electricity. There is no reason why computing services should eventually be viewed any differently to any other utility and outsourced.

Private Finance Initiatives (PFIs) are about the public and private sectors working together in Public/Private Partnerships (PPPs). These are essentially agreements that will bring benefits to both sectors. The private sector expects to earn a return on performing outsourced services and the investments that they may need to make to carry this out. The public sector wants to deliver services to specified standards and to make the best use of public resources.

Central to PFI is a shift in focus away from the public sector purchase of capital assets to the purchase of services associated with those assets. Payment by the public sector for those services is based on the performance of the private sector operator against agreed criteria.

In some countries, some schooling services are outsourced to the private sector. In the UK, for example, Education consultants Nord Anglia and support services company Amey were awarded a £200m contract to run a range of services for 92 schools in the London Borough of Waltham Forest for five years. The contract covered:

- Direct learner services incorporating welfare and special needs
- School development and review, including performance monitoring and development planning
- Literacy and numeracy strategies
- Core support services such as financial management, human resources and information technology.

The work involved in a school or authority owning and maintaining property and buildings contributes nothing to the core mission of providing a schooling service. The real estate taken up by a typical secondary school in the developed world could account for tens of millions of dollars capital, and significant operational costs. But the returns on that asset are restricted to the school day—around 17% of the year. In many cases a better solution would be for schools to sell property and rent back what they need, and find ways to derive additional revenues from facility use outside standard school hours.

Under Public Private Partnerships it's common for an organisation that specialises in this property development and management to own or lease a property and to provide a set of services to an agreed standard to a schooling operation. This happens most often when a new school is being built, or an old school is being rebuilt. A school or authority selling its property to a service provider, who in effect rents it back to them, creates a pool of capital that can be used in a range of different ways. The spectrum of approaches to PPP is vast—for example, The National College of School Leadership's new "Models of Leadership" includes no fewer than 60 case studies of innovative and entrepreneurial partnerships.

Invest in Early Years

The key to macro level outcomes is macro level targeting of funding to the right places and activities. Take one policy decision that arguably matters more than most—relative spend across different phases of education.

Nobel Prize winner James Heckman, quoted by the National Conference on State Legislatures, concluded that investment in early years education has a much higher impact on human capital than investments in later phases.

"Because skills are accumulated, starting early and over time, investing in young children is an investment in future productivity. Early education and other early interventions can mitigate the effects of poor family environments. Key workforce skills such as motivation, persistence and self-control are developed early."

Heckman concludes that K-12 schooling comes too late, and other remedies are prohibitively costly as well (e.g., job training programmes...) (National Conference on State Legislatures, 2010). This would suggest re-thinking, or even reversing, the current model where the highest rewards and prestige tend to go to those teaching at the highest levels of education.

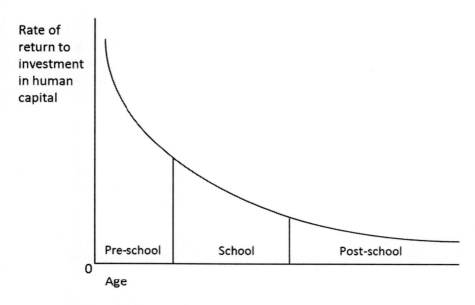

Figure 9. Heckman and Masterov. The Productivity Argument for Investing in Young Children, October 2004.

Prioritise Subject Areas

In the same way that there is limited funding available from the public purse, there is also limited time in the school day into which to squeeze the curriculum. This means that prioritising what gets learned is of enormous importance. Writing in *EducationNext*, Hanushek, Jamison, Woessmann, Jamison, and Ludger concluded that it's not just going to school, but learning something worthwhile that matters most.

> "…But it's not just as simple as providing more schooling. The impact of improved cognitive skills, as measured by the performance of students on Math and Science tests, is considerably larger [than just time spent in school]. When we performed the analysis again, this time also including the average test-score performance of a country in our model, we found that countries with higher test scores experienced far higher growth rates. If one country's test-score performance was 0.5 standard deviations higher than another country during the 1960s … that country's growth rate was, on average, one full percentage point higher annually over the following 40-year period than lower educationally performing country's

growth rates. Further, once the impact of higher levels of cognitive skills are taken into account, the significance for economic growth of additional years of schooling, dwindles to nothing. A country benefits from asking its students to remain in school for a longer period of time only if the students are learning something as a consequence."

Target the Neediest

Learners from more privileged socio-economic backgrounds (in terms of parents' education, occupational status or household wealth) and those with access to books consistently perform better than those from poorer backgrounds or with limited access to reading materials. Learning disparities in Reading, Mathematics and Science among 15-year-olds are also related to immigrant status, language spoken at home and family structure such as two-parent or non-two-parent households.

African and Latin American assessments find strong disparities in favour of urban students, reflecting both higher household incomes and better school provision in urban areas (UNESCO, 2008).

Targeting educational expenditures towards the neediest could also have a strong impact on learning through closing the gap between socio-economic groups. There already are a number of such programmes. For example, a variety of programmes ranging from television programmes to targeted tuition to conditional cash transfers have shown to have an impact in Latin American countries including Brazil, Chile, Mexico, and Columbia (UNESCO, 2006).

Work to Long-Term Plans

Short termism can cause significant difficulties for developing schooling systems and make change more expensive in the longer run. Very often, politicians and their civil servants seek "quick wins" to gain favour with voters. For example, many 1:1 access laptop programmes have been set up with no or little consideration for how the devices are assimilated into the schooling system— e.g. how teachers would be trained, how basic infrastructures would be set up, etc. This inevitably leads to dissatisfaction and has the knock-on effect of making people less willing to take risks. Another problem is turnover of staff in Ministries of Education. Politicians new in post will frequently change ministry staff, losing expertise and continuity. Significant, meaningful structural change takes a long time. Building new schools, for example, can take four years or more from conception to completion.

However, it's possible to make short-term, visible gains that contribute to a longer term strategy by carefully planning each stage and organising complementary work streams that run in parallel. The Government of Queensland, Australia, have a 21-step process for implementing ICT that involves training, curriculum change, infrastructure and learning space development, which all happen before they then provide staff and students with mobile computing. Phasing-in these steps so they occur in parallel ensures that full implementation can happen within two years, but overall the modernisation of schooling in Queensland is a long-term project that transcends short-term political cycles.

Management

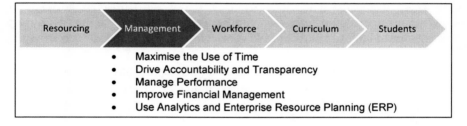

Maximise the Use of Time

Strategic financial and human resource management starts with maximising the use of time—the most critical resource available to managers.

Whilst just being in school isn't sufficient in itself for effective learning, the actual amount of time students are present in school does impact on learning performance. According to UNESCO the time actually spent learning specific subjects, either in school or through homework, positively affects performance, especially in Languages, Mathematics and Science (*Education for All by 2015, Will we make it?* UNESCO).

Many students, especially in developing countries, do not get enough time to learn even the most basic skills. Additionally, governments pay for schools to be open and for teachers to be teaching a given number of instructional hours per year, but the utilisation of this resource varies greatly across different schooling systems.

In the United States, a fierce policy debate has raged over President Obama's advocacy of students spending more time in the classroom. The argument against this centres on the fact that students in the U.S. spend more hours in school (1,146 instructional hours per year) than do students in the Asian countries that persistently outscore the U.S. on Maths and Science tests (Associated Press, 2009). On the other hand, as discussed in detail by Malcolm Gladwell, there are cultural and linguistic reasons why Asian countries outperform not just the US but much of the rest of the world in Maths. Gladwell also cites the success of the KIPP (Knowledge Is Power Programme—www.kippny.org) as being attributable to 50-60% more learning time (Gladwell, 2009). A reasonable conclusion is that the length of time spent in class is likely to have an effect on learning—but only if that time isn't wasted.

Many argue that parts of the long Summer, Easter and Christmas holidays—a throwback to agricultural times—should be used for formal learning. However, there is scope to both add days *and* add contact time in the "standard" school year.

In the example shown in Table 7, if we add 30 extra days and 60 minutes additional daily contact time we gain an additional 24% over a "standard" school year of 200 days at 6hr 40min per day.

"Standard" school year in minutes	200 days x 400 mins = 80,000 mins
Increase number of school days in the year by 30	230 days x 400 mins = 92,000 mins
Add 60 minutes contact time per day	230 days x 460 mins = 105,800 mins
Increase as a percentage of time available in a school year	24%

Table 7. Example of effects of making changes to the school year.

However, just adding time is not necessarily the smartest approach – it's how time is used that matters most. In the same way as having more money doesn't necessarily translate into results, it's how resources are *used* that counts. So let's now take a closer look at how time is spent in a standard schooling system.

Learning is a matter of intensity of engagement, not elapsed time. However, the timetable is the fundamental organising instrument of everyday life of schools. For secondary students and teachers, the division of school time into 'periods', the beginning and end of which is marked by the ringing of a bell, is taken-for-granted. The origins of the secondary timetable can be traced to the "Carnegie Unit", early in the last century in the United States. A Carnegie Unit was defined as a year-long course of five periods a week—each "period" being fifty to fifty-five minutes long. The Carnegie Unit system of academic time-keeping and the division of teachers into faculty departments provided a neat framework at the time.

Thanks to the Carnegie Unit, the bell rings, the corridor fills up like rush hour on the metro; students get to their classrooms, they get out their books and settle down. They start learning and then the bell rings again and the cycle starts over—again and again and again… Does this *really* make sense? Is it the best possible use of our time in schools? Will spending increasing amounts of time in a system organised like this really make as much difference as it could?

Developed Country Example

Let's look at a typical secondary schooling system's use of time. We'll focus on the UK for this example. A typical UK secondary school day is structured as follows (TeachingintheUK):

	Timetabled lesson time	Time out of lessons
09.00—9.20am Morning Registration or Assembly		20
09.20—10.00am Period 1	40	
10.00—10.40 Period 2	40	
10.40—11.00am Break		20
11.00—11.40am Period 3	40	
11.40—12.20 Period 4	40	
12.20—13.20 Lunch		60
13.20—13.40pm Afternoon Registration		20
13.40—14.20 Period 5	40	
14.20—15.00pm Period 6	40	
15.00—15.40pm Period 7	40	
Total:	280	120
	70%	30%

Table 8. How time is spent in a typical school day—part 1

The 6hr and 40 min (400 minute) day is broken into small chunks. During this time, the total percentage of time spent formally engaged in learning is 70% of the school day.

Let's now add some realism to this scenario. Children don't just magically appear in lessons as the bell announcing the changeover between each period rings. Let's assume that the children move to a new classroom each time. There are long corridors to negotiate, distractions along the way, and lining up to do once children arrive at their destination classroom. So let's estimate 5 minutes per changeover and only count changeovers that happen between consecutive lessons. That time has to come from somewhere, so we take it off the next lesson.

	Timetabled lesson time	Time out of lessons	Movements between lessons
09.00— 9.20am Morning Registration or Assembly		20	
09.20—10.00am Period 1	40		
10.00—10.40 Period 2	35		5
10.40—11.00am Break		20	
11.00—11.40am Period 3	40		
11.40—12.20 Period 4	35		5
12.20—13.20 Lunch		60	
13.20—13.40pm Afternoon Registration		20	
13.40—14.20 Period 5	40		
14.20—15.00pm Period 6	35		5
15.00—15.40pm Period 7	35		5
Total:	260	120	20
	65%	30%	5%

Table 9. How time is spent in a typical school day—part 2

So now we're down to 65% actual formal learning time per day in timetabled lessons. This means that by design approximately 1/3rd of a typical school day is used for things other than learning. By the time that you take into account other disruptive factors associated with this mass movement during a school day, the effective formal learning time will be lower still.

We could carry on analysing time inefficiencies, considering factors such as absences and lateness etc. This kind of analysis leads to questions such as "why waste time with registration periods?"

Indeed, why assemble children in one class only to send them to another—a minimum of 200 times a year! Morning registration can happen in the first lesson of the day and, again, at the start of periods 2 and 3. Notices that would have otherwise been given out in registration time could be delivered via ICT.

Changing the length of lesson times in 'Block Scheduling' reduces the amount of movements across the school, and replaces walking between classrooms and disruptions to learning time.

Governments and authorities pay teacher salaries and school expenses regardless of time, so the inefficient use of time costs money to governments—and therefore tax payers. The issue is particularly serious when resources are few.

"Deputy Head Jonathan Boyle outlines the timetable in use in Walsall Academy. The day is divided into three sections: morning, afternoon and after school. The morning and afternoon programmes last for approximately three hours. The advantages for a teacher are that they are with students for a period of time that allows them to monitor progress and build deeper relationships. The advantage for a student is that they can engage in a range of activities in that time period—they don't just work on one topic for three hours. They are engaged in a range of diverse tasks and obviously personalised learning is a big part of this.

As in the primary schools, changing timetable changes the pedagogy. No one can lecture a group for that length of time and teachers can spend real time with students who need it. Jonathan explains: 'At the beginning of the lesson is the exposition where you can share with all the students what the aims and objectives are for the day. They know the objectives: the route they choose to get there is largely dependent on them. They know where they can get the resources for a new task because everything is online and they are empowered to make those decisions. I don't mind as long as they get an outcome. This all lends itself to mixed ability teaching. Teachers can interact with all the students over a three-hour period, can sit with them and record what they are doing. We have an effective recording system; we share progress on a report to parents over a three- or four-week period.'

There are other benefits. 'What we have got is a smoothly running school because we have reduced the amount of movement around the school. A lot of time can be wasted in a school day. We don't need any bells. All the staff shares the same vision. We have challenging students here who would probably react badly in other schools. We can cater for students who require more intensive attention, we can look after them better; engage them more'."
(Futurelab, 2006)

Developing Country Example

The economics of classroom time and how to measure classroom "time on task" were recently addressed by the World Bank. The study entitled *The Economics of Classroom Time* (Abadzi, 2003) illustrates schooling inefficiencies with the following example:

Take a legal requirement to deliver 700—1000 total instructional hours per year. This time is reduced by extended holidays, floods; strikes; examinations, etc. In Mali, for example, this represents about 30% of all possible school days. Now reduce the time further through teacher absence—in some parts of India this could be as much as 25% of the time. Now factor-in student absence—in Bangladesh, for example, this could be as much as 50%. The amount of contact time then is where both students' and teachers' presence intersect.

Now consider engagement on learning task within that contact time. For example, students may spend time copying, left unattended or being disciplined, etc., so that the actual in-class time on task may be as low as 15-25%. What is shocking is that the cumulative efficiency of the education systems may be as low as 7% in some countries! As in developed countries, there is no one single easy answer, but making appropriate investments aimed at improving schooling systems holistically—including maximising opportunities for unsupervised schooling—is the only way to approach this problem.

> "If we evaluated how much time a student is actually engaged in learning activities in each of our classrooms, what percentage would that be? Is it 100 percent? Is it 50 percent? Or is it only 25 percent? If we want students to really learn, we, as educators, have to plan for, facilitate, and vigilantly protect our increasingly precious engaged student learning time.

> "Other elements of instruction time we must consider are the things that steal it away from us. Some "time robbers" are of our own doing, while others are interruptions that occur because schools are full of people who need things. Common self-made time robbers include taking roll, lunch counts, passing out papers, and waiting for students to line up, be quiet, or pay attention.

"Others we sometimes don't think about as much are transition times between activities or subjects, instructions dictated to students who should know the routine, poorly designed discipline procedures, poor communication of the day's activities to students, students not being involved in reaching daily goals and objectives, and lack of teacher preparation for student learning activities. There probably are more, but these are sufficient to show that in a typical classroom, we waste extraordinary amounts of time for one reason or another" (Cross, 2005).

Drive Accountability and Transparency

Accountability is a contentious area when applied to schooling. This is because it is often associated with answerability, blameworthiness and liability. Yet accountability is a key lever for achieving learning goals and reducing wasted time.

There are two different views of the role of accountability in education change. One seeks to induce change through extrinsic rewards and sanctions on the assumption that the fundamental problems or lack of will to change on the part of the workforce. The other view seeks to induce change by building knowledge among the school community about alternative methods, and re-thinking approaches. This view assumes that the fundamental problem is lack of knowledge combined with a lack of organisational capacity for change. (Earl, 2006)

In schooling, accountability starts with an acknowledgement that anyone in receipt of public funding—in the form of salary or budget—is accountable to the tax-paying public for how that money is spent. Accountability is about responsibility for actions, services, decisions, and policies including the administration, governance, and implementation within the scope of the role or employment position. It involves the obligation to report, explain and be answerable for resulting outcomes. It should encompass the following:

- Accountability for management's actions
- Accountability for learning performance
- Fiscal accountability
- Transparency in operations and selection of and disclosure of policies
- Board/policymaking body members, as appropriate
- Independence in internal and external audits
- Protection of stakeholder interests, as appropriate.

Core to the concept of accountability in schooling is taking responsibility for the learning outcomes of students. To achieve this, schooling systems need what Michael Fullan calls "cultures of evaluation". "One of the highest yield strategies for educational change recently developed is 'Assessment for Learning'. When school systems increase their collective capacity to engage in ongoing assessment for learning, major improvements are achieved" (Fullan, *Learning to Lead Change*, 2004). Key aspects of assessment for learning are:

- Gathering data on student learning
- Analysing data for more detailed understanding
- Developing action plans based on data in order to make improvements
- Being able to discuss performance with parents, external groups.

Jim Collins (2002) found in 'great' organizations a commitment to 'confronting the brutal facts', and establishing a culture of disciplined inquiry.

In schooling systems this can be achieved through school-based self-appraisal, benchmarking value-add against other schools, and exposing accurate data showing performance against collectively agreed indicators back to the tax-paying public.

Manage Performance

Performance management has always been a contentious issue in education, but in business it's a standard method for the effective delivery of strategic and operational goals. There is a clear and immediate correlation between using performance management results.

In business, performance management improves employee engagement because everyone understands how they are directly contributing to the organisations high level goals. It enables professional development programmes to be better aligned directly to achieving organisational goals. It also enables improved management control aligned and responsive to management needs.

Improve Financial Management

A wide variety of management actions can be taken to help ensure the highest possible value is derived from investments in schooling.

These could include, for example, financing institutions on the basis of outputs (students completing their course) rather than inputs (numbers of teachers); differential financing depending on the extent to which institutions have challenging circumstances; employing business managers to help institutions to seek additional sources of financing from the private sector as well as through cost recovery; strengthening review of performance; and publishing of information on the quality of institutions' performance.

Improving financial management is also about making sure that financial systems are complaint with the highest standards of financial accountability, GAAP (Generally Accepted Accounting Principles) and completely transparent.

Financial management should cover the following:

- Fiscal health evidenced in the "Fund Balance"
- Low variance between budgeted revenues and expenditure
- Audit issue resolution—drive actions from prior year audit findings
- Management of the acquisition and capacity to service debt
- Ensure optimal compensation to workforce
- Risk management—containing insurance premium and claim costs
- Drive funding to where it most impacts learning
- Control administrative expenses.

The UK Government has a system of mandatory requirements to provide assurance to a range of stakeholders that schools have proper arrangements in place to manage their resources effectively. *Financial Management Standard in Schools* (FMSiS) embodies a set of principles that are transferable into schooling systems as well as individual schools.

Some of the key requirements that schools must demonstrate in order to meet the required FMSiS are:

- Competence at handling finance
- Legally binding accountability for the appropriate use of resources
- Systems for ensuring integrity and dealing with conflicts of interest and reporting misconduct
- Resources have been properly managed
- Effective governance arrangements covering issues of misconduct

- The school has:
    - o Realistic and affordable budgets aligned to the school development plan
    - o Comparison of financial performance with that of similar schools.

(Department for Children Schools and Families, 2009)

Use Analytics and Enterprise Resource Planning (ERP)

Understanding exactly where to invest resource is crucial to making schooling more efficient. The worldwide financial crisis has forced governments to scrutinise public expenditure on schooling, and to drive for maximum impact for every dollar spent.

The use of analytics systems can support "precision spending"—i.e. precisely targeting resources and understanding returns on investment. Imagine a schooling system that has extremely low Science scores. One approach could be to throw resources across the entire system in a national Science programme aimed at raising Science standards. A better approach is to use analytics to deeply understand the causes of the problem and then to use this information to remediate it. Out of the thousands of potential contributory factors, analytics could help identify those factors that have the biggest impact on the results, and enable much more precisely targeted resourcing to address those. The net is raised standards at a fraction of the cost.

Resource management is about improving the "back office" functions, making the internal workings of the organisation more efficient. A Resource Management or Enterprise Resource Planning (ERP) system usually includes financial, supply chain and human resource management sub-systems, together with analytical and programme management tools.

Traditionally schooling systems have computerised their functions in a piecemeal fashion. As a result, most schooling systems have a plethora of different systems, using different information structures, so that each fulfils different tasks. For example, a typical schooling system could have tens of different databases holding basic student record data. Each of these has to be separately maintained, often with its own administrative function, with huge scope for confusion and duplication.

Many systems have different HR systems for different departments and where they do have a single system, it's not necessarily integrated with recruitment, training and payroll functions. Many have different suppliers for their General Ledger, Accounts Payable and Accounts Receivable systems. This makes commitment and accrual accounting cumbersome, and makes it much more difficult to implement e-ordering and e-procurement. ERP provides a unified view of the organisation and its resources—a single view of the "truth." It provides the ability to track, route, analyse and report on the use of resources on an organisation-wide basis.

Economies of scale, in terms of reduced administration, maintenance and training, accrue from consistent business processes and a consolidated technology platform. Common security and information management tools provide improved integrity of data, better business intelligence, increased internal control and significantly reduced potential for fraud. An integrated solution facilitates more coherent and better coordinated planning, and speeds up reporting and scheduled and unscheduled procedures.

Workforce

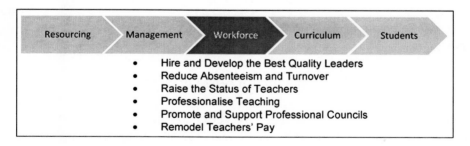

| Resourcing | Management | Workforce | Curriculum | Students |

- Hire and Develop the Best Quality Leaders
- Reduce Absenteeism and Turnover
- Raise the Status of Teachers
- Professionalise Teaching
- Promote and Support Professional Councils
- Remodel Teachers' Pay

"If you don't like change, you are going to like irrelevance even less."
General Eric Shinseki, United States Secretary of Veterans Affairs

Clearly, capacity and motivation of a schooling system workforce will be one of the biggest factors in the success of a schooling organisation.

The schooling workforce is mostly made up of teachers or ex-teachers. There are about 55m teachers worldwide and the number is rising. The number of primary teachers has increased globally from 25.8 million in 1999 to 27.8 million in 2007, according to data released by the UIS.

However, simply adding more teachers isn't necessarily going to make a significant impact. According to Beare (Beare, *Creating the Future School*, 2001), the average cost of teachers is rising above inflation—in part due to the increase in the qualifications needed to become a teacher. Therefore adding more teachers to a schooling system is an expensive way to improve results unless accompanied by a set of measures that improve effectiveness.

In the UK, staffing on average absorbs about 80 per cent of schools' budgets, so the use and deployment of staff is a vital consideration in looking at effectiveness and efficiency in schools.

In improving the effectiveness of the workforce there are six key levers:

- Reducing absenteeism and turnover
- Raising status
- Professionalising teaching
- Changing the mix
- Encouraging the best teachers to work with the youngest students
- Managing performance.

Driving these requires strong leadership.

Hire and Develop the Best Quality Leaders

Jim Collins in *Good to Great* (Collins, 2001) compared "good" companies—strong performance here and there—and "great" companies—those with sustained high performance over a minimum of fifteen years. He found that good companies had good managers who drive performance to a vision and standards, but great companies had 'Executive Leaders' who build enduring greatness. School leaders are no longer expected to be merely good managers. School leadership is increasingly viewed as key to large-scale education reform and to improved educational outcomes.

Motivating people—teachers and students—to work towards goals is the primary task of schooling leaders. The key is creating the conditions in which both teaching and learning become intrinsically motivated.

The OECD set out the following principles for redefining school leadership responsibilities for improved student learning:

- Strategic financial and human resource management
- Supporting, evaluating and developing teacher quality
- Goal-setting, assessment and accountability
- Collaborating with other schools.

The OECD also advocates making school leadership an attractive profession by:

- Professionalising recruitment
- Focus on the relative attractiveness of school leaders' salaries
- Acknowledge the role of professional organisations of school leaders
- Provide options and support for skill and career development.

(OECD, 2008)

Reduce Absenteeism and Turnover

Where the status of teachers is low, there are high levels of absenteeism and turnover. For example, there is 25% absence in some areas of India (Abadzi, 2003), and in Brazil in schools run by state governments 13% of all school days were lost owing to absent teachers in 2006 (The Economist, 2009). Many African schools cannot conform to the official school year due to teacher turnover and late teacher vacancy postings (UNESCO, 2008).

Teachers daily fight uphill battles against overcrowded, factory-like classrooms and assembly-line lessons. It's no wonder that absenteeism is so high. Because there are so many teachers, absenteeism is an extremely expensive drain on schooling systems.

Take, for example, a schooling system with 100k teachers each costing $50k—a 10% absenteeism rate represents a $0.5bn drain on the system. Every percentage point cut from absenteeism effectively adds $50m of value, or an additional 1,000 teachers, back into the system.

Like absenteeism, staff turnover also represents a serious drain on the efficiency of a schooling system.   An estimate for the cost of a member of staff being replaced in industry is approximately one year's salary (Stanford, 1996), but let's be optimistic and say that in education it takes just one term (1/3 year) for the teacher to come fully "up to speed" in a new school. Let's also disregard the fact that some won't be replaced within their notice period. If the same schooling system as above with 100k teachers experiences a (conservative) 10% staff turnover (10,000), it would be the equivalent of losing around "3,000 man years". At $50k per man-year, that's a loss of $150m. Every percentage point cut from turnover effectively adds $15m of value, or an additional 300 teachers, back into the system.

This represents a strong argument for shifting the salary budget to reward staff who attend work regularly and give long service to the same institution, and to help those who persistently spend the least amount of time in work to move into careers where their physical presence is less important. Reallocating budget to cut absenteeism and turnover by just 1% enables a system with 100k teachers to gain the equivalent of 1,300 teachers—enabling the same number of the lowest performing teachers to be helped to improve or find new occupations.

Raise the Status of Teachers

Finland is widely acknowledged as being the country that scores highest in PISA, and many attribute the high status of teachers there as a key driver of excellence.   Whilst teachers are paid reasonably well, it's their standing in society that makes each available post highly sought after. Generally, outside Finland, the status of teachers is lower and entry level for teaching is set lower than for most other professions and occupations.

Having a high status for the teaching profession has a number of key advantages, the main one being competition for jobs which ensures that the most motivated join the profession.

> "The teaching force suffers from a perceived lack of esteem especially in developing countries where a medical career rates as a far higher aspiration that a career as a classroom teacher. Many of the professional judgements of teachers are relatively undervalued by society, largely because those

judgements are hidden—policy tells teachers what to do, teachers rarely directly influence policy. The recruitment of teachers worldwide suffers from this so that it is both hard to attract, and to retain, the best teachers. Judgement about the complexity of learning is undervalued because teachers are not seen as people with authoritative views."

(Heppell, *Professional Doctorate for All Teachers*)

Raising the status of teachers doesn't only mean raising the entry bar. It also means getting the public to appreciate the skills and knowledge involved in delivering sophisticated services to demanding customers, which in turn requires teachers' work to be exposed to wider audience through a range of media.

Professionalise Teaching

Teaching is moving from the characteristics of a trade towards the characteristics of a profession. In a relatively short time, teaching has been elevated from a certificated trade to a graduate profession—in the developed world at least. Compared to people in other occupations, teachers are generally very well qualified—it's not uncommon to find teachers with PhDs, Masters or two degrees on a school staff.

So what is considered professional teaching practice?

According to Beare (Beare, *Creating the Future School*, 2001), teachers are expected to:

- Have content knowledge about the courses he or she is teaching, and there is an expectation that this will be kept up to date. There is also an expectation that the teacher will be able to design programmes of learning and understand the learning theory behind the curriculum and all relevant policies.
- Know how to teach, be able to manage a class, understand different modes of learning, be able to deploy a range of learning and teaching methods, and increasingly be able to exploit technology.
- Regularly evaluate students' work; assess and benchmark; keep records; and report progress constructively and appropriately.
- Contribute constructively to the wider life of the school, formally and informally.

- • Be actively engaged with the teaching profession by participating in the professional development, contributing to the profession's knowledge and skill base, and by being available to assist in the growth of professional colleagues.

Where a real profession operates its work is characterised by a research-based service which is inquiry-driven. Prof Stephen Heppell, a leading figure in schooling modernization, argues for Professional Doctorates for all teachers:

"Most teachers already spend a significant proportion of their initial teaching development in what might be characterised as 'pragmatic micro-research'. They explore much: children's changed behaviour on windy days; their learning on Mondays compared perhaps to Fridays; their ability to handle open ended tasks; their complex behavioural needs, the personalisation of their learning, the impact of their differing intelligences and expectations, and so on."

"Good teachers internalise answers to many complex practical questions about how to teach well and this reflection is very much at a postgraduate level. However, typically schools don't learn so well; all the teachers in a school might be clear that children behave differently on windy days, but the school rarely learns well enough to create 'windy day timetables' for example! Reflective teachers become better teachers but schools do not necessarily improve. This existing reflection is important because it helps us to justify a 'faster track' route to the doctorate for teachers who also remain in full time work" (Heppell, *Professional Doctorate for All Teachers*).

Research and an expanding knowledge base inevitably lead to specialisation within a profession. Delivering professional services of high complexity is a "team sport", requiring sophisticated communication, collaboration and information technology skills. So, a teacher now needs to acquire the full range of 21st Century skills that we are now expecting students to acquire too. This is not only to help students acquire those skills, but to take full advantage of new technologies and modern management methods to deliver ever higher quality services.

Promote and Support Professional Councils

A profession tends to become differentiated, splitting into specialisations, each with its own pay structures. The Medical and Legal professions both exemplify this. If teaching is truly a profession, then the idea of a "standard" teacher is outdated, and teachers, therefore, should no longer expect to be remunerated in a standard way.

Professions tend to set up their own councils to promote best practice and their own acceptable levels performance. Registration and certification—the trades approach to work—is replaced by a code of practice and qualification standards.

So why do teachers tend to be members of trade unions rather than professional councils? The ability of unions to address short term issues and demands may have something to do with it. Teaching union leaders in France, for example, boast that they can put a million people in the streets of Paris to back their calls for bigger salaries and benefits. In terms of advancing the profession as a whole, teacher unions fall into two camps—progressive and obstructive. Obstructive unions are those that do little to help the longer term modernisation of schooling—which would ultimately elevate and open up opportunities for the profession, as has happened for doctors of medicine, for example.

A quick scan through some teacher trade union websites clearly shows where some of their energy is focussed:

- Preventing extending entitlement of education to the early years
- Stopping the introduction of a professional status for teachers specialising in early years
- Opposing the licensing of teachers
- Rejecting new frameworks for inspection.

In a democracy it's critical that matters of public interest are opposed as well as supported. But *just* opposing initiatives is not enough. Imagining a radically better schooling system, and helping put that vision into practice, is much harder—but that's what is needed to really advance schooling for *all* stakeholders.

Obstructive trade unions claim to represent the interests of teachers, but what they really represent is the teacher of the past—teachers practicing a "trade" in schools that operate as factories did in a bygone era. When perpetuating out-dated practices, they do nothing to increase the status of their members or ensure their long-term futures. Strikes don't help increase teacher status much either. Fortunately many unions are evolving into professional associations that offer increasingly sophisticated services for members. There is a clear role for professional organisations in a modernised schooling systems—but not for those organisations that don't link reward and quality of work; strive for the best outcomes for students and the system as a whole; and play a part in radically transforming schooling for the long term good of their members and evolution of the occupation they represent.

None of this amounts to an argument that says teachers should be without representation or endure unfulfilling work, poor conditions, or to be devalued as professionals. When these conditions occur, teachers are less likely to commit to new initiatives—which are against the interests of all stakeholders. Teachers are extremely important stakeholders, who need to be given a chance to break out of their boxes, given more status, reward, incentive, and opportunities to thrive in what should be a post-industrial age of schooling. Teachers should expect a lot from their unions.

Remodel Teachers' Pay

The goal of remodelling teachers' pay should be to attract and retain high quality professionals in an internationally competitive marketplace. To do this, teachers' pay should well reward good professional practice and outcomes, and offer the possibility of excellent incomes at the higher levels of the profession.

As a bureaucracy, a school has a pyramid of authority: the principal at the top, with descending tiers of seniority—from assistant principals, faculty department heads, year level co-ordinators and, finally, classroom teachers at the base level. Teachers are, in turn, often ranked by the number of years they have taught and are rewarded accordingly.

A common model is for teachers to start on a base salary which rises in annual increments.   But automatic pay increases provide no incentive to improve performance or take on additional responsibilities. Across the board pay increases cause an automatic escalation in outlay, often with no apparent benefit—i.e. the same service at a higher price with no demonstrable improvement in outcomes.

Teaching is now, in the developed world at least, largely a graduate profession, and teaching in the 21st Century should involve a far more sophisticated set of working practices than when it was merely a trade. Teachers should be able to design, produce and deliver learning programmes for which there are clear objectives, a negotiated appraisal scheme for outcomes, agreed pay for satisfactory delivery and a bonus scheme for superior delivery. In order to attract and retain the best, pay scales should be flexible and open, and student achievement should be the bottom line (Beare, *How to Pay Teachers in the 21st Century*, 2007).

Salary increases should not be about pacifying unions, but should be linked to better performance and accountability, starting with easily measured outcomes— such as reduced absenteeism—and continuing to more sophisticated measures of "value added". They should also be linked to learning standards and the cultural changes needed to transform schooling for the good of all stakeholders.

Curriculum

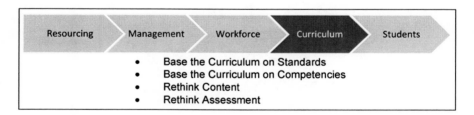

Resourcing   Management   Workforce   Curriculum   Students

- Base the Curriculum on Standards
- Base the Curriculum on Competencies
- Rethink Content
- Rethink Assessment

The word *curriculum* is derived from the Latin word for 'race course'—the course of learning experiences through which children grow to become mature adults. As with a physical race course, its quality and design is going to have a huge impact on the effectiveness of those racing on it. The curriculum defines the learning outcomes required from a schooling system, so there's no surprise that curriculum designers have to reconcile a range of conflicting forces, tensions and dilemmas.

One key dilemma is whether to have a standardised curriculum across a schooling system or not. On the one hand, there are strong arguments for having a curriculum that is open-ended and adapted to local needs, as opposed to it being linear and closed. On the other hand, there is equally a strong argument for having a curriculum that is sufficiently well defined for national or state level consensus about what counts as good or bad. It is, however, possible to have both. A core curriculum based on standards that everybody agrees on, can be applied at country level, whilst at the same time, schools can be given the freedom to add more open-ended and localised extensions.

Figure 10. The curriculum at Hermit Park School, Queensland, Australia, reflects environmental topics including water harvesting—crucial for students growing up in a drought area.

Base the Curriculum on Standards

No two countries have the same needs, and will therefore approach curriculum design in different ways. Some governments leave curriculum design and testing entirely to schools; other governments implement national testing or examination standards and allow schooling systems freedom to teach whatever they feel necessary to enable students to pass these; others have introduced prescriptive, standards based curricula with clear descriptors of what is expected from students.

There are many arguments both for and against large scale standards based curricula. The point is that if a government wants to have some control over the efficiency, effectiveness and relevance of its schooling system, then having standards based curricula is a key asset.

The purpose of standards based curricula is to have agreement between all stakeholders about what counts as meaningful learning outcomes. Only when everyone can agree on what counts as good or bad, acceptable or unacceptable, can meaningful discussions about improvements and developments take place.

Carr and Harris (Carr, 1996) explain the benefits of using standards for the following stakeholders:

- For **the state or country**, standards provide common reference points and a defined framework for national testing and comparison. With standards, governments can more accurately target investments and interventions.
- For **districts and schools**, standards provide the basis for data driven decision-making and planning.
- Standards enable **teachers** to make expectations clear to learners, which improves their learning. They help teachers design learning activities and assessment on the basis of what it is important to learn.
- For **students**, standards set clear performance expectations, helping them understand what they need to do in order to succeed.
- Standards communicate shared expectations for learning, so it enables **parents** to know how their children are progressing in their education, and how their progress compares to expected norms.

The English National Curriculum

The purpose of the English National Curriculum was to standardise the content taught across schools in order to enable assessment, which in turn enabled the compilation of league tables detailing the assessment statistics for each school. These league tables, together with the provision to parents of some degree of choice of the school for their child, were intended to encourage a 'free market' by allowing parents to choose schools based on their ability to teach the National Curriculum.

In England, there is a legal requirement for schools to deliver the National Curriculum. It applies to learners of compulsory school age in State Schools, and is organised on the basis of four "key stages".

- Key stage 1: Ages 5-7 (Years 1-2)
- Key stage 2: Ages 7-11 (Years 3-6)
- Key stage 3: Ages 11-14 (Years 7-9)
- Key stage 4: Ages 14-16 (Years 10-11).

The subjects that students have to be able to take at school are as follows:

Key stage 1 & 2 (5-11)	Key stage 3 (11-14)	Key stage 4 (14-16)
Art and Design	Art and Design	Citizenship
Design and Technology	Citizenship	English
English	Design and Technology	IT
Geography	English	Mathematics
History	Geography	Physical Education
IT (ICT)	History	Science
Mathematics	IT (ICT)	Careers Education
Music	Mathematics	Sex Education
Physical Education	Modern Foreign Languages	Work-Related Learning
Religious Education	Music	Religious Education
Science	Physical Education	
	Science	
	Sex Education	
	Religious Education	

Table 10. The English National Curriculum

For each subject and for each key stage, programmes of study set out what learners should be taught, and attainment targets set out the expected standards of learners' performance. It is for schools to choose how they organise their school curriculum to include the programmes of study.

Programmes of study

The programmes of study set out what learners should be taught in each subject at each key stage, and provide the basis for planning schemes of work. When planning, schools should also consider the four general teaching requirements (use of language, use of ICT, health and safety, and inclusion) that apply across the programmes of study.

Attainment targets and level descriptions

An attainment target sets out the "knowledge, skills and understanding which learners of different abilities and maturities are expected to have by the end of each key stage" (Education Act, 1996, section 353a). Attainment targets consist of eight-level descriptions of increasing difficulty, plus a description for exceptional performance above level 8. Each level description describes the types and range of performance that learners working at that level should characteristically demonstrate.

The level descriptions provide the basis for making judgements about learners' performance at the end of key stages 1, 2 and 3. At key stage 4, national qualifications are the main means of assessing attainment in National Curriculum subjects.

The majority of learners are expected to work at:

- Levels 1-3 in key stage 1 and attain level 2 at the end of the key stage
- Levels 2-5 in key stage 2 and attain level 4 at the end of the key stage
- Levels 3-7 in key stage 3 and attain level 5/6 at the end of the key stage.

Using level descriptions

In deciding on a learner's level of attainment at the end of a key stage, teachers should judge which description best fits the learner's performance. When doing so, each description should be considered alongside descriptions for adjacent levels.

The level descriptions are not designed to assess individual pieces of work. They list aspects of attainment, based on the programmes of study, which teachers need to assess to build up a picture of a learner's performance over time in a range of contexts.

Example level descriptors

Take, for example, Mathematics in Key Stages 1 and 2. The curriculum is broken down into the following attainment targets:

- Using and applying Mathematics
- Number and Algebra
- Shape, Space and Measures
- Handling Data

Take, for example, the "Number and Algebra" attainment target. At the lowest level, Level 1, the descriptor is as follows:

Learners count, order, add and subtract numbers when solving problems involving up to 10 objects. They read and write the numbers involved.

Working up through the levels, take level 4, for example:

> Learners use their understanding of place value to multiply and divide whole numbers by 10 or 100. In solving number problems, learners use a range of mental methods of computation with the four operations, including mental recall of multiplication facts up to 10 x 10 and quick derivation of corresponding division facts. They use efficient written methods of addition and subtraction and of short multiplication and division. They add and subtract decimals to two places and order decimals to three places. In solving problems with or without a calculator, learners check the reasonableness of their results by reference to their knowledge of the context or to the size of the numbers. They recognise approximate proportions of a whole and use simple fractions and percentages to describe these. Learners recognise and describe number patterns, and relationships including multiple, factor and square. They begin to use simple formulae expressed in words. Learners use and interpret coordinates in the first quadrant.

Then take, for example, the highest level, Level 8:

> Learners solve problems involving calculating with powers, roots and numbers expressed in standard form, checking for correct order of

magnitude. They choose to use fractions or percentages to solve problems involving repeated proportional changes or the calculation of the original quantity given the result of a proportional change. They evaluate algebraic formulae, substituting fractions, decimals and negative numbers. They calculate one variable, given the others, in formulae such as $V = \pi r2h$. Learners manipulate algebraic formulae, equations and expressions, finding common factors and multiplying two linear expressions. They know that a $2 - b\ 2 = (a + b)(a - b)$. They solve inequalities in two variables. Learners sketch and interpret graphs of linear, quadratic, cubic and reciprocal functions, and graphs that model real situations.

Beyond this level, is another level descriptor, "Exceptional Performance".

Each Attainment Target has its own set of descriptors.

Base the Curriculum on Competencies

The notion of basing the curriculum on demonstrable competencies rather than just memorised facts has gained a lot of ground in the past few years. It's possible to combine both standards and competencies. You can find competency based curricula in operation in many countries including, for example, Indonesia.

In the United Kingdom recent research has found the Royal Society of Arts' (RSA) "Opening Minds" competencies based curriculum to be effective (Boyle, 2006), (RSA, 2008).

Opening Minds aims to help schools to provide young people with real world skills. It is a broad framework through which schools can deliver the content of the English National Curriculum. The RSA developed this in response to a belief that the way students were being educated was becoming increasingly detached from their needs as citizens of the 21st Century. Opening Minds is now being used in over 200 schools across the UK and is growing rapidly. It encourages the following:

- Teaching subjects from outside the normal school curriculum
- Half-termly modules
- Combination of subjects

- Student led learning
- Longer lessons
- Team teaching
- End of module celebration
- Larger groups

One school, John Cabot in Bristol, uses the Opening Minds curriculum extensively in year 7. Here the students work on cross curricular projects based around a central theme over a period of five terms. The themes are:

- Learning to Learn
- Community and Environment
- Communications
- Lifestyles and Health
- Finance and Enterprise

They did this to address the issues of:

- Transitioning from primary to secondary schooling
- Developing curriculum pathways that help personalise learning
- To enable students to deal with the ever-increasing demands of adult life in a society driven by information and technology
- To develop more independent and confident learners.

Cambridge Education Associates have a programme called PbyP (Personalisation by Pieces) which enables schools to personalise learning and take children through a competencies based curriculum.

Key principles include:

- Making it clear to learners what they need to do to be successful
- Trusting learners with increasing responsibility in controlled and appropriate ways
- Focusing learning around lifelong competencies so that schools become places where children collaborate and learn by taking an active role in their communities

- Encouraging teachers to model good learning behaviour by providing them with opportunities for reflective learning, action research and professional sharing
- Removing age and stage restrictions on achievement so that learners are compared to themselves and not notional averages.

In order to support learners and teachers in applying these principles, PbyP uses "skill ladders" and structured peer assessment within a learning cycle.

The PbyP approach involves breaking skills down into 9 levels, each with a target statement of increasing difficulty and complexity, displayed to the students using ICT as a ladder. This provides a framework for personal target setting, and the wider framework for managing the curriculum.

A second component of PbyP is 'peer assessment'. A web tool used in the PbyP system allows peer assessment across the Internet. Completed work is automatically sent to peer assessors in other schools. These peer assessors have already achieved the target that the learner has sent to them, so are 'experts'. When marked and commented on, the work is automatically returned to the learner. The system ensures that peer assessors are qualified, fair and constructive in their comments through a combination of moderation and a ratings system familiar to users of eBay.

A third component of PbyP is a "learning cycle" which gives learners of all ages and stages a way of taking greater responsibility for their own learning. It simplifies learning into five steps and presents it in a cycle:

> Inspiring problem to solve → aspiration → goals → do learning task and demonstrate new competencies → peer recognition.

Learners can see the excellent work of others in any of the component skills of any of the four capacities at any level and be inspired by this. The skills ladder structures achievable goals. Support is given to mentors, recognising that these may be parents and friends. Secure peer assessment then completes the cycle.

(Buckley)

According to Merlin John, a leading education journalist, PbyP has "the potential to take a huge burden from teachers".

Rethink Content

The ease with which ideas, concepts and knowledge are assimilated by learners is a function of the quality of the content used. We will all be familiar with good books used in our schooling that helped us understand and retain better, and which supplemented what our teachers were teaching us.

The advent of the printing press enabled the top-down process of curriculum "transmission" through textbooks, but now of course technology is changing all that. Whilst there is still a role for professionally produced content, it's now possible for teachers to take content "building blocks" and reassemble them relatively easily to meet their teaching needs. But the real advantage with using information technology is that the learners themselves can become the content producers. Students learn much more by teaching other students than by just listening to teachers. IT also makes it easy for children to distribute learning content and to get it to be assessed relatively easily by other students.

So the ease with which ideas, concepts and knowledge is assimilated by learners is no longer just a function of the content itself, but also a function of how that content was produced. So, setting the best conditions for success involves giving students a range of digital tools to gather information, edit it and use creativity and productivity tools to develop and distribute learning content. Ideally, portal technologies would be used to provide a digital library and reviewing system.

Advances in technology are also changing views about what actually counts as content. For example, it could be argued that threads of dialogue through blogs, wikis and instant messaging are forms of content production.

Rethink Assessment

There are different ways of knowing, so logically, there should be different ways of demonstrating understanding. In the Internet era, when information is so readily available, the relevance and cost effectiveness of mass scale memory tests has to be questioned. For example, public examinations are a huge industry. In England, for instance, PricewaterhouseCoopers estimated that the cost of running the examination system in 2003-04 was $915 million.

(QCDA, 2005).

ICT has become a necessary and powerful tool in our work on assessment as it makes it possible to access and analyse student achievement data on an on-going basis, take corrective action, and share best practice. ICT can cheaply open up new ways for students to demonstrate and authenticate their understanding, skills and abilities. E-portfolios, distance peer assessment, electronic testing, assessments and video presentations are all readily accessible to many students, especially in the developed world.

Whilst energy is expended keeping mobile phones out of assessments, some enlightened organisations explore ways to use mobile phone technology *for* assessment—e.g., a project in Ireland recently used mobile learning for Irish Language learning and assessment (FON).

Both *what* we assess and *how* we assess need to be rethought.

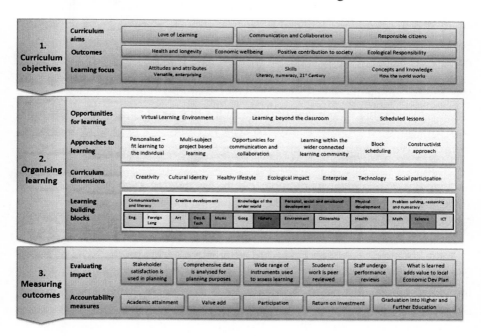

Figure 11. Planning the curriculum—high level overview example

Students

Resourcing	Management	Workforce	Curriculum	Students

- Promote Equity
- Accelerate Learning
- Personalise Learning
- Promote Learning Beyond the Classroom
- Involve Parents and the Community

Promote Equity

Top performing schooling systems tend to have strong equity. In Finland, for example, strong special needs inputs and processes ensure that their outputs are consistently high across groups with different needs. In OECD countries, most equity driven reforms are targeted at "at-risk" groups, whereas in the developing world they tend to be targeted at low income groups, women and rural populations.

But equity cannot be achieved by treating everyone equally. Clearly, every student, teacher and school is different—so treating them all in exactly the same way isn't going to promote equity. To achieve equity, we need to make a break from the old industrial-era model of mass-producing identical students in identical classrooms and identical schools. Through using Information Technology, schooling can promote equity by treating each school and each student, differently as needs require. IT gives us the means to accurately adjust levels of different resources as each school and each student requires.

In some countries, selection is used to segregate students on the basis of ability or religion. Selection undoubtedly works to help deliver high standards for those individual schools that get to choose the students who are likely to perform best, but selection tends to lower the overall performance of a schooling system as a whole. The findings from PISA 2000 show that education systems with the lowest degree of differentiation achieve the highest mean student performance in reading literacy. Non-selective systems are actually more flexible in matching curriculum content to students' needs than selective education. This ability to better deal with individual differences among students might explain the higher performance levels in PISA for these countries (OECD, 2005).

The reality for the vast majority of the world is that students are taught in classes, and class size has a real impact.

Rather than wholesale reduction of class size, an effective approach would be to lower class sizes selectively, especially for disadvantaged children in primary grades 1 to 3, encourage the best teachers to migrate to these grades and implement training programmes to change classroom pedagogy (UNESCO, 2006).

Accelerate Learning

"You don't understand anything until you have learnt it more than one way."
Marvin Minsky, artificial intelligence pioneer.

If learning is the core operation of a schooling system, then accelerating learning is a core lever to pull. Over a lifetime, human beings have the potential to think more thoughts than there are particles in the universe! The human brain is composed of billions of brain cells, which are linked together by trillions of connections. Yet scientists estimate that we don't use all of our brain capacity. In other words, a vast well of potential remains to be untapped. Imagine the impact on learning and achievement if every schoolchild was able to use just a fraction of this untapped potential. Many schools are looking at how we exploit what we know about the brain and learning in the classroom.

Based on the work of Dunn and Dunn, Barbara Prashnig suggests that in a standard, factory-style school:

- Only 30% remember even 75% of what they hear in class
- Only 40% retain even 75% of what they read in class.

Furthermore, Holland (1998) reported that boys—in schools in which she researched—revealed that they spent between 25-70% of their time listening passively to teachers.

Accelerating learning is essentially about understanding and exploiting the way people learn, to make it more natural, effective and fun. In the UK, a highly regarded approach to this is ALPs—Accelerated Learning in Primary Schools, by Alistair Smith and Nicola Call. (Alistair Smith, 1999). Key features of the ALPs approach are:

Addressing Visual Auditory and Kinaesthetic learning styles	Create the right environment for learning
Ensuring children are in the right physical state to learn	Develop 'Emotional Intelligence'
Setting up the classroom to maximise learning opportunities	Use mind mapping techniques.
Discovering and utilising learners' individual learning preferences to improve their learning performance and understanding	Be aware of the different forms of intelligence as you plan for children's learning
Using the right techniques to input information so it sticks	Use rhythm, rhyme and music to enrich learning
Using optimal questioning strategies for meaningful class interaction	Use motivation systems such as RAP (Recognition, Affirmation and Praise)
Creating independent learners, and equipping children to manage their own learning	Teach children to understand how they learn

Table 11. Key features of the ALPs approach

Basing the process of schooling on the science of learning is another way to accelerate learning. One school that does this brilliantly is Monkseaton School in North England. In his book—*Making Minds*—Dr Paul Kelley, Monkseaton's Principal, describes learning as neuroscience (Kelley, 2008). Paul and his staff consistently develop and apply their scientific understanding of the science of learning to significantly improve the performance of their students. For example, the school takes advantage of its understanding of Circadian Rhythms to provide a staggered timetable for children. Some children learn better earlier in the day than others, so adjusting the timetable to fit optimal learning patterns makes sense. Another example is using short repetitive bursts of content delivery interspersed with quick bursts of physical exercise to help students memorise facts. The real brilliance of Monkseaton lies in the fact that they deeply analyse whether they have been effective or not, look for wider patterns from data gathered from multiple activities across the school, and use data to make informed decisions to innovate and drive improvement.

Research has given us new understandings of intelligence and thankfully in recent years we've moved from a single concept of intelligence—Intelligence Quotient—to the concept of multiple intelligences. A step towards making schooling more intrinsically motivating is to customise learning to match the way each child learns best.

Harvard psychologist Howard Gardner pioneered multiple intelligence theory. Gardner defines intelligence as follows:

- The ability to solve problems that one encounters in real life
- The ability to generate new problems to solve
- The ability to make something or offer a service that is valued within one's culture.

Gardner shows that people possess eight distinct intelligences:

- **Linguistic**—the ability to think in words and to use language to express complex meanings
- **Logical-mathematical**—the ability to calculate, quantify, consider propositions and hypotheses and perform complex mathematical operations
- **Spatial**—the ability to think in three-dimensional ways; perceive external and internal imagery; create, transform, or modify images; navigate oneself and objects through space; and produce or use graphic information
- **Bodily-kinaesthetic**—the ability to manipulate objects and fine-tune physical skills
- **Musical**—the ability to distinguish and create pitch, melody, rhythm, and tone
- **Interpersonal**—the ability to understand and interact effectively with other people
- **Intrapersonal**—the ability to construct an accurate self-perception and to use this knowledge in planning and directing one's life
- **Naturalist**—the ability to observe patterns in nature, identify and classify objects, and understand natural and human-made systems.

Gardner's research highlights the need to both align learning with individual strengths, but also to develop all intelligences in an individual. New City School, in St. Louis, Missouri has been using MI theory since 1988. The school has hosted four conferences, each attracting educators from around the world, and published books and papers.

"Waldorf Education", which is based on the educational philosophy of Rudolf Steiner, has similar theoretical underpinnings, i.e.—learning is interdisciplinary and integrating as well as practical, artistic, and conceptual.

Accelerated learning can also be achieved by using a wide range learning modalities. These include:

- Project Based Learning (PBL)
- Independent study
- Peer tutoring
- Team collaboration
- Lecture
- Virtual tutoring
- Asynchronous instruction
- Small group projects
- Individual tutoring

Using information technology opens a range of possibilities for offering a wider range of learning modes, for example:

Mode	Activities	Methods	
Face to Face	Get together; Live it, Do it; Build Learning Communities & Relationships	Learning Labs, Classroom, Mentoring, Role Playing, Coaching,	
Collaboration	Discuss it, Practice it with Others	Live Virtual Classrooms, e-Labs, Collaborative Sessions, Real-time - Live Conferences, Project Based Learning	
Interaction	Examine it, Try it, Play it	Self-Directed Learning, Interactive – Real Time Team Challenges, Coaching and Simulations	
Consumption	Read it, See it, Hear it, Experience it	Web based instruction, eBooks, Interactive web pages, Videos	

Figure 12. ICT opens up possibilities for a range of learning modes

Another key aspect of accelerating learning is to address students' different learning styles. There are principally three key learning styles:

- **Visual**—A person with a visual learning style tendency may need to have a concept explained using drawings, pictures, diagrams, scribbles, video, photographs, etc.
- **Auditory**—A person who learns best through an auditory style will respond well to being taught through the spoken or written word. Schooling has traditionally favoured this kind of learner—somebody who is comfortable listening to a teacher talk and writing in books
- **Kinaesthetic**—A kinaesthetic learner needs to be able to model their learning physically. This could involve making models, acting something out, or even just moving around. Traditional learning environments disadvantage kinaesthetic learners—how many times do teachers in a traditional classroom have to say "keep still" or "sit down"? Very often, a student who appears to be disrupting a class could simply be a kinaesthetic learner needing to move in order to assimilate what he or she is supposed to be learning.

We all have a unique blend of all these three learning styles, but one is likely to be more prominent than others.

So how do we apply this understanding in the schooling process? Imagine you were given the task of getting a group of students to understand how the heart works and you have to choose between the following three approaches:

Method 1. Take an unlabelled diagram of a heart, photocopy it, then give it to the students and ask them to label the diagram and annotate it to explain how it works. They hand in the sheet of paper; you mark it and give it back to them.

Method 2. You ask the students to go online and explore a multimedia model of a working heart, then write an explanation of how the heart works using diagrams.

Method 3. You give the students a real heart in a tray and ask them to shoot a video of a heart being dissected, and then narrate an audio track on top of the video. When complete, the video is posted on a website and reviewed by the students' peers.

Which of these three methods do you think would have the most impact? Award winning Eggbuckland School in Cornwall, UK, would argue that the third method is the most effective. Why? Because it engages all three learning styles. 'Visual' because the students are shooting a video; 'Auditory' because they are narrating a soundtrack; and 'Kinaesthetic' because they have to handle and dissect a real heart. All three learning styles are being engaged, making learning more engaging and effective.

A similar process is at play when students produce clay animations. At Otterton School, Devon, students produced an animated film based on a journey along their local river—a kind of scaled down version of the "Wallace and Grommet" animation. Again, all learning styles are engaged—visual in the analysis of the artwork and shooting the video; auditory in writing a story and narrating a soundtrack; kinaesthetic in making the scenery, and building and moving the clay animation objects (BBC).

This is not to suggest that every single learning activity needs to engage every single learning style. What it does suggest is that effective and efficient learning comes from engaging a range of learning styles and choosing the right style at the right time for the individual students.

Personalise Learning

Whether we agree with the concepts of Multiple Intelligence and Learning Styles or not, there can be no doubt that everyone is fundamentally different. We need schooling that is organised around the individual ways in which human beings learn and grow. For years we have been trying to change, adjust, and tweak the existing mass education system, when what we need is a fundamentally different system.

In schooling systems across the world, there is a constant struggle over who is eligible for "special" consideration, and, because those costs soak up so many resources (lower staff ratios, special spaces, tailored instructional approaches), schools tend to standardize for everyone else. But here is the dilemma: because students have different types of intelligence, learning styles, varying paces, and starting points, all students have special learning needs. It is not just students we label who have special learning needs (Christensen).

When students walk into a classroom, they bring very different sets of attributes, abilities, knowledge, skills, understandings and attitudes with them. People learn different things at different speeds. Each student necessarily learns differently, so why do schools struggle to teach differently? It's time we rethought the role of learners. Learning, by definition, is personal—no one else can learn for you.

Over recent years, the concept of personalising learning has gained considerable ground. The problem is that changing schooling systems so they deliver a more personalised learning experience is very complex. But 'complex' isn't the same as 'impossible'. Personalising learning starts with an understanding that schools are ecosystems. Attempting to personalise learning through programmes, initiatives or by means other than those that are completely holistic just won't work.

If you look at some of the best performing countries in PISA, you will see that these countries have combined comprehensive schooling with highly individualised learning opportunities. That enables them to compensate for differences in abilities and learning dispositions. They have established bridges from prescribed forms of teaching, curriculum and assessment towards enabling every student to reach their potential. The education systems of Victoria in Australia, Alberta in Canada and Finland drive to make such practices systemic, through the establishment of clear learning pathways and fostering the motivation of students to become independent and lifelong learners.

Teachers in these systems use data to evaluate the learning needs of their students, and are consistently expanding their range of pedagogic strategies to address the diversity in students' interests and abilities. To do this well, schools need to adopt innovative approaches to timetabling and the deployment of increasingly differentiated staffing models.

(Schleicher, 2009)

Personalising learning is a subject that could take a book in its own right to explore, but essentially it reduces down to three main factors:

- Extending choice
- Intelligent intervention
- Expanding opportunities to collaborate

Extending choice

Imagine walking into a restaurant and the menu has just one item on it. That's hardly what you would call personalised. On the other hand, imagine a restaurant with not just a wide choice of food and drink on the menu but the ability to customise your dining experience so that it is exactly as you want it.

Now apply the same idea to schooling. Imagine on the one hand a class of 30 children all learning to remember texts in a written examination—one source of content; one learning pathway; one learning modality; and a single form of assessment. Contrast that with a system which provides a wide choice of learning experiences, modalities, pathways and assessments, and engages the learner in helping design the learning experience. This second scenario is perfectly possible, providing the entire schooling system is set up to deliver this, and that technology is fully exploited.

Intelligent intervention

This is essentially about using data to make well informed decisions about what students need to learn next. To fully personalise the learning experience students would be constantly assessed as they move through the learning programme, and the pathways that they take through the learning programme would continuously evolve as they work their way through. This relies on highly effective feedback loops and systems which can dynamically adapt to the twists and turns of the learning process, and set challenging learning goals and tasks. This is extremely difficult to do within a standardised setup. But it can be made a lot easier through using sophisticated IT systems that provide powerful analytic and workflow capabilities. Intelligent tutoring systems, and managed learning environments, are becoming more commonplace and increasingly sophisticated.

Expanding opportunities to collaborate

Personalised learning is not about learning in isolation. It is quite the opposite in, fact. Learning is a social activity and personalising the learning experience is to do with providing opportunities to collaborate as well as to learn independently. A learning task that has been personalised for somebody could involve them working in a team, and part of the assessment could be how well they have managed to collaborate with other people. The extent to which a learning task has been personalised is a function of the extent to which that individual's prior knowledge, skills, preferred learning styles, and attitudes have been taken into account when assigning the task.

Promote Learning Beyond the Classroom

All learners "should have the opportunity to learn beyond the school gates working with businesses, primary schools, charities or other local organisations. Learning in appropriate contexts not only allows the student to have access to experts in their chosen area, it also recognises the value and power of learning through doing and that different people learn better in different settings. One of the drawbacks of the current education system is that students have to learn in isolation from reality and often in removed and inappropriate environments. The increasingly wide availability of personalised mobile digital technologies enhances learning in these out-of-school settings and creates links between these and school-based experiences" (Futurelab, 2005).

At best, students only spend around 15% of their time in school. Even if that were doubled, they would still spend 70% outside school, so what they add to their learning outside school is crucial.

The demand for customised learning that schools can't provide is being serviced by a rapidly growing industry that delivers learning services to students outside school time. Students can now select from a vast array of services including:

- Phone based tutoring—particularly for English and Mathematics, e.g. premiertutoring.com
- Online tutoring and homework help —e.g. tutor.com; Cramster.com, eduFire.com and TutorVista.com
- Online managed learning—extend the formal lessons into the home by setting homework that is mediated online e.g. mymaths.co.uk
- Computer-supported collaborative learning (CSCL) is a promising method of supporting collaborative learning over the internet. The use of CSCL tools such as wikis, blogs, learning management systems (LMS), online image/video sharing, video-conferencing/chat/file sharing, collaborative work spaces; online whiteboards and virtual worlds, is increasing

- Minimally Invasive Education (or MIE), e.g. "The Hole in the Wall" (http://www.hole-in-the-wall.com) where students learn unsupervised at 'learning stations'—a computer workstation built into walls similar to cash dispensers (ATMs).

"Student of Fortune" http://www.studentoffortune.com has an interesting approach. "The concept is simple: post your homework problem on the site with a price you want to pay for help, and either wait for experts to accept or raise your bid, or let the site match you with a tutorial that is already available" (Reuters India, 2009).

Online learning is gaining hold in the advanced courses that many schools are unable to offer, in small, rural, and urban schools that are unable to offer breadth, in remedial courses for students who must retake courses in order to graduate, with home-schooled students and those who can't keep up with the regular schedule of school, and for those who need tutoring. Online enrolments are up from 45,000 in 2000 to 1 million today, as organizations like Florida Virtual School and Apex Learning lead the way (Clayton Christensen, 2008).

In recent times, there has been a steady growth in home schooling, especially in countries such as the UK, US, Sweden and Germany—despite the risk of prosecution by the authorities (The Economist, 2010).

Home schooling was the original "mass schooling". Before publically funded schooling, the vast majorities of parents who couldn't afford to pay for private schooling had no choice other than to home school their children, so why fight this trend? Rather than detecting and prosecuting people for not sending their children to school, wouldn't it be more effective to support them and ensure high quality learning happens? Again, technology can play a crucial role. For example, Notschool is a successful online learning community for young people for whom traditional education has not worked. This might include those who are sick, pregnant, disaffected, excluded, travellers' children and young offenders. Notschool has supported over 5,500 young people, helping over 98% back into life-long learning and employment.

For more information on Notschool go to:
http://www.channel4.com/life/microsites/U/unteachables/inclusive3.html

Involve Parents and the Community

Parents can and do contribute significantly to learning, so should be considered a resource. To achieve the best results, teachers, parents and students all need to work together.

> "Research clearly indicates that good schools become better schools when there is a strong connection with parents as part of the learning community. The positive results of a genuine partnership between parents and schools include improved student achievement, reduced absenteeism, better behaviour, and restored confidence among parents in their children's schooling" (Ontario Ministry of Education).

In Bowring School, Liverpool, success has been achieved by engaging parents in a range of ways including involving them in setting individual targets for students.

At the least, parents should have the ability to see the latest attendance information, homework assignments, structured feedback, disciplinary reports, and related information via a secured Internet school portal.

Ideally, parents should be able to:

- See what their child is doing in school
- See how their child is doing in school
- Communicate with teachers easily
- See teachers' feedback
- Learn how to help their child learn specific subject matter (through on-line resources)
- Purchase items and services from a school-vetted list to help their child succeed
- Stay informed about school activities
- Learn how their local school is performing relative to other schools.

Case Studies

Standards Based Curricular

Australia

From 1998—1992, the Australian Board of Education phased-in a completely new senior secondary curriculum. Victoria, a leading state in Australia, subsequently implemented the VCE—Victorian Certificate of Education—which is not based on testing, but rather on the completion of work requirements. Instead of twelfth grade learners preparing obsessively for final exams, they are required to complete work requirements, known as the Common Assessment Tasks, or CATs.

Although some CATs are assessed under exam conditions, over half of each learner's grades, and well over half of a learner's work, involve conducting research and writing reports, making oral or audio-visual presentations, constructing working models or preparing design briefs. The Victorian Curriculum and Assessment Board, therefore, built clear standards and high expectations into the system's curriculum and codified these standards in terms of grading criteria for the CATs.

South Korea

South Korea has a national curriculum, which has been revised regularly since the first revision in 1954. The national curriculum is mandatory for all schools from kindergarten to upper secondary, including private schools. It sets strict regulations for the number of schooldays, the subjects to be taught for each school year, and the time allocation for each subject in each school year, but there is some room for modification either by local education authorities or individual schools. The South Korean national curriculum provides criteria for the development of textbooks and general guidelines for teaching-learning activities and methods of assessment.

Singapore

In Singapore, the curriculum is divided up into the following phases:

- Pre-compulsory, age 0—6/7
- Primary, age 6/7—12
- Lower secondary, age 12—16/17
- Upper secondary, age 16/17—18-20

There is a national curriculum in place for primary and lower secondary. In upper secondary, the curriculum is largely defined by external examination syllabuses.

Sweden

There is a statutory national curriculum (Grundskola) for compulsory school—7 to 16-year-olds. This is linked to the two other national curricula for pre-school and upper secondary education (ages 16+ to 19/20), which all take a common view of curriculum, development and learning.

The "Grundskola" curriculum gives prominence to the core subjects, which are Swedish, or Swedish as a second language, Mathematics and English, which children normally begin to learn from around age 9. The statutory curriculum also includes practical arts subjects (Art, Domestic Science, Sport/Physical and Health Education, Music, Crafts), Social Sciences (Geography, History, Civics, Religious Studies), Sciences (Biology, Physics, Chemistry and Technology), a second Foreign language (from around age 13) and some optional subjects.

The Government sets out a total minimum teaching time in the various subjects for the whole nine-year period of Grundskola. Schools may then determine exactly how these hours should be allocated.

Uganda

Factors that influence effectiveness vary considerably across the world. Uganda provides a great example of thoughtful reflection on success factors. Free primary schooling was introduced in the 1990's, and National Assessment reports between 1996 and 2000 list the following factors which affect achievement there:

- **Learners' age**—learners join primary at about six years of age
- **Learners' gender**—boys and girls interact in a gender friendly environment and no gender stereotyping
- **Lunch**—learner takes solid food, or other than just porridge, or a drink at lunchtime on school days
- **Reading and writing skills**—learners read textbooks and supplementary readers
- **Home environment**—parents allow children enough space and time for doing homework
- **Parental participation**—parents visit the school and check on child's attendance and class work
- **Instructional materials**—parents and Ministry of Education and Sports buy enough instructional materials
- **Use of instructional materials**—headteacher releases and ensures effective use of materials
- **Monitoring and supervision**—inspectors and the education standards agency monitor teaching in schools
- **Time management**—headteacher emphasises proper time management by teachers and learners
- **Teacher's housing**—teacher lives in or near the schooling in a house of at least two rooms
- **Assessment practice**—teacher gives planned tests, marks and gives immediate feedback
- **Teaching load**—there is some subject specialisation at the school level so a teacher does not teach more than two subjects
- **Teaching methods**—teacher allows learners to actively participate in class activities
- **Teachers' experience**—after teaching for about five years, teacher attends refresher courses regularly
- **Teachers' qualifications**—teacher has a grade three or four teaching qualification or holds a degree in education.

(Acana, 2006)

Jordan Education Initiative UNESCO

The Jordan Education Initiative (JEI) is a case study on how to do private public partnerships to improve education. The JEI is one of several education initiatives run by the World Economic Forum, others being the Egyptian Palestinian and Rajasthan Education initiatives.

The JEI has four key objectives:

- Improve the development and delivery of education to Jordan's citizens through public-private partnerships, and in the process help the government of Jordan achieve its vision for education as a catalyst for social and economic development
- Encourage the development of an efficient public-private model for the acceleration of educational reforms in developing countries based on unleashing the innovation of teachers and students through the effective use of ICT
- Build the capacity of the local information technology industry for the development of innovative learning solutions in partnership with world class firms, creating economic value that will lead to mutually beneficial business opportunities
- Leverage an environment of national government commitment and corporate citizenship to build a model of reform that can be exported to and replicated in other countries.

The JEI has 17 global corporations, 17 Jordanian entities, and 11 governmental and non-governmental organizations all working together to achieve these objectives, in partnership with the Government of Jordan. Direct contributions to the Initiative from global and local partners have reached over US$ 25 million.

This PPP has enabled JEI to improve learning for 80,000 students, 3200 teachers in 100 "Discovery Schools". Each Discovery School is fully networked, Internet connected and has access to computer labs and online curricula.

Jordan participated in PISA for the first time in 2006, and found that scores for Maths, Science and Reading were higher in the "Discovery Schools". Whilst these differences could potentially be caused by other factors, it's reasonable to conclude that the initiative will have an overall positive effect. In 2007, the JEI received the UNESCO prize on ICT use in Education.

Key learning from the JEI includes:

- Never lose focus on education
- Ensure the technology is scalable
- PPP is the backbone with clear roles and responsibilities for each partner
- Strong governance and organizational structure
- Correct scale of programme
- Monitoring and impact assessment is critical
- Communication and PR plays a role
- Change management vs. training
- Continuity.

(The World Economic Forum)

McKinsey and Company published an analysis of the JEI in 2005, and concluded that effective global-local, public-private partnerships should have the following key elements:

1. Clear vision and objectives, powerfully articulated in appropriate forums
2. Attractive governmental, social and geo-strategic conditions
3. Motivated partners, whose interests are aligned with initiative, providing sufficient inputs
4. Programme activities that leverage appropriate partner competences
5. Well-supported coordinating mechanisms
6. Consistent monitoring and evaluation
7. Effective governance to set strategic direction and align partners.

(McKinsey & Company, 2005)

4. RE-ORGANISING SCHOOLING

Schools' "Kafka-like rituals enforce sensory deprivation on classes of children held in featureless rooms ... sort children into rigid categories by the use of fantastic measures such as age-grading, or standardized test scores ... train children to drop whatever they are occupied with and to move as a body from room to room at the sound of a bell, buzzer, horn, or klaxon ... keep children under constant surveillance, depriving them of private time and space."

John Taylor Gatto, A Different Kind of Teacher

The purpose of this chapter is to give you an understanding of the following:

- Different operating modes and their relative merits
- The interconnectedness between each organisational layer
- What are the key ways in which waste can be driven out of the schooling process
- What's the difference between a time and a performance-based system
- How management systems can be structured for maximum effectiveness
- Different options for school building and learning space design
- How funding should be re-organised to maximise opportunities.

The key points made in this chapter are:

- The key to improving effectiveness is to move from time to performance-based schooling systems
- There are seven layers of structure that all have to be changed simultaneously to get the maximum effect
- Seeing students as customers is an essential component in changing the paradigm
- Devolving power down to school level improves effectiveness
- Changing the workforce mix gives flexibility to innovate
- Modernised schooling systems are networked enterprises
- Physical changes to school buildings are crucial but need not be prohibitively expensive
- Form follows function
- Multi-layered funding and public private partnerships enable optimal funding.

C hapter 3 helped us identify those factors that contribute to effective schooling, and outlined a set of levers that policy makers can pull to improve outputs. The next challenge is to work out how to make the kind of changes necessary to get much bigger outcomes—how can we change the paradigm so we go beyond making incremental improvements? Incremental change is hard enough, so how can we possibly go about re-organising schooling—while it is still in operation?

Organisations behave the way they are designed to behave, so this is essentially a design question. Schooling systems are ecosystems so cannot be changed one piece at a time. Affect one part and all other parts are affected too. There are at least seven layers of that structure that each needs to be organised and re-organised when introducing change.

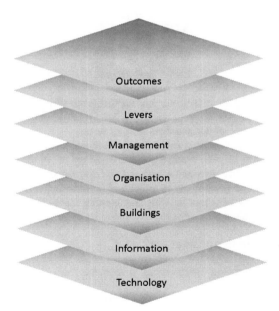

Figure 13. The interconnected layers of a schooling system

The truth is there are few people on the planet who have attempted schooling system transformation and succeeded—especially whilst running a schooling operation at the same time. One person who has succeeded is Richard De Lorenzo, who transformed the Chugach School District in Alaska. If the US is one of the countries that most requires an overhaul of its schooling system, then the Chugach District in Alaska was a microcosm of all that was wrong in US schooling—but amplified to the point that it became a "burning platform".

What Richard and his colleagues did in Alaska was truly remarkable. They took a system that was dysfunctional in the extreme, and completely re-organised it through smart insights, clear vision, and tenacity. Ironically, the "advantage" that Richard and his colleagues had was that the situation in Alaska was so bad that something radical simply had to be done. In some ways it's harder to bring about transformation where schooling systems are performing reasonably well—where there is no "burning" demand to make radical changes. "Good is the enemy of great."

The key insight offered by Richard De Lorenzo and his colleagues in the Re-inventing Schools Coalition (RISC) is that in order to get an order-of-magnitude change in outcomes, you need an organisational paradigm shift. From the Alaska experience, Richard De Lorenzo provides an extremely powerful insight—

"The traditional schooling system is primarily a passive learning environment. The energy and momentum of schooling moves from the teachers to students" (DeLorenzo, Battino, Schreiber, & Carrio, 2009). The end goal of re-organising schooling has to be to redress this so the energy and momentum of schooling is balanced across all stakeholders.

Based on what can be gleaned from the most promising references for across the world, there are four key dimensions for re-organising schooling:

- Moving from Time to Performance-Based systems
- Restructuring
- Changing the physical environment
- Taking a fresh approach to funding

Moving from Time to Performance-Based Systems

Time To Performance-Based Systems	Restructuring	Physical Environment Options	Re-organising Funding

- Eliminating Waste from the Learning Process
- Performance Based Learning Management
- Changing the Paradigm

Eliminating Waste from the Learning Process

So what do we mean by performance when we talk about "performance"-based schooling systems? One way to think about this is to imagine the perfect schooling system where 100% of students learn 100% of what they are expected to learn for 100% of the time—that gives us 100% performance.

But what happens in reality? In the United States, for example, despite $50bn expenditure, 40% of students lack basic reading skills. Even in excellent schooling systems it's virtually impossible to get 100% of students learning 100% of what they should learn for 100% of the time. So why does this happen? The people at RISC would argue that it's because schooling systems are time-based, when they should be performance-based.

In a time-based system, massive inefficiencies occur simply because learning is bounded within blocks of time.

Take a subject area such as Maths in a secondary school, for example. Let's imagine an average student achieving scores of 50% in all of their Maths assessments throughout their secondary schooling. In any one year, then, an average of 50% of possible achievement is wasted. In a time-based system, the vast majority of students will progress to the next year regardless of how well they have done in the previous year—even if that year's learning requires prior understanding. In a time-based system, wasted learning performance is tolerated because the system is driven by the calendar and timetables. Eliminating the difference between what students *can* achieve and what they *do* achieve is a fundamental principle of performance-based systems.

The systems developed by RISC shifts the organisational paradigm from

- one in which students progress on mass by following uniform methods of earning credits or seat time and reaching relatively low levels of academic performance...
- ...to one in which students progress individually by demonstrating in a variety of ways that they have reached high levels of academic performance.

This allows them to stack blocks of learning on top of one another, driving out the waste and ensuring learning progression and continuity. Students don't move up from one block of learning to the next until they have demonstrated proficiency. In a RISC system there are only 3 grades—A, B and "try again".

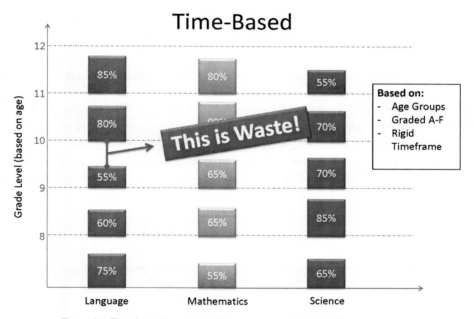

Figure 14. Time-based system—example of achieved learning versus potential

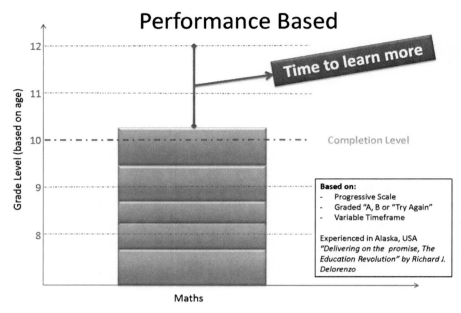

Figure 15. Performance-based system—"stacking" achievements drives out waste.

In a traditional system, time is the constant and learning is the variable. Factory schools organise learning so that when a class is ready to move on to a new concept, all students move on, regardless of how many had mastered the previous concept. Progression to the next block of learning happens regardless of whether proficiency can be demonstrated—even though it might have been a prerequisite for understanding what comes next.

In a RISC system the reverse is true—learning is the constant and time is the variable. Students move at their own pace (as fast or slow as needed) through standards based attainment levels rather than age related grade or stage levels.

Performance Based Learning Management

Controlling students is one of the main workloads of a factory school. Dictating where they are supposed to be; controlling their movement through the building; lining them up outside the classroom; managing behaviour; escalating behaviour issues; punishing bad behaviour; detentions; verbal warnings; seclusions; suspensions; writing lines, etc—all activities needed to enforce time-based regimes. Some schools go to extreme measures to control students. It's hard to believe, but even in 2010 there are some countries that are considered modern where it is still acceptable to beat students with sticks, or to inflict other forms of physical punishment.

The overheads associated with controlling students in schools add no real value to the learning process, and are therefore a serious drag on efficiency. An interesting exercise would be to understand the real costs of controlling students—and determine the return on that investment. What percent of teaching time—the single biggest schooling budget item—is dedicated to keeping order?

So why do schooling systems invest so much in keeping control? Is it the nightmare vision of St Trinian's, the fictional girls boarding school immortalised in numerous films but based on a real school which allegedly let the girls do whatever they liked? The prospect of losing control is something that will have terrified all teachers at some point in the career.

But there are successful models of schooling where the control is transferred from teachers to students—where students are taught self-control and are given responsibility for their learning. The "Sudbury Schooling Model" is perhaps at the extreme opposite of regimented factory schools. A Sudbury school is one in which students individually decide what to do with their time, and learn as a by-product of ordinary experience rather than by standardised "instruction".

There are about 40 schools of this type around the world with the following features in common:

- De-emphasis of classes
- Students studying what they want to study
- Age mixing
- Autonomous democracy

(Marano, 2006)

Kunskapsskolan schools, where students achieve higher than average results, are another example. In Kunskapsskolan schools, students have a teacher as their personal tutor, who follows them through their schooling and helps them learn how to plan and develop their own learning strategies. The tutor follows progress and is there to give support. As the students learn to set their own goals and plan their time, they are given increasing responsibility to manage their own studies. In other words learning how to conduct yourself, how to behave, how to learn and how to use your time productively are treated as competencies to be mastered and demonstrated.

The Council at Richmond upon Thames in London were sufficiently convinced that the Kunskapsskolan model works that they approved plans for two Kunskapsskolan Academies to be built in the borough.

In another example, the Lumiar Institute in Brazil is developing a Learning Management System called "Mosaic" to help students and their teachers make decisions about where to spend their learning time.

Mosaic has three key basic components:

- A **Competency Matrix**—the curriculum of Lumiar School. This determines what students should (or could) learn.
- A **Project Database**. Students develop competencies by working on projects, and the Project Database establishes "how" they will learn. It connects learning projects to people in the community who have something to offer and can contribute time to the school.
- The **Learning Portfolio** is the learning roadmap of students at Lumiar, and helps guide them to the projects that best match their learning needs.

Lumiar is very much a work in progress, and opinion is divided over whether their approach works or not. Either way, they are pushing forward with new approaches to learning from which everyone can learn.

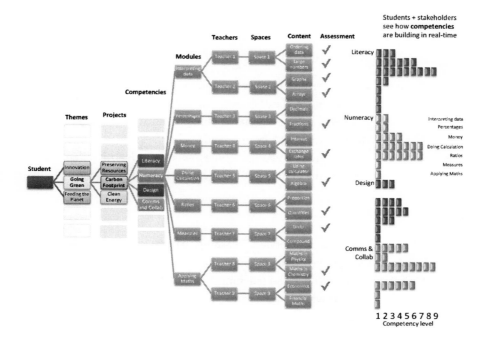

Figure 16. Modularising the curriculum—essential to managing learning in a performance-based system

Changing the Paradigm

Shifting from a time-based to a performance-based paradigm requires a range of changes. Changing the system, whilst operating it at the same time, means balancing the introduction of new activities, whilst still running some old ones. Blue Ocean Strategy is a tried and tested method used in business and public sector to create new value, and can be a very useful planning tool here. A key principle in Blue Ocean Strategy is that meaningful change involves creating some new approaches; raising the emphasis on some existing processes; reducing the emphasis on some existing processes; and eliminating other processes altogether.

(W. Chan Kim, Renée Mauborgne)

Shifting from a time-based to a performance-based system, using the Blue Ocean Strategy approach could involve these types of changes:

Create
- Acceptance that learning is more important than teaching
- Acceptance that a standards-based curriculum is at the heart of the system; agreement on the standards students must reach; agreement on how students will learn and be assessed
- Processes by which students co-design their learning and make decisions about the kinds of assessments used to measure their competence.

Raise
- The emphasis on independent learning where students know exactly what they need to be doing
- Consistency in learning and teaching
- The system's orientation towards dealing with student's individual learning needs
- Project based learning.

Reduce
- The emphasis of teaching over learning
- Classes in favour of work groups
- Uniformity, in favour of creativity and innovation
- Decisions based on gut feel, in favour of data-driven decision-making.

Eliminate
- Students being grouped to work together by their age, rather than the work they need to be doing
- Acceptance of wasted learning performance
- Bells and buzzers signalling the end or start of classes.

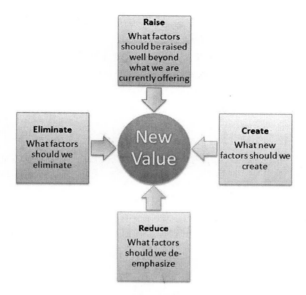

Figure 17. Blue Ocean Strategy

Restructuring

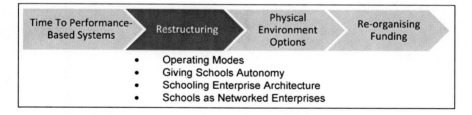

Operating Modes

Schooling operates in national and regional contexts. Publicly funded schools will always exist in some larger policy and administrative context that affects their operations.   At national level there are four main "centres of gravity" around which schooling is organised.

- **National Government.** Power is concentrated at a National level Ministry of Education. Examples include Russia

- **State**. Power resides with Ministries of Education at state level. Examples include Australia and Brazil
- **Local Authorities.** Local Government has Education Departments in which power resides. Examples include France (Rectorats)
- **Schools.** Through School Based Management (SBM), schools are given the power to manage themselves.

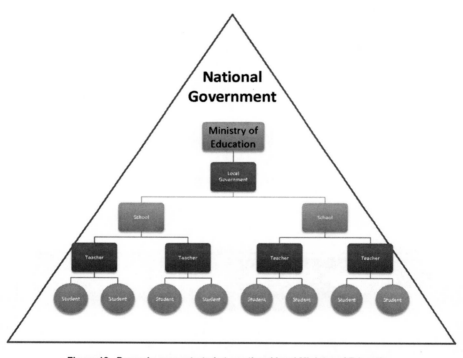

Figure 18. Power is concentrated at a national level Ministry of Education.

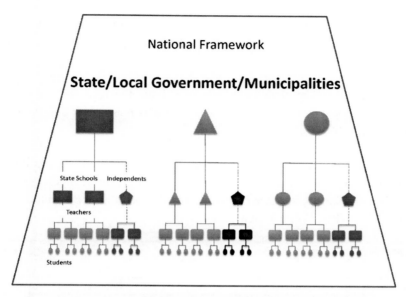

Figure 19. Power resides with Ministries of Education at state level or Education Departments in Local Governments.

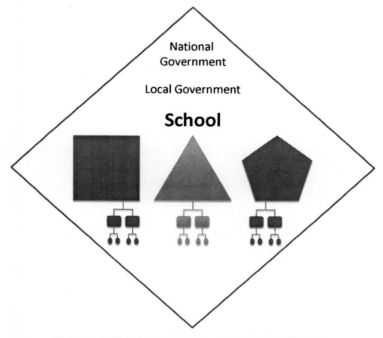

Figure 20. Through School Based Management (SBM), schools are given the power to manage themselves.

The most common model is for power to be concentrated at National Government level. Where countries are federated, regional bodies tend to be more influential.

In some countries, central governments may have the lead role in planning, structures and personnel management while schools make most decisions about the organisation of learning.

In the area of resource allocation and use, the central government is the most common level for decision-making in WEI countries. However, in countries with School Based Management, decision-making happens at local authority and school level (UNESCO-UIS/OECD, 2002).

Planning and structures	Resource allocation/use	Personnel management
Central	State	Local
State	Local	School
Local	School	School
School	School	School

Table 12. Common Decision Making Models.

Another approach again is to the devolve power down to the school level, but enable schools to form consortia. In the UK, where schools have a high degree of autonomy, the following models operate:

Single Schools

This is the most common model, with one headteacher, one school and one governing body.

Federations

A federation has a single governing body for two or more schools, and will often share a headteacher too. Federations may consist of either primary or secondary schools or both. The advantages of federations include collective purchasing power, resource and best practice sharing, management at lower cost.

Collaborations and Partnerships

In a collaboration or partnership, schools and organisations choose to join forces but maintain separate governing bodies. Partnerships are less formal arrangements which may involve other non-education partners.

Of all these models, School Based Management (SBM) is more connected and responsive to the needs of its local stakeholders and has become a very popular movement. SMB means transferring responsibility and decision-making to a combination of principals, teachers, parents, students, and other school community members.

A number of countries including New Zealand, the United States, the United Kingdom, El Salvador, Nicaragua, Guatemala, the Netherlands, Hong Kong (SAR), Thailand and Israel have instituted SBM. Within the SMB model, sub-structures of Single School, Federation and Collaboration/Partnership models can operate.

Giving Schools Autonomy

A trend amongst many of the best performing schooling systems is to enable *schools* to become the driver of educational improvement. In Finland, for example, strategic thinking and planning takes place at every level of the system and every decision is made at the level of those most able to implement them in practice.

PISA assessments found better reading scores in those schools that have more autonomy. The OECD concluded that "decentralised education systems are more advantageous for students than centralised systems" (OECD, 2005). In the latest PISA assessments there was a 22% advantage in science scores in schools that had autonomy in selecting their teachers.

Devolved decision-making, which makes schools the main drivers of educational development, needs to be combined with "intelligent accountability". This means moving from a system based on nationally determined approaches to a system based on building capacity within clearly defined national objectives. In this context, intervention and support means diagnosing problems in each school and tailoring solutions accordingly.

External accountability systems are often a key part of the agenda, but they are not enough. According to Andres Schleicher from the OECD "among OECD countries, we find countless tests and reforms that have resulted in giving schools more money or taking money away from them, developing greater prescription on school standards or less prescription, making classes larger or smaller, often without measurable effects. What distinguishes the top-performer Finland is that it places the emphasis on building various ways in which networks of schools stimulate and spread innovation as well as collaborate to provide curriculum diversity, extended services and professional support.

The balance between national prescription and schools leading reform is not an "all-or-nothing" matter. In fact, most school systems have started out with highly prescriptive education systems, but have gradually moved towards enabling schools to assume greater responsibility (Schleicher, 2009).

Giving schools more autonomy means giving them increased legal and professional responsibilities; wide discretion over funding; the responsibility to select their own staff and to fill their senior positions from the principal down; the power to handle the management and upkeep of their physical infrastructure, and so on.

School Based Management has the potential to be a low cost means of making public spending on schooling more efficient by increasing the accountability at all levels, and empowering teachers in the "front line" to improve learning outcomes. Benefits can include:

- More input and resources from parents
- More effective use of resources because those making the decisions for each school best understand its needs
- A higher quality of schooling as a result of more efficient and transparent use of resources
- A more open and welcoming school environment because the community is involved in its management
- Increased participation of all local stakeholders in the decision-making processes, leading to better relationships and increased satisfaction
- Improved student performance as a result of reduced repetition rates, reduced dropout rates, and (eventually) better learning outcomes.

(World Bank, 2009)

Devolving Managerial Functions

The wide variation in school size and local circumstances means that no one management structure will fit all schools. However, it's common to find a core set of management tasks including:

Leadership	Personnel Management
• Policy-making • Teaching and learning • Curriculum and progression • Attainment and assessment—internal and external • Social inclusion • Student welfare • Culture and behaviour	• Performance management • Paying staff salaries • Professional development • New teacher probation and student teachers • Establishing incentives for teaching staff • Hiring/firing teaching and administrative staff • Supervising and evaluating teachers • Funding teacher training
Pedagogy	**Maintenance and infrastructure**
• Timetabling • Selecting content—textbooks, e-learning resources • Prescribing approaches to teaching • Setting the school calendar	• Building/maintenance • Buying school materials
Finance	**Consultation and communication**
• Overseeing budget • Allocating budget • Driving school income • Monitoring and evaluation • Statutory record-keeping and reporting	• Links with the community, the local education authority, other schools, external agencies, employers, higher and further education • Student councils • Partnerships with parents and the community • Staff professional associations
Quality Assurance	
• Monitoring and evaluating teaching and learning • Self-evaluation • Planning for improvement • School development plans	

Table 13. Core set of school level management tasks.

A key question is who should have responsibility for these devolved functions? There are four typical models:

1. Administrative-control — in which the authority is devolved to the school principal
2. Professional-control — in which teachers hold the main decision-making authority
3. Community-control — in which parents have the major decision-making authority
4. Balanced-control — in which decision-making authority is shared by parents and teachers.

Decision making happens on several levels. In the UK, for example, school management is generally hierarchical. At the top level are the school governors, the chairperson being the highest level of authority. The Board of Governors will include parent, teacher and community representation. Cascading down, authority goes to the headteacher (principal), deputy-headteachers, a layer of middle managers (department heads) and a "grass-roots" level of classroom practitioners.

It's common to find two higher-level tiers of decision-making in school-based management:

School Councils/Board of Governors

The role of the Board of Governors or council ranges from monitoring the school's performance; raising funds; appointing, suspending and dismissing teachers; ensuring the teachers' salaries are paid regularly; approve annual budgets; monitor compliance with financial and legal requirements. There tends to be four levels of governance:

- Weak—Limited autonomy over school affairs, mainly for planning and instruction—e.g. Mexico (PEC programme)
- Moderate—School councils serve only an advisory role e.g. Canada, Senegal, and Thailand
- Somewhat strong—Councils receive funds and have autonomy to hire and fire teachers and principals, set curricula, and control substantial resources—e.g. EDUCO programme in El Salvador

- Strong—Parents or community can create and control schools—e.g. New Zealand, Netherlands.

Senior Leadership Team (SLT)

The SLT is usually made up of the school's most senior teachers, including the headteacher or principal. The SLT will have an executive function and responsibilities for the day-to-day operations including areas such as:

- Implementing the overall strategic direction, as identified by the governing body
- Leading initiatives in the school
- Setting policies, exploring innovative ideas, resource sharing and best practice
- Monitoring of the progress of strategic initiatives and the impact of these on teaching and learning and the development of staff.

Rethink the School Structure

The National College for School Leadership proposes an interesting way to rethink how roles are organised.

"One way to rethink the structure is to divide accountabilities into operational, support/advisory and co-ordination/partnership roles at different levels in the organisation.

- **Operational roles**: taking tactical decisions to achieve objectives; setting targets; monitoring achievements; coaching, appraising and generally managing the performance of staff within their defined areas; ensuring customers are properly served; and securing the resources necessary for achieving all of these things. These roles require job holders who can lead a team, hold people accountable, influence others across the school and display high degrees of self-confidence.
- **Support/advisory roles**: providing support to the operational roles and requiring a different mindset orientated much more towards new ideas for the longer term and a willingness to challenge with integrity proposed courses of action. These roles require organisational understanding, empathy with internal customers and conceptual thinking.

- **Co-ordination/partnership roles**: accountable for achieving business results but have to rely on others, for whom they are not directly responsible. These roles require an ability to indirectly influence others, work in a team and understand others' perspectives."

(National College for School Leadership, 2004)

Change the Workforce Mix

Beare (2001) argues that as teaching became a graduate profession in the developed world, these graduate teachers sought and were paid salaries commensurate with a graduate status. Now graduate teachers expect that when they enter school they will be supported by auxiliary staff, and sophisticated materials and facilities. In Australia at the turn of the 20th Century only 1 person in every 800 was a teacher, but by the 1980s 1 person in every 70 was a teacher. There comes a point in this escalation when teachers will price themselves out of the market if present trends continue, so serious consideration has to be given to remodelling how teachers are thought of and used.

(Beare, *Creating the Future School*, 2001)

A large secondary school in the developed world could have a salary bill in the order of $3m/year. Given that teachers' salaries are such a high proportion of overall schooling costs, a key lever that needs to be considered is changing the workforce mix. In a factory model, where most teachers tend to do pretty much the same kind of job, there is little reason to have significantly different roles. A typical primary school staff will comprise mainly of teachers whose responsibilities are pretty much the same, led by a headteacher, and assisted by a small number of senior teachers. Same goes for secondary schools. In both cases there are likely to be a small number of ancillary staff to support in areas such as admin, reprographics, lunch and break time supervision, etc. However, with the advent of new technology, which means the teacher no longer needs to be the source of all knowledge, new models that are much more cost effective can emerge.

For example, where perhaps a block of 6 standard classrooms require 6 full-time teachers to each run a class, new organisational structures such as bigger spaces and longer periods could see that mix change to say 1 very senior (Master) teacher (equivalent to a "Consultant" in the Healthcare industry), 1 mid ranking teacher and 2 junior teachers, supported by 4 or more classroom assistants. This gives managers financial flexibility to significantly differentiate the responsibilities and pay levels between each of these grades—within or below current budgets. This approach can also lead to students being able to benefit from having more responsible adults working with them.

Scenario 1 "Standard" classroom block of 6 classrooms, 1 teacher per 30 student	People	Cost	Scenario 2 6 classrooms combined into 1 large space, team of responsible adults teaching and supervising	People	Cost
6 standard teachers @ $50k each	6	$300k	"Master" teacher	1	$80k
			"Mid-rank" teacher	1	$50k
			Junior teachers @$35k each	2	$70k
			Assistants @ $25k each	4	$100k
Total	6	$300k	Total	8	$300k

Table 14. Comparative costs of alternative resource use models

Schooling Enterprise Architecture

Schooling systems tend to be organised on principles of scientific management to reflect economies of scale and standardisation of work. These traditional structures, largely stemming from the late 1800s, are no longer valid because they are based on a set of principles that are no longer true, i.e.:

- There is a single best structure for any type of organisation
- Management control and coordination are essential for maintaining productivity and performance
- Specialisation and division of labour increase the quality and quantity of production.

Whilst there is no single model that will work for all schooling systems, it's essential to search for a framework approach that is more appropriate for the age we live in—i.e. of the 2000's, not the 1800's. One such approach is "schooling as enterprise".

Many question the idea of schooling as enterprise, but most schools are a long way towards being enterprises anyway. If you take the total running costs of an average secondary school—staff and other operational costs—and add the capital value of the buildings and equipment, it emerges as an enterprise with a multi-million dollar annual turnover. Compared with any other local business, the school is usually the largest enterprise in a locality.

Schooling as enterprise strongly favours SBM where schools are forced to be responsive to their local community, but with a national and regional framework. Where schooling is run as an enterprise, schools are self-managing, with their own budgets. School boards or councils not only represent the stakeholders but are accountable to them. Schools compete for resources (especially funds), in order to provide an in-demand, high quality service. They have to demonstrate the quality of their educational services to survive and evolve. Underperforming schools and teachers at first receive support, but those that continually underperform will not be allowed to continue. Evolving is about constantly innovating, on the hunt for additional resources, and making smart decisions. In short, schools are expected to be enterprising.

In an enterprise model, school managers are no longer subordinate parts of a bureaucracy, but rather they are among the most highly skilled and qualified executives (or Chief Executive Officers, CEOs) in the community. The enterprise they run is much more complicated than any other local business because its purposes are more complex, more public and more politically sensitive directly affecting daily a far larger proportion of the community than any other enterprise.

Many do not like the enterprise model of schooling. Many—especially students—don't like the factory metaphor either, but have had to get used to it. The single biggest advantage with the enterprise approach is that it inverts the hierarchical pyramid which placed learners at the base of the power pyramid, and places their interests below that of the organisation.

The enterprise metaphor makes us begin with the student, and then to build out from the support they need to enable them to reach their full potential. It places the student at the centre of the power equation, and those in receipt of public money in the position of service provider. As the philosopher Seneca said—"to govern is to serve, not to rule."

Students as Customers

The idea of treating school students as customers is hotly contested and emotive. Whether we call students 'customers' or something else, is largely a matter of semantics. The bottom-line is that students *behave* like customers—they vote with their presence, attention, engagement and behaviour. This isn't surprising given that they get treated like customers in other aspects of their lives—so why should they expect to be treated as anything less during the 15% of their time that they spend in schools?

In a schooling enterprise, where effectiveness is core, students consume a learning service. In order to be effective, that service needs to deliver a highly satisfactory experience to the student.

A key argument against the "student as customer" approach is that students are not capable of understanding what is in their best interest, and therefore what learning to choose.   But supporting students through the decision-making process; guiding them through their choices; and helping them learn how to act in their own, and others', best interests, are in themselves services—and in consuming those services students are customers.

Before the advent of the Internet and advanced learning and communication technologies, students had no choice other than to attend school in order to learn. But things are very different now. In *Disrupting Class* (Clayton Christensen, 2008), Clayton Christensen argues a brilliant case which can be summarised as "treat your students as customers within the schooling system before a technology enabled organisation outside the formal schooling system does instead".

Governments may compel young people to go to school, with all the costs associated with it, but the rise of customer orientated, tailored, electronically mediated learning services available beyond the school boundaries is rising unstoppably. Those who think that the rightful place of a student is at the bottom of the "food chain" should check to see if their "lunch is being eaten" by enterprises that are more prepared to treat students as customers.

Schooling as Networked Enterprises

In a schooling enterprise model, formerly centralised education bureaucracies no longer take day-to-day control of individual schools but instead, put into place accountability, regular audit, and quality control—and then leave the school to carry on. They have downsized, and carry only monitoring functions and global policy-making roles. They have shrunk to being a strategic core.

The proliferation of networking technologies has brought about a complete transformation to not only the business world but to most public sector enterprises—apart from schooling.

The modern Networked Enterprise organisation has a strategic core which becomes the intelligence centre of a group of organisations. Through a network of relationships, relatively autonomous contractual units deliver goods or services where they are needed. The small and lean strategic core provides a leadership service to the rest of the organisation. A modern organisation need employ only a small number of core staff. The rest of the organisation's activities are separable functions which can be contracted or franchised out to specialist units, vendors, or subsidiary firms.

The network organisation which has replaced so much conventional bureaucracy the world over has the following characteristics:

- Operating units are expected to be enterprising—i.e. pro-active and innovative, rather than reacting to orders and events
- The units operate on a provision-of-service basis rather than on a control basis
- Staff at the core provides leadership as a service to the rest of the organisation. The enterprise is therefore much more egalitarian than the bureaucracy
- The unit managers have to manage by consensus, because their units are professionals hired on the basis of their expertise
- Information technology allows mainstream data to be accessed and analysed by anyone anywhere in the network. The flow of information is not dominated by hierarchy
- The networked enterprise is an 'ecology'—an environment for interrelated activities.

The networked enterprise model applied to schooling systems replaces the traditional bureaucratic hierarchical system with one of interconnecting, semi-autonomous, operating units, each of which is relatively small and whose arrangements and modes of operating are self-determined.

These units have a contract to provide a service of a required quality for the enterprise. It is not necessary for the schooling organisation to own all the units; they can be spin-off companies, or units to whom a function can be franchised out, or schools within schools. The parent organisation ensures that it gets value for money through accountability systems, which use mutually negotiated performance indicators and audits or quality checks. There are formal reporting-back procedures, an agreed format for giving that feedback, and a core that handles these regular audits. The units are judged on outputs, on the quality of the services they contribute to the whole.

The 'strategic core' does not control the units in the traditional, command and control, sense, but it does co-ordinate them by providing the broad frameworks within which the whole organisation operates.

That core:

- Makes the strategic decisions for the whole
- Raises the enterprise's global budget, and then apportions it
- Undertakes long-range planning
- Co-ordinates and represents the enterprise
- Institutes quality controls
- Ensures staff development is provided throughout the whole organization
- Manages the enterprise's culture.

The enterprise model of management seems particularly well suited to schooling. Schools, after all, are the ultimate 'knowledge organisation'. However, moving to this model involves substantial change including accepting principles such as:

- Education is an industry
- Schooling is part of the service sector of the economy
- Students are customers of that service
- Government is the regulator of an essential service

- Schools are providers of the schooling process
- Some aspects of education will be provided by bodies which until now have not been regarded as 'schools'
- Schools are or will become brokers of educational services
- Every service, including an essential service, has to be paid for
- The term *teacher* will undergo re-definition as the teaching service professionalises
- The funding of education and meeting the costs of schooling will become split-level and more complicated.

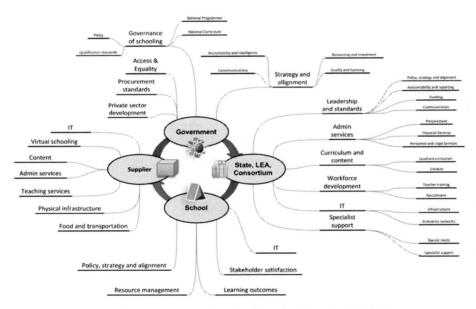

Figure 21. Organisational elements in a Schooling Enterprise Architecture.

Physical Environment Options

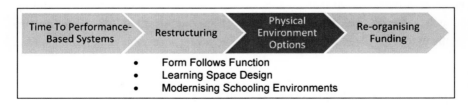

"We shape our buildings; thereafter they shape us." Winston Churchill.

The standard mode of schooling operation assumes that a predetermined number of students will all learn the same thing at the same time from the same person in the same way in the same place for several hours each day. The new paradigm is a model where different students, of various ages, learn different things from different people in different places in different ways and at different times (Prakash Nair, 2009).

As demands on schooling systems evolve, there is a need to redesign school buildings and the learning spaces within.

There is nothing new in this. Over the centuries, a vast array of different models of the physical environment of schools has been successfully used. For example:

- The Ottoman system of Kulliye—a building complex containing a mosque, a hospital, madrassa, and public kitchen and dining areas, revolutionized the education system, making learning accessible to a wider public through its free meals, health care and sometimes free accommodation;
- Mobile, tent schools—these are still used in remote parts of Russia to teach students in remote areas. In Kenya 91 mobile schools—sometimes a teacher with a group of children under a tree—serve students from nomadic tribes;
- One-room-schools—common in the US before factory school, where a single teacher taught seven grades of boys and girls in the same classroom. These still exist in rural areas in most parts of the world.

Whilst it's clear that learning can happen anytime anywhere, we have been locked into thinking of schools as monolithic buildings with classrooms and corridors.

In the one-room-school, learning *had* to be personalised. But as "economies of scale" schooling factories became the dominant model, personalisation was replaced with standardisation, and production-line classrooms. The question now is whether the physical architecture of systems that were designed to process students in standardised ways can be adapted to make learning more individualised, particularly through exploiting new technology.

Form Follows Function

The idea of form following function is that the design of a building should be based on its intended purpose. As the purpose of schooling should reflect local, regional and national interests, it's no longer possible to claim that there is a single form which suits all schooling.

A key question then is what purpose we want school buildings to fulfil, and this in turn traces back to what we want from schooling.

These can generally be summarised as:

- Academic Qualifications
- Vocational Qualifications
- 21st Century Skills

But it's not just the outcomes we need to consider, it's *how* we want students to acquire these that matters. The challenge isn't just to make it more personalised but to orchestrate the learning in a way that helps develop 21st Century Skills. Project Based Learning (PBL) fits the 21st Century Skills model very well, and is increasingly used in the United States—with the backing of organisations such as the George Lucas Foundation and the Bill and Melinda Gates Foundation. PBL success stories include PROMOTE Georgia; GenYes and High Tech High.

> "There is strong evidence that project-based learning is a highly motivating way for many students to synthesize what they are learning as well as to identify gaps in their knowledge that need to be filled. But many schools can't adopt widespread project-based learning because the layout of their buildings simply can't accommodate it" (Clayton Christensen, 2008).

Christensen has a point. But it is possible, with some careful consideration, to adapt most schools—at least in part—to accommodate PBL. The challenge is to enable PBL through low cost changes—i.e. not knocking down schools and starting again, but adapting the stock of schools that we've got.

So what "function" would we want our "form" to follow? What functions should the physical environment enable?

Firstly, PBL, which involves developing and using the following kinds of 21st Century Skills:

- Creativity and Innovation
- Critical thinking, problem solving and decision-making
- Learning to learn and metacognition
- Communication
- Collaboration and teamwork
- Information literacy
- ICT literacy.

Additionally, learning should be:

- Outcomes-based—produce an artefact, presentation, or action
- Based on open-ended questions or issues that are challenging, real and relevant to the students' lives
- Student-directed or co-designed
- Multi-disciplinary
- Long term, as opposed to being based on short periods.

The physical environment should also enable accelerated learning through addressing:

- Visual Auditory and Kinaesthetic (VAK) learning styles
- Multiple Intelligences
- Individual learning preferences to improve their learning performance and understanding
- Independent learning and equipping children to manage their own learning.

We also need the environment to support different learning modes including:

- Face-to-Face
- Collaboration
- Interaction
- Content consumption.

Finally, we need to ensure that the learning goes beyond—and is from beyond—the classroom, e.g. external expert input and deep connection with parents and the wider community.

Learning Space Design

The next step is to think about how these functions can be applied to learning spaces. The core processes in Project-Based Learning can be broken down into the following sequence:

- **Analyse**—research the question; define the problem to be solved; define the approach to solving it
- **Synthesise**—acquire the data, information and knowledge needed to address the problem; and combine materials from different sources to address the problem
- **Deliver**—produce an artefact, presentation, or action that solves the problem, and demonstrates new knowledge and skills.

The kinds of learning that you'd expect to see in each of these sequences can be clustered around learning spaces, for example:

Analyse		Synthesise		Deliver	
Receive (content)	Theatre	Write	"Knowledge Workbench"	Prototype	Practical Workbench
Search	Research station	Calculate		Evaluate	
Gather		Model		Construct	
Classify		Reflect		Film	Media Station
Discuss	"Collaboration Station"	Resolve	Breakout Area	Record	
Decide		Ponder		Edit	
Test	Science pod	Imagine	"Creation Station"	Present	Presentation Suite
Experiment		Consider		Propose	
Hypothesise		Conclude		Assess	

Table 15. Different kinds of learning need different kinds of spaces.

So how do we begin to implement this type of approach in existing, operating schools?

Beech Williamson, Design Manager at Partnerships for Schools, says that flexibility is the key when adapting spaces in an old school to a 21st Century educational vision (Hinds, 2010).   So let's take a standard block of six classrooms with a corridor in a secondary school, each built to house 30 students and a teacher. At one end of the "flexibility spectrum", a single learning space combining all of the different approaches to learning can be created from this. This approach is essentially going back to the one-room-school, but within the setting of a much larger collection of buildings.

Students and teachers spend the first weeks of the year learning how to work effectively and how to minimize disruption. Students are divided into different groups to undertake learning modules. The learning module they undertake is not determined by their age, but by what they need to be learning at any specific moment. The students then work in small collaborative groups to achieve their assigned goal at their own pace and in the learning style that best suits them.

This type of environment mirrors many modern workplaces, and requires completely different sets of disciplines and skills on the part of both students and teachers in order to succeed.

There are many places where this approach works. One, for example, is New Line Learning in Kent.

> "If we believe that transformation involves providing children with a wide range of learning opportunities, among which sitting still and listening to the teacher is one of the least important, then the concept of the 'Learning Plaza' immediately looks like an entirely logical solution. There, children can consult more than one teacher. Teachers can consult each other. Children can work in groups—of any size from two to ninety—or independently, and they can do all of this in comfortable, decidedly non-institutional surroundings with their technology to hand."

The figures show that the children who use the Learning Plazas are less likely to be absent from school, and much less likely to be excluded for misbehaviour (Haigh).

The Learning Plaza concept delivers increased value for money in terms of building costs and therefore enables greater investment to be made in upgrading furniture, acoustics and lighting, which further enhances the effectiveness of the learning space provided.

For some people, working in a single room with 180 children simultaneously could be a big ask, so consideration should be given to reducing the size of the spaces to say two standard class sizes (plus corridor)—housing 60 children. In the example given of a six classroom block, this can give three large spaces, and each one could be dedicated to either areas of the curriculum or a part of the learning process—analyse, synthesise, deliver.

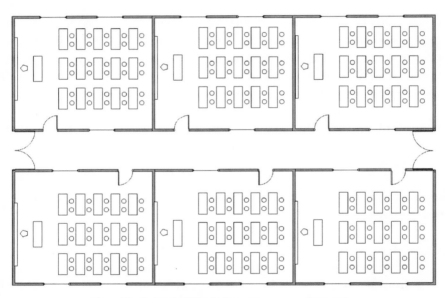

Figure 22. A standard block of six classrooms with corridor.

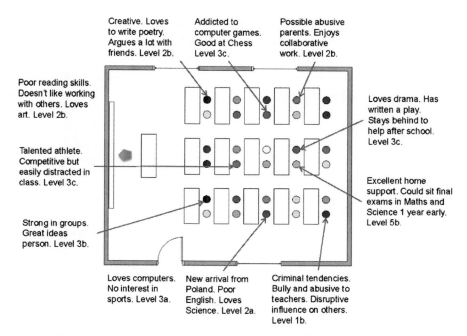

Creative. Loves to write poetry. Argues a lot with friends. Level 2b.

Addicted to computer games. Good at Chess Level 3c.

Possible abusive parents. Enjoys collaborative work. Level 2b.

Poor reading skills. Doesn't like working with others. Loves art. Level 2b.

Loves drama. Has written a play. Stays behind to help after school. Level 3c.

Talented athlete. Competitive but easily distracted in class. Level 3c.

Excellent home support. Could sit final exams in Maths and Science 1 year early. Level 5b.

Strong in groups. Great ideas person. Level 3b.

Loves computers. No interest in sports. Level 3a.

New arrival from Poland. Poor English. Loves Science. Level 2a.

Criminal tendencies. Bully and abusive to teachers. Disruptive influence on others. Level 1b.

Figure 23. First design principle is to recognise that classes are populated with individual students, each with unique needs.

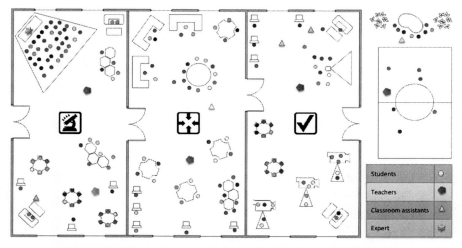

Students	
Teachers	
Classroom assistants	
Expert	

Figure 24. With the same space, create three large spaces, each dedicated to a different part of the 21st Century Learning Process.

Dr Kenn Fisher, Director of Learning Futures at Rubida Research Pty Ltd, proposes that the "centre of gravity" for a student's days in school is a "home base". This is an area that an individual student can personalise, use for storage, and work and study in.   It provides a sense of ownership and teaches independent learning but also enables group discussions.

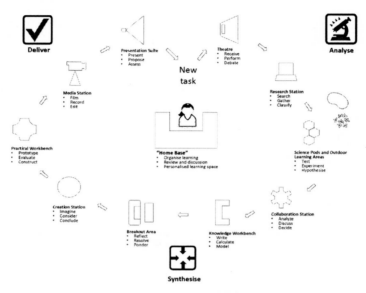

Figure 25. The Home Base Approach.

From this "Home Base"—which can resemble a typical individual "cubicle" workspace in a modern work environment—students go to work in a range of different learning spaces according to what they need to be working on at any one time. For example, the stage of a project they are working on could call for them to be in any one of the following types of spaces:

- Learning studios—Multi-media; Science + Technology; Performing Arts; Art + Design
- Collaboration incubator
- Project space
- Group learning
- Wet areas
- Presentation space
- Outdoor learning resources

- Individual pod [place to think]
- Specialised focus lab
- Breakout space
- Display space
- Open resources
- Floor sitting area

These spaces are set up for various modes and group sizes—they are multi-modal and clustered to allow students to move around the various learning environments to suit the particular learning task (Fisher, 2005).

Schools with open, transparent spaces will enable classes to work within the same proximity, promoting more effective student-teacher interaction.

Design is critical to create an atmosphere that feels open and trusting, while providing maximum security and supervision. Using hidden structures that use 'safe-by-design' concepts will help achieve this.

Any school constructing new spaces must ensure they can accommodate such environments as well as any increase in staff and student numbers. One way in which schools can ensure that any new buildings are fully flexible is to design larger spaces, first with the structural walls and core services, then divide these into smaller spaces by building solid but non-structural walls. These walls can then be removed (during the summer holidays for example) if the larger space is required. Alternatively, a school could use movable partitions in these spaces, but equipping these with the required acoustic properties makes this an expensive option.

Modernising Schooling Environments

There are only a handful of countries worldwide that have the resources and the long term commitment to rebuild their entire secondary school stock. There are fantastic showcase schools across the world—some of which resemble the most modern possible workplaces. But the reality for most is that a capital reinvestment programme means small amounts of expenditure used to refurbish the oldest and most out of date schools.

So the question is how do we re-organise learning in mainstream schools without having to completely rebuild them? How do we take the "form" that we already have, and make it deliver the function that we really need?

One approach is remodelling. Peter Maxwell, head of enabling at the Commission for Architecture and the Built Environment (Cabe) believes remodelled schools can have much better space than would be possible in a new build.

Remodelling a school also has considerable advantages in terms of sustainability and cost since some materials will be reused and less energy will be expended in manufacture and transport.

So having established the kinds of learning environments that we'd like, and the principle that remodelling is better than rebuild, the next consideration is what kind of schooling environments we want.

A useful set of models comes from Stephen Heppell (Heppell, *Building Learning Futures*, 2004) and the OECD's *Think Scenarios* (OECD, 2006).

School as Fortress/Closed Schools

The model that most of us will be familiar with is the "school as fortress". In this model the school is the single validator of learning for the community, it is mechanistic, based on learning "cells" and "delivery" based. Students are managed in terms of flows from grade to grade. Tight integration, co-ordination, and control aim to ensure stability, which become ends in themselves rather than means to an end.

Architecturally the "Fortress School" may sound quite seductive because the integrity of the school campus is a straightforward design task, but the artificiality of the environment thus created too is sterile and divorced from the community that schools are there to serve to adequately prepare learners for the real world beyond school.

To move from fortress/closed schools to more open models means building institutions that on the one hand provide   students with a secure schooling environment, but on the other hand doesn't isolate them from the community that the school serves.

The Extended School

The Extended School embraces most of the major functions of the community, drawing them in to its campus—functions, like sports, police, health or libraries, small scale start-up enterprise support and even subsidised housing for teachers, nurses and other public service workers. An architecturally extended school is a vision of a very large campus with its own "street life" and an all-embracing view of learning that reaches out into the local community, and is very much the central heart of that community. With the students learning about citizenship and citizens rediscovering learning, the extended school comes to define and redefine the community it serves.

The Dissolved School

The idea of the dissolved school is that there is no central campus or single location and the schooling system "dissolves" into the local community in a way that is familiar in many university towns. Faculty centres are clustered near to local specialist functions. Each of these centres is a base for the specialist staff who teach the specialism that they house: Engineering, Performance, Sport, Health, Media, and Science, for example. In many cases the local resource becomes shared as a school resource too, so that perhaps the local radio station shares the facilities of the school's media faculty, or the public library becomes a place of work for school students. The school still has buildings and working spaces, but these are scattered away from each other and embedded in many places within the community. The school has literally dissolved into the community.

Moving towards this model requires radical restructuring of timetabling. Children learn in far longer blocks of time, often spread over days, and their teachers are based at each of these specialist function locations. It also requires the exploitation of ICT to facilitate effective communications across the learning community.

This offers the considerable advantage that work-based learning can actually happen where the work is located.

Multi-Age Campus

Another interesting model is the Multi-Age Campus, exemplified by Caroline Springs—a rapidly growing suburban community located twenty kilometres west of Melbourne, Australia.

Caroline Springs College is a government funded college providing for students through kindergarten, primary and secondary education, spanning fourteen years of learning. Its enrolment is growing and is expected to stabilise at over 3200 students. Graduates move on to a range of tertiary educational settings or employment. The college is a four-campus institution, each aligned to a set of "whole college" expectations and policies, which provides seamless transition for students.

Re-organising Funding

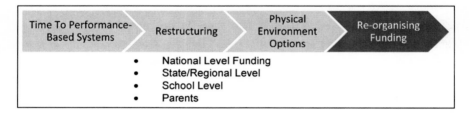

Time To Performance-Based Systems	Restructuring	Physical Environment Options	Re-organising Funding

- National Level Funding
- State/Regional Level
- School Level
- Parents

An important policy issue trend is fiscal decentralisation, i.e. shifting responsibilities for education finance to lower levels of government. There are several levels of government which have an intense interest in what happens in schooling. But it is solely sectorial interest and they are prepared only to finance the part of education operations which affect their interests. What is developing, therefore, is split level funding, and possibly also split level provision.

(Beare, *Creating the Future School*, 2001)

National Level Funding

A national government tends to be deeply concerned with those aspects of education which affect the country's economy, the productivity of its workforce, it's relationships with its neighbours and its health—over each of which it has accountability. A national government will take a keen interest in certain parts of schooling, but not all of it. A national government will also want to lead the policy agenda by funding changes to the system that lead to long term improvements. E.g. national level programmes to improve literacy, or grants for improving attainment in subjects that have high impacts on the economy—such as Science, Technology and Maths.

Interestingly, not all funding for schooling at national level will necessarily come from the Ministry of Education either. In Portugal, for example, the equipping of primary school children with laptop computers was funded by the Ministry of Transport and Telecommunication. In other countries, the development of ICT in schools can be supported by a range of Ministries, including "Innovation"; Trade and Industry; Skills and Employment, etc. There is no reason why relevant aspects for schooling couldn't be paid for by Health, Sports, Culture or Law and Order Ministries.

State/Regional Level Funding

State or regional governments—including local authorities, districts or municipalities—are directly concerned about community wellbeing and should be prepared to provide funding for those aspects of schooling that make for social harmony, for the skills of the workforce, the understanding of political systems, and the process of government, etc. They should support the provision of education in key learning areas, in the domains which make for good citizenship, social responsibility, and a sense of community.

Regional government should also be prepared to fund those aspects of schooling that contribute to regional economic development plans. For example, where schooling can help change the basis of the regional economy by building skills and capacity in areas such as 21st Century Skills. Whilst this may align with national level government, regional government will necessarily have its own unique sets of circumstances and demands that need to be addressed.

School Level Funding

Schools should be expected to be entrepreneurial, aggressively seeking grants and private finance to develop their services and grow as organisations. There is a myriad of ways in which income can be generated, besides obvious approaches such as renting facilities. In the UK, the government is encouraging schools to hire a business manager to oversee income generation.

ICT opens up a very wide range of opportunities, for example computer courses for parents and the community, or using the school as a base for selling software and computer supplies to parents and the community.

In developing countries, the computer facilities at a school can be opened up to the local community and become a catalyst for local trade, enabling buyers and sellers to connect in new ways. Some schools in Uganda are used as community access points. Traders from different villages communicate with each other over email to find out what supplies are required before departing, thus ensuring that the demand and supply is in equilibrium. Small charges could be made which help with recovering costs of the facilities.

There's also no reason why schools shouldn't sell their services to other schools, for example:

- Curriculum content production and delivery
- Staff training
- Assessment
- Hosting ICT-based services.

Funding From Parents

Governments are often not particularly interested in funding those educational provisions which are clearly personal. Ensuring that every child meets his or her *full* potential, in reality, tends to be a parental concern. Parents are generally expected to subsidise those aspects of schooling such as specialist organised sport, or specialist study of arts, that sit outside the curriculum.

Within this organisational model, each school can expect to receive split-level funding from a plurality of financing bodies, including different levels of governments, different government departments and a spectrum of private funding.

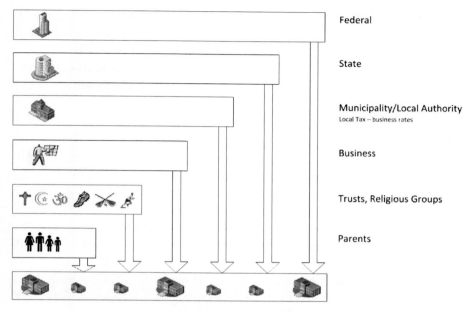

Federal

State

Municipality/Local Authority
Local Tax – business rates

Business

Trusts, Religious Groups

Parents

Figure 26. A split level funding approach.

Case Studies

High Tech High

This high school is part of an innovative charter school organization with a specific focus on international studies. By completely renovating a former Navy building, the project team—led by architects Carrier Johnson—created a collaborative learning space that reinforces the school's emphasis on team teaching, use of technology, and assessment through delivery and demonstrated competence.

Launched in September 2004 by an industry and education coalition, this small, diverse learning community is founded on three design principles:

- Personalisation—the structure allows teachers to know their students well

- Adult World Connection—through community service and projects, students develop an awareness of the world beyond their school walls and a practical understanding of both local and international issues
- Common Intellectual Mission—school leadership expects all students to graduate well prepared for post-secondary work, education, and world citizenship.

Students learn about issues that are shared around the globe, such as world trade, environmental concerns, health care, war, poverty, population growth, immigration and border issues, human rights, political systems, globalization, nuclear proliferation, etc.

Each faculty member serves as an advisor to approximately twelve students. Working in teams of varying size, teachers are responsible for the academic achievement of the 50-60 students in their group. Overall, the faculty represents a diverse mix of master teachers, newly trained teachers, and individuals from industry with strong content knowledge. The team approach helps teachers make the most of their varied talents, knowledge, and experience.

Pedagogic functions that are supported by the architectural design of the school include:

- Performance-based assessment
- Project-based learning
- Highly available technology
- Distance learning partnerships with schools both nationally and internationally
- Community-based internship experiences for all students
- Opportunities for international travel and exchange.

Internally, the school is a series of open spaces that allow for both structured and informal interaction between students and teachers—from classrooms and studios, to informal seating areas and multi-purpose function spaces. Furniture is arranged to resemble modern "knowledge economy" workplaces, with cubicles, workstations and presentation areas (Designshare.com).

Duke School

In 2005, Duke School, a centre for innovation in education linked to Duke University, consolidated its elementary and middle schools on one campus. In the process it created true 21st Century learning environments predicated on personalised learning. Stage one of the building project opened in February 2009.

The key to the development was setting up two personalised learning communities (PLCs)—5th & 6th and 7th & 8th Grade. This provides opportunities for personalized, project-based learning.

The design breaks down the campus into small learning communities so that all students are individually acknowledged by their peers and by caring adults which means that every student now has an opportunity to succeed no matter what his or her preferred learning style or particular strength.

Each of these buildings comprises a range of open and discreet spaces for a wide range of different learning modalities as defined by Nair & Fielding in *The Language of School Design* (Nair & Feilding, 2005). The design ensured that each learning modality would be fully available to students as independent learners. This means that if a student needs to access a particular resource such as an outdoor space, a teacher or student in another class, a computer or a handheld device, they are able to without needing to be led by an adult.

The entire middle school is planned without any corridors or hallway, meaning that every space can be used for learning. This enables small teams of teachers and support staff to have the flexibility to coordinate interdisciplinary studies (Designshare.com).

Figure 27. Commons/Café space in Duke School. Fielding Nair International/DTW Architects.

Scotch Oakburn College

In 2005 Scotch Oakburn College began planning for a new paradigm of education. This model would be more collaborative, more interdisciplinary, more hands-on, and more focused on sustainable futures, all the while attending to students' social, emotional and spiritual needs.

The process of envisioning change began by engaging reputed educational facility planning and design firm Fielding Nair International. This generated ground-breaking designs, two of which are described below:

Scotch Oakburn Colleges' Senior School converted their existing gymnasium into two learning communities of 100 students each on two floors of the building with visual and physical connections between the two communities.

Scotch Oakburn Colleges' Middle School developed three distinct Personalized Learning Communities (PLC) in the form of Learning Studios—(Da Vinci Studios). A high volume of glazing and several mobile walls meant that each

PLC could easily be transformed into an Advisory or Community Centre. This approach provides groups of students and their teachers with a variety of spaces for a range of different teaching and learning modalities. Teachers and students in the Middle School are no longer limited to conducting classes in a box. Instead, there are larger and smaller rooms, so team teaching and student-led activities can take place. "Da Vinci Studios" are always available for hands-on projects in any discipline, and ICT is ubiquitous.

The Middle School building is located on one of the steepest parts of the campus, and the architects exploited this to enhance the surrounding outdoor learning areas, most significantly incorporating a large amphitheatre immediately adjacent the main entrance (Designshare.com).

Figure 28. Interdisciplinary "Da Vinci" studios at Scotch Oakburn College. Fielding Nair International in association with Philp Lighton Architects.

The School that Business Built

Napa New Technology High is situated in Napa town centre, at the northern tip of the Bay Area, California. In the mid-1990s, it was recognised that the town needed a new high school, and the authorities wanted to make sure it was going to equip youngsters to exploit the explosion of 'high-tech' industry in the area.

The founders of Napa New Technology High School realised that technology companies were paying head-hunters up to 30% of an entry-level salary in order to fill one vacancy. This fee did not include training for the new employee. The amount that these businesses paid each year in head-hunting fees could pay a student's tuition for four years at New Technology High School, where students were learning the skills that businesses were searching for. So, the founders persuaded businesses in and beyond the area to divert money from head-hunting agencies into the school, and they ended up with over 40 sponsors including multinationals such as Hewlett-Packard. This allowed them to change the paradigm of school architecture from school as classrooms to school as network.

The critical principle here is that the school didn't approach business with a begging bowl—it offered a fair exchange based on real value-add.

Eltham College, Melbourne, Australia

Eltham College has 1200 students aged between five and eighteen years old. Principal David Warner has remodelled Eltham College so it is based on the principle of teachers working with students to create knowledge, as opposed to teachers passing on knowledge.

Key elements that were remodelled include the use of time, space and technology.

Time

Time has always been over-controlled in schools, particularly in secondary schools. This is largely because we teach a multitude of subjects to large numbers of young people and also have reasonably large workforces of teachers. Traditionally it has all been managed through a timetable where the two principle issues for secondary schools are, the importance of the subject and, the teacher-directed nature of curriculum and schools. Schools therefore control learning by allocating periods of time to subjects. When time is less of an issue, learning engagement and schooling enjoyment are attainable.

Imagine how unproductive the modern workforce would be if it still worked to the Taylorist factory time whistles. However, schools do! Why would you allow yourself to become totally engrossed in a project knowing that a bell will imminently force you to break away?

Because of the teacher-directed nature of much secondary schooling, most teachers prefer managed and limited time periods on the presumption that young people cannot listen or watch for long periods of time. When schools focus on engaging students, then time is less of an issue. We need to see a shift from both the importance of the subject and the importance of teacher direction if we are going to create the time to engage young people, particularly those in the middle years.

Space

Using the physical space available can be a factor in teachers wanting to do things differently and being prepared to take risks. Part of it also is about being prepared to collaborate with colleagues as well as students.

Eltham College uses its space to support effective learning. One walk around the Years 7-8 cluster areas will show some students in class working with the teacher, some in the cluster common room working as a small group, some in one of the IT areas, and some in the library. The major thing you notice is that they will be engaged in the learning and generally working as a team. On another occasion you will see some students in a science lab with the teacher, others working outside building science experiments or models and others in a senior science lab working with a lab technician or senior students. If you look closely, you might also see some Year 3-4 students who have come down to check something out with the science teacher. In fact, their learning spaces align space, time and collaboration.

You won't hear any bells. Teachers and students manage their own time.

Young people respect each other much more when they have some space and time and a culture that rewards working together.

Technology

The school recognises that a fundamental change in the learning environment is required in order to prepare its students for a new working environment. Rather than emphasizing the importance of hardware which quickly becomes obsolete, the knowledge era school invests in creating easy access to information and groups and individuals to an online programme that supports learning in an open and collaborative environment.

An example of creating this environment at Eltham College was the development and introduction of the Knowledge Network with Corskill

Australia, with the support of the National Office for the Information Economy (NOIE) (now the Australian Government Information Management Office).

The knowledge network has allowed:

- Students easy access to information as part of their education including:
    o   Individuals studied profiles and access to subject information
    o   Personal development reports
    o   E-mail access to their teachers

- Teachers have a direct links to:
    o   Class groups and individual students
    o   Parents
    o   Coursework and continuous student online reporting and assessment

- Parents can view their child's progress with the access to:
    o   Curriculum content
    o   Assessment reports
    o   E-mail access to teachers and school administration

The network was a core infrastructure upgrade as part of the college's commitment to knowledge era schooling, which over the past two years have seen the school:

- Create open and collaborative learning environments
- Install multimedia technology, e-learning systems, electronic students mark books, sound systems, data projectors etc.
- Work with teachers to recognise the skills that students possess and those strengths to encourage independent self-learning and network-learning skills.

                                                              (Warner, 2006)

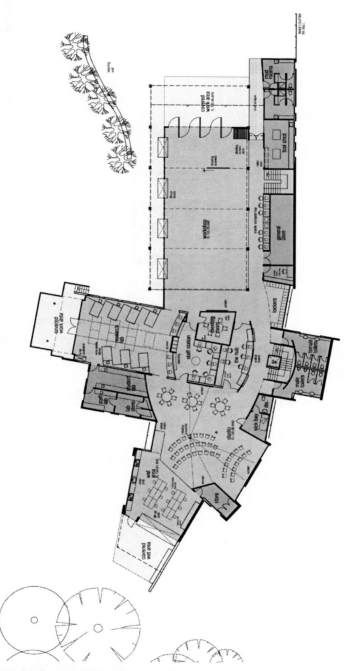

Figure 29. Learning Spaces at Eltham College, Australia. Designed by Clark Hopkins Clark Architects.

5. LEADING SYSTEM-WIDE TRANSFORMATION

For more than 100 years the lack of a school management methodology has been the cause of countless complaints. But it has been only in the last 30 years that efforts have been made to find a solution to this problem. And, what has resulted so far? Schools continue exactly the same as before.

Jan Amos Comenius, 1632

The purpose of this chapter is to give you an understanding of the following:

- How to achieve change at scale
- How to overcome inertia
- Methods for driving change and performance
- How to build the change leadership team
- Planning—process and ingredients
- The role of quality and different quality models
- How to maximise leadership and overcome obstacles
- How to build a culture of performance
- Measuring Return on Investment (ROI).

The key points made in this chapter are:

- There are many great individual examples of excellence but achieving transformational change at scale requires the application of disciplined thinking, planning and execution
- It's essential to apply pressure whilst at the same time giving support
- Agreeing on measurements and deciding on the right quality model is an important part of planning
- Without engaging stakeholders the change process will fail
- Leadership needs to be distributed to be successful
- Knowing and acting on Return on Investment is a key effectiveness driver.

n chapter 4 we learned how each layer of organisation needs to be re-arranged to bring about greater levels of effectiveness. Whilst this is most easily achieved under a strong leader, or in a "green field" site, achieving significant levels of re-organisation at scale is complex and requires sophisticated planning and disciplined execution.

Achieving Change at Scale

Achieving Change At Scale	Plan	Prepare	Implement	Embed	Review

- Overcoming Inertia
- Pressure and Support
- Driving Performance
- Driving Change

There are many leading practitioners bravely pushing the boundaries of schooling—some already mentioned here—but the problem is that there are far too few people determined and able enough to drive the kind of change needed to make schooling what it should be.

So the question is how to drive systemic change in a way that doesn't rely on driven individuals but, instead, is predicated on the organised, co-ordinated and collective effort of the workforce and stakeholders.

Overcoming Inertia

State funded schooling is a vast web of complex hierarchical interdependencies; national and state mandates; union dictated work rules; contracts and policies. Changes to schools and schooling are always accompanied by deep resistances—from conservative and traditionalists from the top to the bottom of the decision-making process.

Different stakeholders develop different, perhaps conflicting, interpretations filtered through their experiences of schooling, and their own values as former students. The fact that practically everyone went to school, and probably knows a teacher, makes everyone an "expert" on schooling.

External resistance to change comes from parents who often hold a kind of nostalgia for the kind of schooling which seemed to serve them so well when they were young. The media often don't help either—all too often, coverage of new approaches to schooling focus on the dips in performance that inevitably accompany early stages of innovation.

The press report below highlights a failure to think-through a laptop implementation. However, the clear message readers are left with is that laptops in schools are in themselves a bad thing, and that schooling is better without mobile technology and the internet.

"LIVERPOOL, N.Y. — The students at Liverpool High have used their school-issued laptops to exchange answers on tests, download pornography and hack into local businesses. When the school tightened its network security, a 10th grader not only found a way around it but also posted step-by-step instructions on the Web for others to follow (which they did).

Chris Barry, 16, carrying his laptop at Liverpool High School in Liverpool, N.Y., where they are being phased out. Scores of the leased laptops break down each month, and every other morning, when the entire school has study hall, the network inevitably freezes because of the sheer number of students roaming the Internet instead of getting help from teachers.

So the Liverpool Central School District, just outside Syracuse, has decided to phase out laptops starting this fall, joining a handful of other schools around the country that adopted one-to-one computing programmes and are now abandoning them as educationally empty—and worse..."

New York Times, May 4, 2007

There are many who have quaint ideas that there once was a golden age of education, and things would be so much better if we just went back to it. There's the "back to basics" brigade—those who want to see more forcefully imposed extrinsic discipline; respect for authority; and an emphasis on traditional subjects.

Resistance to change comes from within the system as well. One of the biggest internal inhibitors to change is the school timetable. Tyack and Cuban contend that the timetable has become so firmly established in the routines of secondary schools that virtually all attempts to dislodge it have been unsuccessful (Tyack and Cuban, 1995).

So often, leaders come up against forces that are dedicated to perpetuating the bureaucracy or status quo (Schleicher, 2009). "One possible reason for education's resistance to change is that substantive change means "going from a society of authority based on societal position to one where authority must constantly be earned" which in turn "increases the demands on the system itself" (OECD, 2006).

In the world of business, bureaucratic overheads like the Carnegie Unit (the over management of time) don't survive long because in business the pain of inefficiency is felt by all—falling financial performance quickly results in reorganisations and lay-offs.   In schooling, the pain of inefficiency, or underperformance, is rarely accompanied by the same consequences. Ultimately, people only change their habits when the pain involved in keeping that habit exceeds the pain of making the change.

In March 2010, David Cameron, now UK Prime Minister, made an attack on bureaucratic waste in the UK education system. In a leading British newspaper, Cameron saw an advert that had been "asking people 'to put questions to the National Strategies for primary children's writing.'"

"Just think of the bureaucratic carnival of waste behind an advertisement like this. A group of civil servants emerge, with a novel idea. They want to set up a taskforce for primary reading. The taskforce books a weekend away to devise a strategy. The strategy needs further thought so they hire consultants. Then there's the branding; the auditing; the monitoring. The strategy needs to be legally reviewed; peer reviewed; benchmarked; mentored and mainstreamed but not before there's a resource allocation impact assessment. Then they call the communications department to create a website, design an ad and get it placed. I could have saved them all that bother and all that money. Writing is about the imagination. What you need is some great teachers, some good books, some pencils and some paper. Is that really too difficult?" (David Cameron MP, 2010)

Whilst Cameron over-simplifies to make a political point, the key point is that there is little purpose to inclusiveness if there's a failure to deliver efficiently.

For publically funded schools—which sit outside a market-based system—the fact that schooling is compulsory gives them a captive market. This gives them a false and dominant position and a lack of genuine competition. This in turn leads to organisations becoming over-managed and under-led. This kind of organisation tends to hire and promote managers, not leaders, to cope with a growing bureaucracy, according to Dr John Kotter, in his book *Leading Change*. The pressures on managers come mostly from inside the organisation. Building and staffing a bureaucracy that can cope with growth is the biggest challenge, and external interests tend to be neglected. Managers fail to prioritise customers and external stakeholders and behave in an insular, sometimes political fashion. They also fail to acknowledge the value of leadership and the fact that employees at all levels and can provide it.(Kotter, 1996).

Pressure and Support

There is a great deal of inertia in *all* social systems—not just schooling systems—which means that new forces are required to change direction. Overcoming the forces of inertia through large scale transformation involves the judicious use of pressure and support.

Pressure means ambitious targets, transparent evaluation and monitoring, calling upon moral purpose, and the like. Support involves developing new competencies, access to new ideas, more time for learning and collaboration. The more that pressure and support become seamless, the more effective the change process at getting things to happen. As the drivers of change begin to operate in concert, pressure and support get built into the on-going culture of interaction (Fullan, *Learning to Lead Change*, 2004).

> "Where our ambitions are low and teachers and schools are poorly supported, nobody would expect much. But increasing the challenges through new standards, new tests, new school inspection, new publication of school test scores and so on without backing them up with a better support often just leads to conflict and demoralisation.
>
> On the other hand, strong support systems without clear ambitions tend to just strengthen schools that are already good while not raising performance systemically. The point is that it is the combination of challenge *and* support that characterises the best performing education systems" (Schleicher, 2009).

Pressure and support are delivered through leadership and management. The terms *leadership* and *management* are often used interchangeably, but there are big differences between them.

Management is a set of processes that can keep a complicated system of people and technology running smoothly. The most important aspects of management include planning, budgeting, organising, staffing, controlling, and problem solving. Leadership is a set of processes that creates organisations in the first place or encourages them to significantly change in circumstances. Leadership defines what the future should look like and aligns people with that vision and inspires them to make it happen despite the obstacles (Kotter, 1996).

The most challenging aspect of large scale transformation in schooling systems is altering the organisation whilst it is still operational. To do this requires two sets of activities in parallel: driving performance—a management job; whilst at the same time driving change—a leadership job.

Driving Performance

Performance management in schooling systems is contentious, but the question is not whether schooling systems will take steps to manage performance; it's a question of how serious they take performance and how well they'll do it. Even without a formal performance management strategy and systems in place, schooling systems have some method, process, or habits they've developed to manage performance. Whether this is simply done via informal, status-update conversations; quarterly reporting to board, staff and parents; bonus-pay incentives; or a formal management-by-objectives method—it's just the degree to which they are effective that varies.

In *Driving Business Performance* (Joey Fitts and Bruno Aziza, 2008), Joey Fitts and Bruno Aziza outline six steps that organisations—public or private sector—can take to improve results through performance management. These are:

- Increasing visibility
- Moving beyond gut feel
- Planning for success
- Executing on strategy
- Competing
- Culture of performance

Driving Large Scale Change

Large scale transformational change in any kind of large organisation, leave alone schooling, is complex and difficult. Harvard University professor, Dr John Kotter, in his book *Leading Change*, simplifies this by breaking down the difficulties into key components, then proposing specific types of actions that can be phased-in to address these and drive the change process:

Difficulty	Solution
Allowing too much complacency	Establishing a sense of urgency
Failing to create a sufficiently powerful leadership team	Creating the leadership team
Underestimating the power of vision	Developing a vision and strategy
Under-communicating the vision	Communicate the change vision
Permitting obstacles to block the new vision	Empowering broad-based action
Failing to create short-term wins	Generating short-term wins
Declaring victory too soon	Consolidating gains and producing more change
Neglecting to anchor changes firmly in the corporate culture	Anchoring new approaches in the culture

Table 16. Difficulties and solutions in managing transformation.

(Kotter, 1996)

Taking the most transferable principles and methodologies used in business, and applying them in a schooling system transformation context, we end up with five stages of development:

- Plan
- Prepare
- Implement
- Embed
- Review

Plan

Achieving Change At Scale	Plan	Prepare	Implement	Embed	Review

- Create the Change Leadership Team
- Design and Execute a Planning Process
- Decide on a Model of Quality Management
- Agree on Measurements
- Build a Detailed Budget

The term "planning" is used interchangeably for a vast array of activities, so what do we mean by planning in the context of managing system wide change?

In this section, we think of planning as the exercise that an organisation goes through to determine what its goals are and, more importantly, what its actions are to make the plan a reality.

Create the Change Leadership Team

The first step in the planning process is to build the change leadership team. This is about pulling together a group with enough power to lead change and getting it to work together as a team.

Four characteristics are essential for the leadership team to be effective:

1. **Position power**: Are enough key players on board, especially the main line managers, so that those left out cannot easily block process?
2. **Expertise**: Are the various points of view—in terms of discipline, experience etc.—relevant to the task in hand, and adequately represented so that informed, intelligent decisions will be made?
3. **Credibility**: Does the group have enough people with good reputations in the organisation so that its pronouncements will be taken seriously by other employees?
4. **Leadership**: does the group include enough proven leaders to be able to drive the change process?

The leadership team should have management as well as leadership disciplines—vision and strategies are created through leadership disciplines, whilst plans and budgets are created through management disciplines.

The "Belbin Team Model" is used widely to guide the formation of balanced teams. When people who exhibit the following characteristics are brought together they generally form effective workgroups due to the degree to which they complement one another:

Role	Characteristic
Plant	Creative, imaginative, unorthodox. Solves difficult problems.
Resource Investigator	Extrovert, enthusiastic, communicative. Explores opportunities. Develops contacts.
Co-ordinator	Mature, confident. Clarifies goals. Brings other people together to promote team discussions.
Shaper	Challenging, dynamic, thrives on pressure. Has the drive and courage to overcome obstacles.
Monitor Evaluator	Serious minded, strategic and discerning. Sees all options. Judges accurately.
Teamworker	Co-operative, mild, perceptive and diplomatic. Listens, builds, averts friction.
Implementer	Disciplined, reliable, conservative in habits. A capacity for taking practical steps and actions.
Completer Finisher	Painstaking, conscientious, anxious. Searches out errors and omissions. Delivers on time.
Specialist	Single-minded, self-starting, dedicated. Provides knowledge and skills in rare supply.

Table 17. Belbin Team Model.

Design and Execute a Planning Process

There is an overabundance of planning theories and methods, and it's very easy to overcomplicate this area or turn it into a bureaucratic quagmire. Ultimately, planning comes down to running through a set of processes, considering some key factors, and arriving at a set of intended outcomes and actions that can be communicated clearly and effectively to all. In planning for schooling transformation, the following can serve as a high level planning template.

Outcomes	Factors	Planning Processes
Vision and Mission— Define a vision that specifies the intended future state of the organisation. Define a mission that specifies the purpose of the organisation.	Establish and agree the ideal future state. Make it bold, ambitious, worth getting out of bed for, achievable and time-bound.	• Envisioning • Legacy analysis • SWOT • PESTLE analysis • Force field analysis
Goals—Specific, time-bound and measurable outcomes.	Establishing what stakeholders want from schooling: • Who are the stakeholders? • What do they want? • What is schooling for? • What should students learn? • Economic outcomes • Financial outcomes • Social outcomes	• Stakeholder map • Stakeholder perception analysis • Stakeholder needs analysis • Outcome map—define outcomes against stakeholder needs • Curriculum planning • Benchmarking
Policy—Define clearly the stakeholders and required outcomes for each stakeholder group. Guide the decisions that will achieve the required outcomes through: • Legislation—legally binding obligations • Intentions—high level goals and statements of values • Procedural—state how something will be done and by whom • Guideline: Non-binding information that assists in implementing procedures	Define The Levers Of Change and prioritise resources and investments— e.g.: • Early years • Prioritised subject areas • Targeting the neediest • Maximise the use of time • Use analytics and Enterprise Resource Planning (ERP) • Hire and develop the best quality leaders • Reduce absenteeism and turnover • Raise the status of teachers • Remodel teachers' pay • Accelerate and personalise learning • Promote learning beyond the classroom • Involve parents and the community	• Root cause analysis • Map needs vs. system requirements • Strategic canvas Policy checklist: • Outcomes are clearly stated • Assumptions are explicit • There are links to government strategic plan and direction • Stakeholders have been included • Student interest has been given the highest priority • Political expectations have been met • The policy is likely to be effective • There is measurability • Evaluation is possible • There is accountability

		• It is lawful and enforceable • Ideas have been tested
Strategy—Plans of action designed to achieve specific goals **Budgets**—Allocations of capital and resources to operations and projects **Architectures**—Organisational, information and technological systems, and physical environments **Actions**—Prioritised organisational objectives; workgroup and individual performance goals; culture and group processes	This is about doing what it takes to restructure schooling so it delivers the vision, and includes, e.g: • Moving from time to performance-based systems • Eliminating waste from the learning process • Managing learning in a performance based system • Giving schools autonomy • Building a schooling enterprise architecture • Modernising schooling environments • Re-organising funding	• Blue Ocean Strategy—decide what to stop, start, reduce and increase • Choose the operating model and organisational structures • Plan changes to physical, information and technology architectures • Decide who funds what, and to what extent

Table 18. The schooling modernisation planning process.

As you work through the process it's important to build a summary that enables the main building blocks to be viewed together. This enables stakeholders to quickly grasp the key concepts. For example:

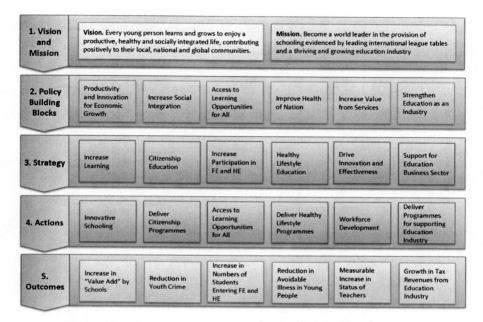

Figure 30. Pulling the plan together into a single "building block" representation.

Decide on a Model of Quality Management

A key decision to be made is how to address quality management. Basu describes four stages in a hierarchy of quality (Basu, 2009).

Inspection

- Checking work after the event
- Identify sources of non-conformance
- Take corrective action

This is an expensive method for achieving a basic level of quality. It requires the employment of people to check on the operation. Inspection and supervision don't add value to the service, they merely add to the cost.

Quality Control (QC)

- Self-inspection
- Quality planning and procedures
- Use of process performance data

In QC, control relies more on the use of data. In schooling, QC is about analysing outcomes, monitoring learning processes and sampling work.

Quality Assurance (QA)

- Develop quality systems
- Use of quality data
- Quality planning
- Control through the use of statistical processes

Whilst inspection and QC is about detecting error or low performance after the event, QA is about preventing mistakes or poor performance. It's largely about training and process improvement.

Total Quality Management (TQM)

- Teamwork
- Employee involvement
- Process management
- Performance measurement
- Involves:
    - All functions
    - Suppliers
    - Customers

TQM, defined by the International Standards Organisation (ISO) as the "management approach centred on quality, based on the participation of all its members and aiming at long-term success through customer satisfaction, and benefits to all members of the organisation", supports the idea that quality is the responsibility of the entire workforce.

Agree on Measurements

You can only manage what you can measure, so at this stage getting agreement about what gets measured is the key. There are five categories where measurement should be applied:

- **Academic**—Qualifications, acquisition of 21st Century skills, test results and Value Added.
- **Operational Excellence**—return on investment, value for money, exploitation of ICT
- **Stakeholder Satisfaction**—parents, students and staff satisfaction
- **People**—organisational health, staff retention, staff qualifications
- **Building Management**—energy use, carbon reduction, water use, electricity generation and area occupation and use.

Build a Detailed Budget

Strategies are broken down into actionable activities, the total costs of which can be predicted. Costs need to include everything required to deliver a particular programme—including people, materials, and all other related expenses.

Gauging the optimal funding level is about understanding the upper and lower limits of effectiveness. One approach is to map expenditure against known ROI from pilot projects. At the lower limits, rate of ROI accelerates with investment. As investment levels approach the upper limits, ROI starts to decelerate. The trick is to set investment between these turning points.

Activity Based Costing

Activity Based Costing (ABC) is an accounting technique that allows an organisation to assign more accurate service costs by understanding activities that create cost. ABC is based on the concept that services give rise to activities, which in turn drive costs.

Traditional cost report	Activity based cost report
Teaching salaries $5.0m	Classroom teaching $2.5m
	Managing discipline $0.8
	Examination and testing $0.7
	Administration $0.6
	Absence and illness $0.3
	Insurances $0.1
$5.0m	$5.0m

Table 19. Activity Based Costing example.

In providing more accurate allocation of costs ABC has proved to be useful in identifying cost reduction or resource allocation opportunities.

Prepare

| Achieving Change At Scale | Plan | **Prepare** | Implement | Embed | Review |

- Prepare your Organisation for Change
- Prepare for Improved Decision Making
- Communicate the Change Vision

Prepare your Organisation for Change

The fear of change is normal. At the beginning of the change process the 'losses' are specific and tangible (it is clear what is being left behind), but the gains are theoretical and distant—you cannot realise the gains until they have been implemented. Not everyone will have confidence that the gains will be attained.

Ironically, the clearer the new vision the easier it is for people to see all the specific ways in which they will be incompetent and look silly. Many prefer to be competent at the [old] wrong thing than incompetent at the [new] right thing.

In other words, an additional element of change process involves realising that clear, even inspiring, visions are not sufficient. People need the right combinations of pressure and support to become adept and comfortable with 'the new right way' (Fullan, *Learning to Lead Change*, 2004).

Fullan also talks about engaging educators, community leaders and society as a whole in the moral purpose of schooling reform. For example, a commitment to raising the bar and closing the gap in student achievement is a moral purpose.

How to Establish the Necessity of Change

One of the biggest causes of inertia is the absence of a major and visible crisis. Where there is no acceptance of the need to change, Dr. John Kotter suggests in his book *Leading Change* the following techniques can be used to make everyone realise the change is necessary:

- Expose managers to major weaknesses by making comparisons with other systems. Jim Collins, in *Good to Great* (Collins, 2001) found that 'great' organisations have a commitment to 'confronting the brutal facts'
- Set stakeholder satisfaction targets so high that they can't be reached by conducting "business as usual"
- Stop measuring performance based on narrow functional goals and insist that more people be held accountable for broader measures of performance
- Send more data about stakeholder satisfaction and outcomes to more employees, especially information that demonstrates weaknesses versus other schooling systems
- Insist that people talk directly about unsatisfied stakeholders
- Stop senior management "happy talk" by putting more honest discussion of the organisation's problems into staff communications and senior managers' speeches
- Take every opportunity to provide people with information on future opportunities, and the rewards for capitalising on those opportunities, and on the organisation's current inability to pursue those opportunities.

(Kotter, 1996)

Engage Stakeholders

For change to work you need the energy, ideas, commitment and 'ownership' of all those implicated in implementing improvements.

The goal of stakeholder engagement is to:

- Identify individuals and groups affected by and capable of influencing the design
- Explain the initiative to key stakeholders
- Assess their interest and areas of resistance and how they might help or hinder progress
- Agree their roles and responsibilities within the programme.

As the end customers for proposed changes, it's essential to involve students in the planning process. Students vote with their attention, engagement and participation, so giving them a voice in how their schooling operates is plain common sense.

It's surprising just how articulate some students are when asked to give their perspectives on learning, teaching, and schooling. Their insights warrant not only the attention but also the responses of adults.

Prepare for Improved Decision-Making

To take an organisation through a change management programme requires a step-change in decision-making. Decisions will be larger scale, more complex and more emotionally charged. They will need to be made more quickly, in a less certain environment, and they will require more sacrifice from those implementing the decisions.

Making better decisions starts with data that can be trusted, information that is shared, execution that is aligned, and results that are reported. Leaders, managers and "front line workers" all need data to understand what is going on across the organisation.

Some institutions simply do not know what they don't know. Since they haven't been closely managing their data and performance information, they lack detailed knowledge of their educational effectiveness and are therefore unable to see issues and opportunities. They focus more on activities than on measured progress toward goals. They may not be aware that they are being ineffective, or that they are missing opportunities to increase educational impact because they have not yet developed an analytic capability or implemented the tools to enable rich inquiry.

In cases like these, the institution is not seeking to resolve a performance problem because it doesn't yet know that it has the problem (or opportunity). The benefit of managing performance in this case is that it enables the identification of problems and opportunities the organisation had no knowledge of—and results in the ability to make better decisions to produce improvements.

Ultimately, better performance comes from the entire workforce making better decisions faster. The value chain of information progresses from data to impact in this way:

Data → Information → Insight → Decision → Impact → Results

Making better decisions in schooling systems is about being able to act on relevant, accessible and high quality data. In turn, the ability to trust data is a prerequisite to managing performance.

The value of high quality data is well understood in the world of business where it is common for data to be certified. Companies such as Siemens and Expedia provide quality and accuracy seals for data, to make sure that their systems don't get "garbage in" leading to "garbage out".

A critical point is that making data available is nowhere near enough. Exposing a school as underperforming can be damaging unless the principal has the power to make staffing changes—through performance management, CPD or firing and hiring.

Communicate the Change Vision

If your workforce has a shared sense of purpose it will be easier to initiate the actions to achieve that purpose. Use every vehicle possible to constantly communicate the new vision and strategies. In *Leading Change*, Dr. Kotter outlines some tips on how to communicate this change vision.

Clearly, the vision itself, and not just how it is communicated, needs to be highly effective. Characteristics of an effective vision are as follows:

- **Imaginable:** conveys a clear picture of what the future will look like
- **Desirable:** appeals to the long-term interests of employees, students, stakeholders, and beyond
- **Feasible**: it comprises realistic, attainable goals
- **Focused:** it is clear enough to provide guidance in decision-making
- **Flexible:** is general enough to allow individual initiative and alternative responses in the light of changing conditions
- **Communicable:** it is easy to communicate and can be successfully explained within 5 minutes.

Key elements in the effective communication of the vision are as follows:

- **Simplicity:** all jargon and techno-babble must be eliminated
- **Metaphor, analogy, and example:** a verbal picture is worth 1000 words
- **Multiple forms:** big meetings; small memos; newsletters; bulletins; blogs; wikis; formal and informal interaction—are all effective ways of spreading the word
- **Repetition:** ideas sink in deeply only after they have been heard many times
- **Leadership by example:** behaviour from important people that is inconsistent with the vision overwhelms all other forms of communication
- **Explanation of seeming inconsistencies:** unaddressed inconsistencies undermine the credibility of all communication
- **Give and take:** two-way communication is always more powerful than one-way communication.

If people don't accept the vision, the next steps in the transformation process will fail. Even worse, if they accept and then attempt to implement a poorly formulated vision, precious time and resources will be wasted and many people will suffer the consequences. The downside to two-way communication is that feedback may suggest that we are on the wrong course and that the vision needs to be reformulated. But in the long run, swallowing pride and re-working the vision will be much more productive than heading off to the wrong direction—or in a direction that others won't follow (Kotter, 1996).

People affected by change go through several phases—contact; awareness; understanding; buy-in; trial use; limited adoption; use; institutionalisation. Each of these phases requires different types of communication:

Communication tactics to support change adoption	
Stage of change adoption	*Communications activities*
Awareness and understanding	Familiarisation for regular information flow: meetings, emails, print etc.
Buy-in	Persuasion—personal and group meetings, demonstrations
Adoption	Training and support, continued information support
Use	Information sharing, development and more sophisticated messages that encourage people to identify with and advocate the new organisation design

Table 20. Communication tactics to support change adoption.

Implement

| Achieving Change At Scale | Plan | Prepare | Implement | Embed | Review |

- Execute on Strategy
- Move Beyond Gut Feel
- Get Rid of Obstacles
- Generate Short Term Wins

Execute on Strategy

Having built a comprehensive plan, the next stage is to ensure that the whole organisation executes it. Best-practice organisations are able to inspire the discipline of execution in their workforce, enabling their people to become the "agents of change" across the organisation. This moves the organisation from disconnected pockets of decisions made in silos and driven by gut feel, to informed decision-making tied to common and aligned objectives.

In executing on strategy, the objective is to create an environment where the myriad of decisions taken every day support and contribute to the overall strategic objectives of the organisation. They want to create an environment where employees are like the third bricklayer in the fabled "Three Bricklayers" story. In the story, the first bricklayer says, "I'm laying bricks," the second says, "I'm making a wall," and the third says, "I'm building a cathedral." The third bricklayer understands the context of the organisational mission and how daily tactics are contributing to the overall goal.

Aligning day-to-day activities to the overall strategy is done *through* performance management because every individual needs to be able and motivated to making better, more informed decisions that are aligned with the organisation's strategy. There are three phases to managing individual people's performance, each of which needs to align to the organisation's strategic goals:

- Planning—where goals and objectives that align to the organisation's strategy are agreed
- Coaching—where managers and peers give feedback
- Appraisal—where individual performance is formally assessed and documented

Fitts and Aziza (Joey Fitts and Bruno Aziza, 2008) talk of a "line of sight" from strategic to operational to tactical decisions as the discipline that drives aligned execution. "Line of sight" means clear visibility of goals, and progress towards them at executive (strategic), management (operational), employees (tactical) levels.

"Clear line of sight" is also about performance metric alignment across organisational layers. This can be thought of as an organisation chart for performance metrics, indicating how the various levels of the organisation's performance metrics relate to one another. At school level, classroom teacher's metrics roll up to their Head of Department, which in turn roll up to Deputy Principals, which in turn roll up to the Principal. In turn, and depending on the mode of operations, performance metrics for Principals should roll up to those of Local Authority Directors, which in turn finally roll up to the MoE.

Move Beyond Gut Feel

In any school or schooling system, any day of the week, hundreds or even thousands of decisions are made. Each of these decisions has an impact, positive or negative, large or small scale. These decisions are the way that the system operates and evolves.

Schooling systems by definition are run and staffed by experts. Cultures with experts sometimes resist a different approach than their expertise dictates. It is understandably the case that experts are often reticent to change to a culture where data can override their judgement. However, improving the quality of decisions necessarily involves moving beyond gut feel and basing decisions on *both* professional judgement and information—i.e. informed professional judgement.

An organization that operates on the basis of facts and validated information benefits not only from making better decisions across the organization, but also from having a more disciplined culture. To improve the quality of decisions, organisations need to first understand how decisions are made. There are three types of decisions that drive performance: strategic, tactical, and operational.

- **Strategic decisions** typically influence the direction of an organisation, or the mission it will try to accomplish. While there tend to be few of these decisions made throughout the year, they require a large amount of information and time. Everyone within the organisation needs to align to them.

- **Operational decisions** are made by managers and are often about allocating resources to accomplish a planned objective. These decisions require relevant information and analytic and forecasting capabilities to be available to the managers.
- **Tactical decisions** occur much more frequently than strategic and operational decisions. In a schooling system they are made mainly by classroom teachers, largely in relation to dealing with individual students, and tend to be made rapidly and on the spot. They are often made on gut feel and habits. Cumulatively, these decisions can determine overall student and parent satisfaction. The quality of these decisions can be greatly improved with real-time, detailed and relevant student information.

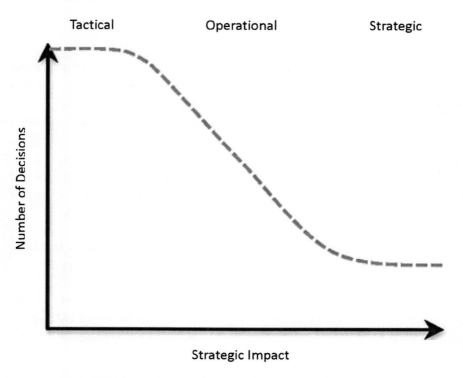

Figure 31. Frequency and impact of decision—courtesy of Aziza and Fitts, *Driving Business Performance*.

The top level of the organisation—where the smallest number of decisions are made—tends to be best serviced with information.   Paradoxically, the classroom—where the vast majority of decisions are made—tends to be least serviced. To move beyond gut feel, the right information needs to be put into the hands of those who are best able to capitalise on it (Kotter, 1996).

Get Rid of Obstacles

Organisational structure can present a series of obstacles, for example:

- Giving more responsibility to lower level employees may be prevented because layers of middle managers second guess and criticise those on the front line
- A desire to speed everything up may be prevented because independent silos don't communicate and thus slow everything down
- A focus on the student could be prevented because the organisation fragments the delivery of its services.

A key way to get rid of obstacles is to align systems to the vision.   Take HR systems for example. These should cover performance appraisal, compensation, promotions, succession planning—all of which need to be aligned to the new vision. If a new vision has an emphasis on student satisfaction for example, that needs to be reflected in the performance evaluation forms. Individual objectives need to be tightly aligned to the organisation's overall objectives; compensation and bonuses need to reflect over achievement against the vision and goals; under/over-achievement again needs to be calibrated against the organisation's overall goals. Recruiting and hiring systems again need to reflect the vision and goals of the organisation.

In transformational change projects, training is usually required in the following areas:

- *Going through the change process itself.* Employees affected by the new design will be at the front line of the change process and therefore must know how to contribute to the changes as effectively as possible and how to work within the changing circumstances.

- *New systems, technologies, processes.* The way in which new systems operate and the technical aspects of doing work with different equipment and in different environments.
- *The work of the organisation when it has been re-engineered.* If the nature of the workforce's activities and responsibilities change, employees will have to acquire new expertise and competencies.

The end goal is a cultural change, and sometimes the only way to change a culture is to change people. Organisational change inevitably brings with it changes in job descriptions and creation of new jobs. This is sensitive and requires the close involvement of the organisation's HR managers, whose knowledge of impact of suggested changes in job descriptions, career paths and succession planning can help to ensure a smooth transition.

Generally approaches to job design should result in:

- Career paths for employees to move to more skilled and higher positions
- Strategies to enable suitably qualified personnel to occupy new positions—sometimes this means staff have to re-apply for their current jobs
- Hiring, promoting and developing people who can implement the change vision
- Identification of training and development needs to meet future staffing requirements.

(Stanford, 1996)

Generate Short Term Wins

Kotter emphasises the importance of short term wins to drive the change process. In schooling, these can often come from pilots—one totally transformed school can act as a showcase for others. Within a school, a block of classes or subject areas can become a pilot for new approaches. The following are Dr John Kotter's ideas for generating and celebrating short term wins from his book *Leading Change*:

- **Provide evidence that sacrifices are worth it:** wins greatly help justify the short term costs involved

- **Reward change agents with a 'pat on the back':** after a lot of hard work, positive feedback builds morale and motivation
- **Help find-tune vision and strategies:** short-term wins give the leadership team concrete data on the validity of their ideas
- **Undermine cynics and self-serving resistors:** clear improvements in performance make it difficult for people to block the need to change
- **Keep bosses on board:** provide those higher in the hierarchy with evidence that transformation is on track
- **Build momentum:** turn neutrals into supporters, and reluctant supporters into active helpers.

(Kotter, 1996)

Embed

Achieving Change At Scale	Plan	Prepare	Implement	Embed	Review

- Leadership Models
- Achieve and Compete
- Build a Culture of Performance
- Sustaining Excellence
- Multi-level Transformation

Leadership Models

Resistance is always waiting to reassert itself. This is why changes need to be anchored into a new culture. In order to embed cultural change, leadership needs to be developed throughout the organisation—not just at the top. Managers need to become managing leaders, and "front line" workers need to be encouraged to demonstrate leadership by trying out new approaches and encouraging others to follow successful strategies.

Many, like Michael Fullan, argue that leadership is *the* most powerful lever in managing change. For the purpose of leading system-wide transformation, we are interested in two areas of leadership:

- Transformational Leadership
- Distributed Leadership

Transformational Leadership

Exeter University's Centre for Leadership Studies, citing Bass and Avolio, state that transformational leaders display behaviours associated with five transformational styles:

Transformational Style	Leader Behaviour
1) Idealised behaviours: living one's ideals	• Talk about their most important values and beliefs • Specify the importance of having a strong sense of purpose • Consider the moral and ethical consequences of decisions • Champion exciting new possibilities • Talk about the importance of trusting each other
2) Inspirational motivation: inspiring others	• Talk optimistically about the future • Talk enthusiastically about what needs to be accomplished • Articulate a compelling vision of the future • Express confidence that goals will be achieved • Take a stand on controversial issues
3) Intellectual stimulation: stimulating others	• Re-examine critical assumptions • Seek differing perspectives when solving problems • Get others to look at problems from many different angles • Suggest new ways of looking at how to complete assignments • Encourage non-traditional thinking to deal with traditional problems • Encourage rethinking those ideas which have never been questioned before
4) Individualised consideration: coaching and development	• Spend time teaching and coaching • Treat others as individuals rather than just as members of the group • Consider individuals as having different needs, abilities, and aspirations from others • Help others to develop their strengths • Listen attentively to others' concerns • Promote self-development
5) Idealised attributes: respect, trust, and faith	• Instil pride in others for being associated with them • Go beyond their self-interests for the good of the group

	• Act in ways that build others' respect
	• Display a sense of power and competence
	• Make personal sacrifices for others' benefit
	• Reassure others that obstacles will be overcome

Table 21. Transformational leadership behaviours

(Bass and Avolio, 1994)

Distributed Leadership

"Leadership, to be effective, must spread throughout the organization... The main mark of a school principal at the end of his or her tenure is not just their impact on the bottom line of student achievement, but rather how many leaders they leave behind who can go even further. Successful managing is not about one's own success but about fostering success in others."

At a practical level, developing leadership in schooling systems is about "enhancing the decision-making capabilities of others" (Fullan, *Learning to Lead Change*, 2004).

The UK's National College for School Leadership has an extensive library of resources to support the development of leadership in schools. In a paper entitled "Everyone a Leader", NCSL identify core principles and practical activities that enable everyone to be a leader and play their part in distributed leadership—e.g.: giving "front line" staff opportunities to:

- Join the senior management team for a specified time and/or purpose
- Lead an initiative in their curriculum area
- Take responsibility outside one's own subject or key stage specialism
- Manage a whole-school theme day
- Set an agenda and chair a staff meeting
- Be a part of an interviewing process
- Make presentations to parents, governors, community partners, etc.
- Take assemblies

(National College for School Leadership, 2006)

Achieve and Compete

In education, the concept of competition is contentious. On the one hand a key goal of schooling is to drive equality of opportunity, which in turn drives social stability. There is no question that a key objective is to narrow the achievement gap between the poorest and the highest performing students.

On the other hand, whether we like it or not, every single student leaving every single school in the world will be thrust into competition—for jobs, for housing, for resources, for their desired lifestyles, etc. At the same time, there isn't a single school that won't be competing for resources, the best staff, the brightest and the best behaved students. Whether we like it or not, parents too are in competition with one another to send their children to the best schools.

The problem occurs when the goal of equality of opportunity is confused with the idea that all schools should be equal. Schools are made of people, people are different—so schools are by definition different and therefore cannot be equal. Fighting this "law of nature" is a waste of resource, so the question is how can we capitalise on it?

A market-based approach can both drive equality of opportunity and capitalise on the fact that schools operate in a competitive environment. In *Think Scenarios, Rethinking Education*, the OECD argues for an information-driven market based approach:

- "First, we can use the information we are gathering from standard tests and other more subtle diagnostic tools to identify the needs of each student, each school, and each district.
- Second, we can allow each school to purchase the supplies, the skills, the personnel it needs to satisfy the needs of its students. Because the information we gather will show that some students have special needs, schools should be allocated special funds to meet those.
- Third, students and their parents can be given the opportunity to shop around for the schools and teachers that best meet their needs.

Funding should follow the flow of student choices. Schools that are chosen by unusually high numbers of students with special needs will be given correspondingly larger budgets.   Those budgets can be spent on increased salaries for those unusually gifted and heroic teachers who can succeed with students at risk.

A system like this will allow market mechanisms to allocate valuable resources far more equitably than the systems now in place. Market forces will reward results—outcomes rather than inputs. Our current system rewards inputs—e.g. years of service, courses taken, credentials—rather than proven effectiveness of teachers or schools. The genius of the market is precisely to process information: information about needs and preferences that a monopoly can afford to neglect" (OECD, 2006).

This broadly makes sense, but three conditions should be met if introducing a more market-led approach:

1. The schooling outcomes being rewarded should be "value-add", not just raw examination or test results. This makes comparing schools a lot fairer and more accurate;
2. The market system must be able to respond quickly to failure. It's no good having to wait for five years to build a new school to take over from one that is failing. To ensure equality of opportunity, failure should be rectified immediately;
3. The market system should reward well those who exceed expectations. A market system should be predicated on encouraging the workforce to push beyond accepted limits of quality, customer satisfaction and professionalism.

In the previous sections—"Increasing Visibility" to "Execute on Strategy"— we've talked about how organisations can manage themselves better internally. But how does any organisation know if its best is good enough? Even if an organisation is predictably achieving 100% of its goals, that still may be 50% short of what is achievable.

Organisations need to have external context to ensure they are not only performing well, but performing better than the competition, and thereby giving students and parents reasons to "vote" for their services. To do this, schools and schooling systems need to benchmark results against value-add standards nationally, and international benchmarks such as PISA and TIMSS.

The Development Bank of Southern Africa (DBSA) competes for public support, government aid, and private-sector sponsorship. The DBSA is a good example of how to align to public objectives that stakeholders have defined as success. Dave Evans, Executive Coordinator, Group Risk Assurance Division for DBSA, explains:

"Our government has a 10-year plan called 'The People's Contract' which was put together in 2004. There are measures that have to do with reducing poverty levels, and the number of households without access to clean water and electricity. We also have the UN Millennium Development Goals which relate to things like reducing mother mortality from childbirth; improving education in particular increasing the percentage of females in school; hygiene; health (with diseases like malaria and AIDS); sanitation, etc. A Balanced Scorecard gives us a framework to see how we're impacting against those goals. The report of how we're doing on our Balanced Scorecard is a separate section in our annual report and is vetted by our external auditors" (Joey Fitts and Bruno Aziza, 2008).

Another aspect of competition is concerned both with whether the school is doing anything that could be better provided by someone else, the strategic use of resources, and getting best value for expenditure.

- Are resources allocated across key spending areas so that high funding in one area does not compromise quality in another?
- Does the school ensure it receives the most economic, efficient and effective service from those who provide services to students and staff?

Build a Culture of Performance, Learning and Evaluation

On one level, culture is easy to change—e.g. relaxing a school uniform or dress code represents a clear cultural shift. Changing behaviours is much harder because they tend to be driven by non-rational factors such as trust, friendship, jealousy, fear, power struggles, ambition and the grapevine.

So, how should we approach developing enterprise cultures out of bureaucratic factory type organisations? First, we have to accept that cultural change comes at the end of the transformation process often when it's very clear that the transformation process has worked and is yielding better results for all. Secondly we need to accept that cultures don't just appear—they have to be developed, and that takes leadership.

To start with, it helps to have everyone working to a common vision, diffused leadership and a focus on outcomes.

Then, it's about pulling the following levers:

- **The Paradigm:** What the organization is about; what it does; its mission; its values
- **Control Systems:** The processes in place to monitor what is going on
- **Organisational Structures:** Reporting lines, hierarchies, and the way that work flows through the organisation
- **Power Structures:** Who makes the decisions, how widely spread is power, and on what is power based?
- **Symbols:** These include organisational logos and designs, but also extend to symbols of power such as parking spaces and even the quality and hierarchy of washrooms
- **Rituals and Routines:** Meetings, reporting structures, the rhythm of the schooling year
- **Stories and Myths:** These build up about people and events, and convey a message about what is valued within the organisation. What gets rewarded, and how visible those rewards are sends very strong signals.

(Johnson, 1988)

To move schooling towards modern, performance driven, customer orientated organisations there are three key cultural behaviours that need to be developed:

Culture of Performance

A culture of performance is goal orientated; results are measured and members—both staff and students—are competitive. A culture of performance is about transparency and predictability, and the ability to adapt to changing conditions. With capabilities to monitor, analyse, and plan, performance orientated organisations can create a culture where information is a prized asset, aligned execution is the norm, and accountability is embedded.

Culture of Learning

An organisation that has a culture of learning will have a set of strategies so that people can learn from each other; other organisations; and the latest theoretical thinking about learning itself—e.g., brain science, motivational theory, and relevant social sciences. This theory is useless on its own but has immense value when used to drive innovation and commitment to improvement.

"One of the most powerful drivers of change involves learning from peers, especially those who are further along in implementing new ideas. Strategies for learning from each other involve developing learning communities at the local, school and community levels, and learning from other schools—local, regional, national and beyond."

(Fullan, *Learning to Lead Change*, 2004)

Aidan McCarthy, an Australian-based education technology expert, recommends that schooling districts use a mentoring system that "embeds" and rotates leading teachers in new departments every 12 months.

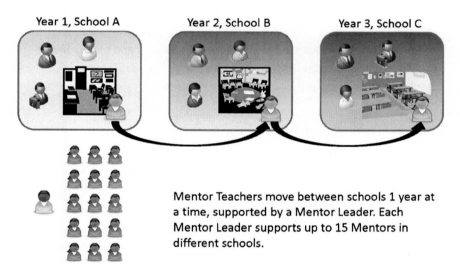

Mentor Teachers move between schools 1 year at a time, supported by a Mentor Leader. Each Mentor Leader supports up to 15 Mentors in different schools.

Figure 32. Using "embedded" mentor teachers.

Culture of Evaluation

One of the highest yield strategies for educational change recently developed is 'Assessment *for* Learning' (not just assessment *of* learning). Assessment for learning incorporates:

- Accessing/gathering data on student learning
- Disaggregating data for more detailed understanding
- Developing action plans based on the previous two points in order to make improvements

- Being able to articulate and discuss performance with parents, internal and external groups

(Fullan, *Learning to Lead Change*, 2004)

Sustaining Excellence

The ultimate goal of the change management process is to create and sustain high performance work practices. The UK Department of Trade and Industry define high performance practices as follows:

- High employee involvement practices, e.g. self-directed teams, quality circles and shared access to information
- Human resource practices, for example sophisticated recruitment processes, performance appraisals, work redesign and mentoring
- Rewards and commitment practices e.g., financial rewards, family friendly policies, job rotation and flexi hours.

The United States Government Accountability Office describes a high performance organisation as follows:

"A high performing organisation has a focus on achieving results and outcomes, and a results-orientated organisation culture. High performing organisations have a clear, well-articulated and compelling mission. They use partnerships strategically; they focus on the needs of clients and customers and strategically manage people. They have a coherent mission, strategic goals for achieving it and a performance management system that aligns with these goals to show employees how their performance can contribute to the overall results of the organisation."

Multi-level Transformation

System transformation needs to happen at three levels. We don't just need to change individuals and schools but entire schooling systems—something that Fullan calls the tri-level model. We need to ask three fundamental questions:

- What has to happen at the school and community level?
- What has to happen at the district level?
- What has to happen at the level of the state?

(Fullan, *Learning to Lead Change*, 2004)

Change management needs to be co-ordinated at the policy level at each layer.

Review

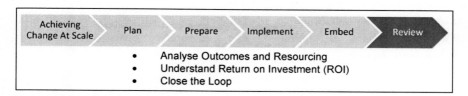

- Analyse Outcomes and Resourcing
- Understand Return on Investment (ROI)
- Close the Loop

At this stage it should be possible to use data to inform short term, tactical decisions and amend longer term strategy and policy. The end-goal of the planning process is to arrive at a course of action that gets ever better results from the money spent. In other words, as more resources are deployed, the resulting outcomes should improve exponentially. Charles Leadbeater offers a simple but powerful illustration of this (Leadbeater, 2005):

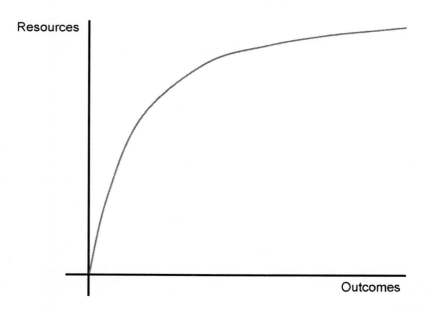

Figure 33. Resource vs. outcomes, Charles Leadbeater, *Shape Of Things To Come*, 2005.

Analyse Outcomes and Resources

Schooling systems should be able to assess current levels and trends against key performance indicators. The organisation should know how these results compare with the performance of comparable organisations and of other appropriate student populations. The comparative costs and resourcing requirements should also be known.

Charlotte Mecklenburg, one of the highest performing school districts in the United States, wanted to maintain its trajectory of high student achievement so tracked the efficacy of its programmes and initiatives so that it could identify which succeeded and which failed to produce desired results. Rather than depend on ad hoc reports manually produced by the central office a few times a year, the Board of Education needed a way to continually monitor and assess programmes in real time. Then it could make informed timely decisions about continuing only those programmes that showed a measurable positive effect on student teacher and the district's operational performance.

For planning purposes, key metrics should include:

- Student learning and improvement
- Stakeholder satisfaction/dissatisfaction
- Budgetary, and financial data

Understand ROI

Bringing our understandings of outputs versus inputs together leads us to Return on Investment. This is a highly contentious issue in education because there are just so many factors and variables to take into account. Understanding ROI is crucial—without it, plans will never evolve to deliver improvements—ultimately, you can't manage what you can't measure.

At a very simple level you could argue that ROI can be broken down into the number of units of learning completed divided by the cost. Whilst a useful idea, schooling systems are ecosystems, so for ROI to be a useful tool, it needs to be more sophisticated than that.

According to Cranfield University School of Management, all benefits can be measured to one degree or another, and the main categories of benefit are:

- Financial—can it be converted to money?
- Observable—can you see it, or find evidence of it?
- Quantifiable—do you have the figures available now, somewhere?

ROI can be thought of in value terms too. For example, economic value, which needs to be understood at the level of contributing human capital to local, regional and national economic development plans. Social value—clearly the domain of schooling—is more complex, but the Harvard Business School offers some useful insights:

"... Social Value is 'about inclusion and access. It is about respect and the openness of institutions. It is about history, knowledge, a sense of heritage and cultural identity...' Value creation in this arena can be measured using a social return on investment metric (SROI), social earnings calculations and other evolving metrics. SROI analysis attempts to identify direct, demonstrable cost savings or revenue contributions that result from... interventions.

(Jed Emerson, Jay Wachowicz, Suzi Chun, 2001)

One clear example would be to connect citizenship programmes with reductions in crime, or healthy eating programmes with reductions in healthcare costs. Whilst always an inexact science, serious attempts need to be made to quantify the contribution of schooling to a wider Social Value.

Steps to Establishing ROI

The London Borough of Hillingdon produced an excellent model for understanding ROI across a range of public services. The following is based on this work (Simon Willis (Editor), 2005).

The first step is to list all the benefits that come from an initiative across all stakeholders. The second step is to categorise those benefits into three groups:

Financial Benefits

Those that will (when delivered) realise hard tangible cost savings, e.g. reduced premises costs or savings in procurement costs.

E.g.

- Reduced recruitment costs from reduced turnover
- Reduced facilities management costs
- Cheaper, faster procurement—enabled by online procurement
- Reduced postage costs—swapping from manual post to email.

Efficiency Benefits

These are productivity improvements in terms of employee time saved, e.g. from web-enabled self-service. They can either be banked as financial savings or alternatively used as 'free' resources to be reallocated elsewhere.

E.g.

- Greater productivity—increased staff motivation from flexible working
- Better use of specialists—focus on value-added tasks via job redesign
- Reduced staff turnover—improved work-life-balance
- Greater efficiency in data handling from access to electronic information
- Reducing resource duplication
- Reduced admin from standardisation of responses—e.g. communication to parents
- Parent and student self-service using online forms/transactions
- Enhanced performance-monitoring through tracking/data
- Simplify supply chains.

Human Capital Benefits

Those benefits that cannot be converted with any degree of reliability into cash or productivity gains, but are the core operation of schooling—i.e. learning:

- Academic Qualifications
- Vocational Qualifications
- 21st Century Skills

ROI Table—Example

An example of how this can then be brought together is as follows:

Programme	Financial Benefits	Efficiency Benefits (cash equivalent)	Human Capital Benefits
Redevelop learning spaces $1.0m	Reduced facilities management -$10,000	Longer periods = 20% more time "on learning tasks" -$1.2m	Academic Qualifications Vocational Qualifications 21st Century Skills Improvement in Contextual Value Add
Staff reorientation $300,000	More flexible staffing - $50,000	Reduced staff turnover -$100,000	
ICT $200,000	Reduction in admin and communication -$40,000	Enhanced staff performance -$100,000	
$1.5m	-$100,000	-$1.4m	500 units of learning output

Table 22. Example modernisation programme, Year 1, ROI.

In this example, for a total investment of $1.5m, during Year 1 of the modernisation project an additional 500 units of learning has been outputted and other benefits to the equivalent amount have accrued. Using this model, you'd expect to see ever increased ROI as capital expenditure decrease whilst the benefits persist.

Setting out the ROI in this way clearly illustrates where more emphasis needs to be placed, and where costs can be reduced and impacts best gained.

Close the Loop

Armed with these insights, the next thing is to re-enter the planning process again and ask the four key Blue Ocean questions:

- What new things do we do?
- What existing things do we need to do better?
- What do we need to do less of?
- What do we need to stop doing?

This should lead to a reinvigoration of the transformation process with new projects, themes and change agents.

In summary then, leading system-wide change can be illustrated as follows:

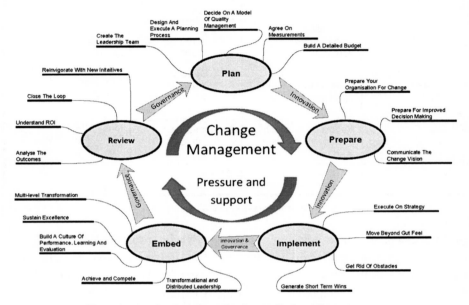

Figure 34. Leading transformation is a cyclical, not linear, process.

Case studies

Queensland, Australia

One of the best planned and executed ICT in schools implementations in the world is Queensland, Australia.

Queensland's strategy is making a big impact. Their change management programme is called Smart Classrooms, which is about driving the use of ICT in Queensland schools. The effects include:

- Automating and streamlining administration within schools
- Developing stronger partnerships between everyone who can make a difference to the educational outcomes of students

- Rolling out superior technical support for well-engineered ICT systems
- Providing more teachers with a tool-of-trade that most knowledge workers have had for years: a computer
- Helping schools engage the digital generation

These impacts are a result of careful planning, and there are a number of distinguishing features that make Queensland's planning world class:

- The planning process is thoroughly organised, highly inclusive and openly available to the public
- It is explicitly connected to the Queensland Government's objectives
- Guidance is detailed but easy to follow

The Smart Classrooms program is made up of the following sub-programs, each of which makes a different contribution:

- Smart Classrooms Professional Development Framework. This enables teachers to get formal recognition for their ICT skills:
  - ICT Certificate
  - Digital Pedagogy Licence
  - Digital Pedagogy Advanced Licence
- Student ICT Expectations
  - A specification for what for all state school students from Prep to Year 10 need to learn with regard to ICT
- OnePortal
  - A new intranet site that will become the 'virtual front door' to all web-based and departmental content
- The Learning Place
  - eLearning environment providing digital content
- Computers for Teachers
  - Every Queensland state school teacher is being provided with a laptop
- ICT Learning Innovation Centre
  - An ICT Learning Innovation Centre, situated in the University of the Sunshine Coast

The ICT planning cycle is made up of the following elements:

- School ICT Census—an annual survey of schools that provides data that helps establish every school's ICT eLearning Index planning level, calculates annual School ICT Grants and informs strategic planning processes.
- School ICT eLearning Index—a simple indicator that represents the level of interaction between the resources that need to come together to ensure ICT is integral to learning in every school.
- School ICT eLearning Plans—mandatory annual resourcing plans negotiated by all schools, detailing how they intend to allocate resources to meet their individual targets.

Queensland has also embarked on a programme to introduce 1:1 access to mobile computers for students. This type of programme is highly complex and full of potential pitfalls. Queensland's 21 Steps to 21st Century Learning provides an excellent guide to each of the steps required to make a laptop programme work. These programmes tend to fail when computers are distributed too early. Queensland's 21 steps puts distributing the laptops at step number 20 out of 21!

Baldrige National Quality Programme

Every year, the US National Institute of Standards runs an award—the Malcolm Baldrige National Quality Programme Award—which recognises performance excellence and quality achievement across a range of industries, including education.

The "Criteria for Performance Excellence in Education"—which is freely available—provides a comprehensive way to achieve and sustain high performance across a schooling organisation. The Chugach District in Alaska, led by Richard DeLorenzo, was the first schooling organisation to win this prestigious award.

The Baldrige Criteria address all key areas of running a successful schooling organisation and are compatible with other performance improvement initiatives, such as School Improvement Planning, ISO 9000, Lean, and Six Sigma.

The Criteria helps education organizations achieve and sustain the highest national levels of:

- Student learning outcomes
- Customer satisfaction and engagement
- Product and service outcomes, and process efficiency
- Workforce satisfaction and engagement
- Budgetary, financial, and market results
- Social responsibility

(Baldrige National Quality Programme, 2009—2010)

The database of winning applications is well worth looking through, particularly the Chugach application which details their transformational approach and clearly articulates a set of highly transferable principles. http://patapsco.nist. gov/Award_Recipients/AwardRecipients.cfm?sector=Education

England's National Literacy Programme

Michael Fullan writing in "The New Meaning of Education Change" offers this analysis of the English National Literacy and Numeracy Strategy:

> "Governments face a dilemma. Their world is one of wanting a quick solution strategy and problems... Yet bringing about change on a large scale is enormously complex. If it is difficult to manage change in one classroom, one school, or one district, imagine the scale of the problems faced by the state or province a country in which numerous agencies and levels and tens or hundreds or thousands of people are involved."

If we are to achieve large scale reform, governments are essential. They have the potential to be a major force for transformation. The historical evidence to date, however, suggests that few governments have got it right.

In 1997 the government in England set specific targets for improvements in national standards of literacy and numeracy. The baseline percentage of those students scoring an acceptable level in national tests was 63% in literacy and 62% in numeracy in 1997. So the Education Minister set a target for 80% for literacy and 75% in numeracy to be achieved by 2002. This commitment impacted 20,000 primary schools and 7 million students.

Michael Barber, the head of the government initiative, set out the main elements of the implementation strategy, which included:

- A national level project plan for both literacy and numeracy setting out actions, responsibilities, and deadlines through to June 2002
- A substantial investment sustained over at least six years and skewed towards those schools that need the most help
- A project infrastructure that involved several government departments, 15 regional directors and over three hundred expert consultants at local level
- An expectation that any class will have a daily maths lesson and a "literacy hour"
- A detailed teaching programme covering every school a year for children from ages 5-11
- An emphasis on intervention and catch up for learners who fall behind
- Professional development programmes
- The provision of intensive support to half of all schools where the most progress is required
- A problem-solving philosophy involved in the early identification of difficulties as they emerge and the provision of rapid solutions for intervention when necessary
- The provision of extra after-school, weekend and holiday camps to classes for those who need extra help to reach the standard.

The theory behind the strategy was high-challenge—high-support in relation to the following:

- Ambitious standards
- Good data
- Clear targets
- Devolved responsibility
- Access to best practice
- Quality professional development
- Accountability
- Interventions in inverse proportion to success—low improving schools receive extra attention.

The impact of the strategy was that in five years literacy improved to 75% and numeracy improved to 73% (a 12 and 11 point increase). This was a remarkable achievement considering 20,000 schools were involved.

This demonstrates clearly that "it is possible to take a very large system and achieve substantial results over a reasonably short period".

(Fullan, The New Meaning of Educational Change, 2007)

6. MANAGING INFORMATION

"Knowledge is power"—Francis Bacon.

The purpose of this chapter is to give you an understanding of the following:

- Why managing information is critical to effectiveness
- What we need Management Information Systems (MIS) to do
- What we mean by "intelligent intervention" and why it is so important
- How information can be used to make better decisions
- How MIS is used to drive learning outcomes

The key points made in this chapter are:

- Well managed information is the key to making better decisions
- Getting high quality, useful information to the "front line" drives effectiveness
- Management Information Systems can drive administrative efficiencies
- Key Performance Indicators can be used to drive alignment and performance towards strategic goals
- MIS can be used to plan, organise, co-ordinate and control operations

Managing Schooling Information

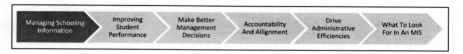

"Some organisations are managing themselves by looking in the past. They are driving while looking out of their rear-view mirrors—on a foggy night with shades on—because they haven't developed the capabilities to effectively manage information."

(Joey Fitts and Bruno Aziza, 2008)

In the best schooling systems you'll find a "web of tensions", defined by the demands of all the key stakeholders—students, teachers, parents, government, employers, governors, examining bodies, and the wider community. The glue that holds them together is the free flow of information.

Providing the right information to everyone in your schooling system in a cost-effective way is potentially a major challenge. Meeting this challenge, however, can bring enormous benefit. A Management Information System (MIS) makes data available to all those who need and are entitled to it, and helps avoid problems, such as:

- Decisions based on historical rather than forward-looking information
- Problems not identified or addressed on a timely basis
- Lack of accountability and transparency
- Poor use of funds, and poor Return on Investment (ROI)
- Inaccurate and unclear performance measurement
- Inability to measure progress or the effect of new programmes or initiatives
- Performance targets not tied to activities that drive the organisation's priorities.

Ultimately, Management Information Systems are about driving effectiveness through:

- Key information and analytical capabilities being made available to "front-line" decision-makers

- Reduced cycles for budgeting, planning, and other key activities
- Agreement and consensus over key metrics through having a "single version of the truth".

The role of an MIS is integrating information to support the tasks of management, research and planning, and to provide information in a synthesized form to end-users. It should provide a global and systemic vision; one capable of ensuring the evolution and adaptability of the entire organisation. An MIS should be designed to strengthen capacities in management, planning and dissemination of information at all levels of the education system for all areas of analysis and decision-making. To attain this goal, it has to:

- Improve capacities for collecting, processing, storing, analysing, and disseminating data in order that decision-makers, administrators and managers can base their judgement on timely and reliable data
- Centralise and coordinate the dispersed efforts in acquiring, processing, analysing and disseminating schooling management information
- Rationalise the nature and flow of information necessary for decision-making by reducing and eliminating duplications, and by filling-in information gaps
- Link and assemble different existing information systems
- Integrate and synthesize in one single system all the required quantitative and qualitative data
- Improve data collection, and the use and dissemination of information for education management, in order to respond to the constantly evolving needs for information.

(UNESCO, 2003)

Across all hierarchical levels, an MIS is typically used for the following:

Discover issues—Reveal the issues and problems that may otherwise remain hidden. Ascertain the needs of stakeholders. Ensure that no students 'fall through the cracks'. Identify strengths and weaknesses.

Diagnose situations—Understand the cause of problems. Comprehend why some students are performing well and why others aren't. Determine eligibility for special programmes. Target the areas to improve. Provide criteria for focusing on high priority goals.

Forecast future conditions—Predict the needs of students, teachers and stakeholders. Suggest possible local, regional, state, or national trends that will affect schooling and the programmes offered. Forecast workforce, resource and budgetary requirements.

Improve policy and practice—Help reform learning and teaching. Enhance teaching and assessment. Guide curriculum development, revision and alignment. Build a culture of enquiry and continuous improvement. Guide the allocation of resources.

Evaluate effectiveness—Understand and describe high quality performance. Provide feedback to students, teachers, and administrators about performance. Measure the programme's effectiveness. Identify practices that produce desired results. Convince stakeholders of the need for change. Highlight successes.

Promote accountability—Monitor and document progress towards achieving goals. Inform internal and external stakeholders of progress. Confirm or discredit assumptions about students or school practices. Develop meaningful responses to criticism. Meet statutory reporting requirements. Ensure that the workforce is focused on student learning (Earl, 2006).

BECTA, the former UK Government's ICT in schools agency offers the following MIS specifications. An MIS should:

Enable users to access the system away from the organisation.	Have an interface that's accessible to all its users.	Be able to import and export admission information.
Support the management and recording of assessments.	Support the measurement and reporting of attendance.	Identify and verify users uniquely.
Manage behaviour information.	Render learner information consistent throughout the system.	Store data securely.
Enable only access to information appropriate to the user's role.	Make it possible for learner information to be imported and exported by the system.	Enable individuals and groups to send messages to each other.
Allow the creation of reports.	Support special educational needs management.	Enable the submission of all statutory returns (information required by law by the government).
Support development and management of a timetable.	Support staff management.	Provide a system for recording and managing assets.

Be capable of managing coursework.	Provide support for curriculum planning.	Manage dinner money.
Enable documents to be managed.	Be compatible with Consistent Financial Reporting (CFR) and support strategic multi-year budgeting.	Integrate with library management.
Manage options for learners (student's choice of subject areas).	Support the creation and maintenance of electronic portfolios for transfer to other organisations.	Be capable of supporting web services protocols.

Table 23. MIS—outline specification from BECTA.

(BECTA, 2006)

Sometimes it is considered sufficient simply to provide teachers with information about students, in the hope that this will automatically improve learning. Of course, there's a lot more to it than that. Schooling systems are ecosystems, so improving learning through MIS comes through integrating a range of interrelated functions. These can be grouped into five functional areas, and a well-designed MIS should be able to deliver all of these:

- **Improve student performance**: Give students, parents, teachers and administrators a clear picture of student performance at an individual or group level so they can adjust and personalise learning accordingly
- **Make better management decisions**: Inform routine decisions and long-range strategic planning across all enablers and disciplines with accurate, readily-available data
- **Increase accountability**: Quickly and easily understand performance across the organisation
- **Manage resources more effectively**: Gain a better understanding of projected revenues and expenditures; keep track of financial health; compare costs against those of other organisations
- **Drive administrative efficiencies**: Improve time and effort taken to collect, process and report data and information. Improve quality and presentation of data and information.

Improving Student Performance

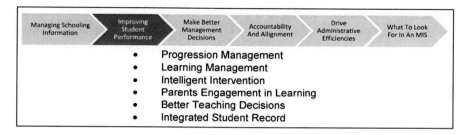

An MIS can support progression and learning management, and enable "intelligent intervention"—using IT to automatically address key risk factors which may otherwise take huge amounts of resource. An MIS should be able to help teachers make better teaching decisions, and help involve parents in the learning process. To enable all of this to happen, an integrated student record is needed.

Progression Management

Critical to the improvement of the learning process is the ability of the individual student, in partnership with their teachers and parents, to manage progression through their learning. Centred around the integrated student record, the right kind of systems and tools should be able to support:

- **Evidence collection:** evidence is collected by the learner and placed in an e-Folio
- **Evaluate:** learners evaluate their current competencies in a particular area—for example "time management"
- **Mentorship:** a meeting with a mentor can review the evidence and work contained within the e-Folio
- **Target setting:** with the mentor's help, the learner sets targets within his/her e-Folio for the coming week. For example, the skill 'time management' may require the learner to provide evidence of planning and managing a project
- **Planning:** IT resources, such as dynamic timetabling, can help learners to plan how they will collect the evidence they need to show their progress. Precise identification of users enables students to access the right resources for their competencies and skill sets.

Learning Management

To support progression management—Learning Management can automate some of the work involved, taking out a lot of the low-grade and administrative work which teachers often complain about having to do. Learning Management systems need to provide:

- Clarity about what has been, and what needs to be, learned and achieved
- Customised learning pathways that take into account specific needs, learning styles and abilities
- A timetable which allows learning resources to be made available as and when needed by the individual student.

A Learning Management System (LMS) will generally manage the following:

- **Content**—teachers can create, store, share and repurpose resources; coursework can be accessed online and synchronised to a personal learning device so it's accessible offline too
- **Workflows**—content can be precisely assigned as a learning task to individual or groups of students
- **Grading and feedback**—responses to the learning tasks can be auto graded in subjects such as Maths. In other cases teachers can provide written feedback with the returned assignments
- **Reporting**—grades can be aggregated and reported.

Intelligent Intervention

Intelligent Intervention uses data to correlate factors that affect learning with individuals or groups of students. For example, low reading ability at an early age may be an indicator of future test/examination results. An intelligent intervention here could involve identifying the students who have the lowest reading abilities, and automatically providing them with additional reading support; assigning them appropriate level reading tasks; suggesting reading activities to parents to do with their child at home; requesting teachers to focus on reading skills for these particular students; inviting students to attend extra reading classes etc. To set up a paper-based programme to the same effect would be massively inefficient by comparison.

Other examples of intelligent interventions include:

- Interventions set up to help broaden the student's social and educational horizons based on analysis of student interests and friendship groups
- Health and wellbeing alerts based on analysis of foodstuffs bought via cashless vending, and correlated against attendance and attainment
- Recommendations for additional learning activities, based on analysis of attainment results and learning style.

Parents Engagement in Learning

To achieve the best results, teachers, parents and students all need to work together. In Bowring School, Liverpool, success has been achieved by engaging parents in a range of ways including involving them in setting individual targets for students.

At the very least, parents should have the ability to see the latest attendance information, homework assignments, structured feedback, disciplinary reports, and related information via a secured Internet school portal.

Ideally, parents should be able to:

- See what their child is doing in school
- See how their child is doing in school
- Communicate with teachers easily
- See teachers' feedback
- Learn how to help their child learn specific subject matter (through on-line resources)
- Purchase items and services from a school-vetted list to help their child succeed
- Stay informed about school activities
- Learn how their local school is performing relative to other schools

Better Teaching Decisions

Teachers should be able to base their teaching decisions on high quality, relevant information on each individual student. For example:

- Grades actual and predicted by subject
- Teachers' comments
- Targets, and progress towards them
- Performance data
- Attendance
- Social, geographic
- Family background
- Attitudinal data
- History of formal interventions
- Timetable

Having this information enables teachers to differentiate learning according to the relevant factors.

Teachers should have immediate access to all their class lists in one place with main KPIs and needs/risks displayed. They should also be alerted to students that are at risk of missing targets with prompts for what action to be taken.

Integrated Student Record

To provide the kind of information needed to improving student performance, the availability of an integrated student record is the key. This should contain all relevant data for each student. Depending on their role, stakeholders should have access to an integrated set of fields to capture and view marks/comments on students. The integrated student record should contain the following information:

Academic	Organisational	Personal
Learning Styles	Attendance	Name, Address, etc.
Individual Learning Plan	Behaviour	Photo
Links to e-Portfolios	Catering	Contacts
Targets	Transportation	Health information
Performance	Access—who is permitted to go where	Social background information
Feedback	Risk profile—real or potential problems	Special needs

Table 24. Key components in an Integrated Student Record.

Make Better Management Decisions

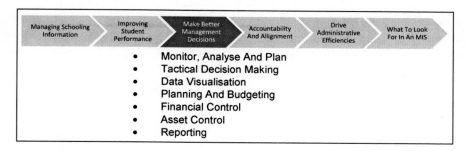

- Monitor, Analyse And Plan
- Tactical Decision Making
- Data Visualisation
- Planning And Budgeting
- Financial Control
- Asset Control
- Reporting

Managing schooling systems is a complex business extending way beyond the classroom. For example, teacher workforce development; transportation systems; lunch and nutritional programmes and student medical welfare are all within the domain of schooling systems and are dependent on the best decisions being made. High quality, insightful and accurate information is needed to analyse outcomes and guide inputs towards continual improvement.

Monitor, Analyse and Plan

In order to manage performance, organizations must be able answer three fundamental questions:

- Monitoring: What has happened? What is happening?
- Analytics: Why is this happening?
- Planning: What do we want to see happen?

Monitor: This capability provides managers with the ability to know "what is happening" and "what has happened." Organisations implement dashboards, scorecards, or reports to monitor their performance. These visual applications allow managers to keep an eye on important indicators of their organisation's health.

Analyse: This capability provides managers with the ability to know what is happening and why. To analyse performance, organisations implement solutions that are often very interactive in nature and allow managers to investigate the root cause of issues they see in their dashboards, scorecards, or reports.

Plan: This capability provides the organisation with the ability to model what should happen. Organisations develop processes and tools to conduct the essential planning, budgeting, and forecasting exercises. These processes allow managers to align groups and individuals around the metrics that drive the organisation—for instance, "What is our examination result target?" "What is our spend versus our revenue?"

(Joey Fitts and Bruno Aziza, 2008)

Tactical Decision-Making

On a day-to-day basis, school managers are faced with having to make quick decisions on matters such as staff deployment or behavioural issues. Having the right information to hand can help enormously in this area, E.g.:

- Automatic notification of teacher illness, with associated capabilities to arrange class coverage
- Online resourcing of supply/substitute staff
- Timetable scheduling for rooms, teaching staff, learning resources and students
- Customisable and extensible alerting, for example, learner non-attendance, dropping attainment level, bullying, behavioural issues, etc.
- Dynamic device and resource tracking, alerts generated by incorrect position or use related to time of day, room booking data.

Data Visualisation

Access to decision-making information, combined with the ability to view and interpret the data graphically, enables easier identification of trends.

Generally, education data views are most impactful when they can be provided as a high-level aggregate summary, such as at the school district level, then broken down into organisational and operational components. For example, a school principal may have a view displaying a summary of standardised assessment results by level. It should be easy to expand the view, showing multiple levels of information such as assessment outcomes by school, class, teacher, period or student.

Location or "Geo" data can be used to visualise school buildings, neighbourhoods, attendance patterns, transportation systems, emergency services, etc. providing stakeholders with a pictorial representation of school district data and administration. Geographic processing can also be integrated with admissions and transfers, transport and population forecasting.

Latest software technologies allow highly pictorial views to be generated. Districts, schools, classrooms, resources, groups of students, classes, teachers and individual students can all be represented photographically, making it easier to connect data with real participants.

Planning and Budgeting

The schooling organisation needs to have an annual budget that:

- Is realistic and affordable in relation to available resources and cash flows
- Is approved by its governing body on a timely basis
- Reflects the organisation's development plan
- Is consistent with longer term financial plans (including recovery of deficits or saving up for future developments).

The system should enable managers to understand and communicate the relationship between resource allocation and attainment (Return on Investment—ROI) and expenditure per student. It should allow managers to compare the schooling system's financial performance with others, examine reasons for differences, and support decisions about what actions to take.

Financial Control

ICT can play a major role in improving the financial management of schooling systems, driving accountability and transparency, and driving down the cost of administration.

At all levels, effective financial management of a schooling system requires effective control over:

- Income received
- Payroll
- Purchasing
- The banking system
- Petty cash holdings and payments
- Taxation system
- Voluntary funds
- Assets

Key features of schooling financial management systems should include:

- General Ledger
- Accounts Payable
- Accounts Received
- Equipment Register
- Budget Planning
- Cash Management
- Personnel
- Compensation
- Grants Management
- Risk Management

Key functions should include:

- Reporting and statement preparation in accordance with generally accepted accounting principles (GAAP)
- Flexible Chart of Accounts (COA)—managers can set up their own cost centres
- Integrated finance and human resource management system, from which it should be possible to forecast staffing and related requirements
- Expenditure can be monitored through an extensive range of reports
- Future years' budgets can be modelled, taking into account different scenarios
- Assets held by individual schools can be allocated to members of staff and/or rooms.

Asset Control

Controlling how assets are used is an important part of controlling costs. An MIS should provide a system for recording and managing assets. This should include the tracking of property assets, equipment, furniture, learning resources, ICT and other "tangibles". The MIS should also be able to track automated e-procurements of goods and services.

Reporting

It's critical that MIS enables the schooling organisation to meet its statutory reporting requirements and address financial management accountability. The organisation needs to provide the appropriate stakeholders with timely, accurate, relevant and up to date information that complies with financial reporting requirements. It needs to have documented and approved detailed financial procedures that are tailored to the organisation's needs and implemented consistently.

An excellent guide to financial management for schools can be found here: http://www.standards.dcsf.gov.uk/vfm/

Accountability and Alignment

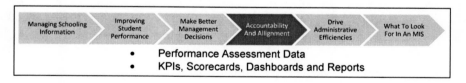

Many governments across the world are mandating stronger accountability. Being accountable in schooling is about being able to correlate outputs with inputs, and results against investments. Key questions for any schooling system include:

- Which schools are adding the most value—i.e. making the most difference to students in their care—and what lessons can others learn from them?
- Which schools are lowest performing and what measures need to be applied to improve standards?

- What inputs—e.g. content, equipment, training etc.—get the best learning impacts?

Alignment means being able to set and execute a policy at any level. Knowing if a policy is being implemented or not requires accountability systems, and this in turn requires automatic real-time reporting on the organisation's Key Performance Indicators (KPI) including educational, financial and legislative commitments.

Performance and Assessment Data

Performance and assessment data can be used to help individual children; staff development; tackling underperformance; transmitting knowledge about good practice; teaching and learning; and care and guidance. Performance and assessment data can be categorised as follows:

- **Academic**: e.g., test scores, exam results or competencies attained, and longitudinal data—i.e. student information collected over multiple years in multiple schools. Assessment data is a vital part of a teacher's toolkit. It greatly informs professional judgement about learning and student support and enables personalised learning.
- **Behaviours**: incident logging for both good and bad behaviour; progress rates; targets met and failed; peer-to-peer report logging; behaviour analysis patterns; health information; secure access to health and social services data; such as medication and home situation; alerts; access; catering.
- **Teaching**: Academic performance by different subject areas, or by teacher.
- **Management**: How well is the institution managed as indicated by absenteeism; stakeholder satisfaction; enrolment; dropout and graduation; expenditure per student, etc.

With sufficient data, managers can ask "what if" questions, and model solutions to problems. E.g. can poor behaviour be correlated to geographic areas, or areas within individual schools—if so, then controls can be put in place to rectify the problems.

To make ever better management decisions requires the following:

- Organisation-wide access to relevant information
- Role-based delivery of performance-related information
- Scorecards, dashboards, and strategy maps that identify performance drivers
- Automated workflow for simpler consolidation and reporting
- Standardized KPIs to align with goals and initiatives.

KPIs, Scorecards, Dashboards and Reports

Key Performance Indicators (KPIs)

A Key Performance Indicator is a summary definition of a specific data point, such as attendance. Progress against KPIs are generally visualised in the form of a target value, actual value, a status indicator of actual performance vs. target goal and a trend indicator that defines progress towards or away from the goal.

Scorecards

These illustrate a collection of KPIs for a specific data point across multiple organisational units, such as schools or classes. Scorecards are used to easily access and compare the performance or status of organisational units. Figure 35 on page 228 is an example of data visualization of a schools' scorecard which is mapped to its strategy.

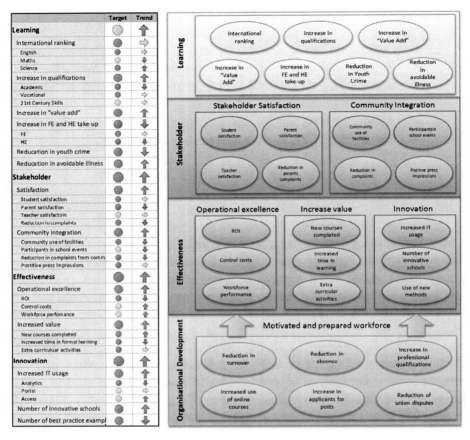

Figure 35. School level strategy map.

Dashboards

A collection of scorecards showing multiple data points, that when combined, provides a summary view of varying elements. The user has the capability to drill down on a specific data element to gain greater insight into overall organizational performance.

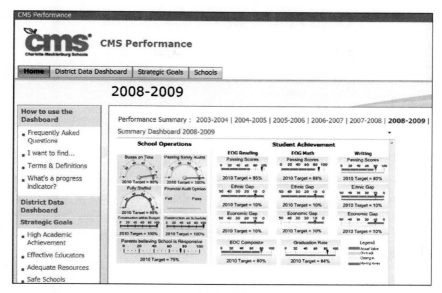

Figure 36. Stakeholder Dashboard for the Charlotte Mecklenburg School District.

Reports

Reports are detailed views of data and information typically summarised into groupings of KPIs. Depending on a user's role, reports may include drill down capabilities allowing the user to disaggregate information from the dashboard view. For example, when a district-level administrator wants to further understand a certain condition, such as declining attendance at a particular school, he/she can select that school's attendance KPI on a scorecard, and then easily open and access a detailed attendance report for that specific school.

Figure 37. Stakeholder Dashboard—Charlotte Mecklenburg School District lets users drill down into specific areas of interest such as academic performance against national standards.

Drive Administrative Efficiencies

Managing Schooling Information	Improving Student Performance	Make Better Management Decisions	Accountability And Alignment	Drive Administrative Efficiencies	What To Look For In An MIS

- Planning
- Organising
- Controlling
- Co-ordinating
- Essential Data

An MIS should reduce time and effort taken to collect, process and report data and information, and increase the quality of data, information and knowledge across and between schooling systems. Administrative processes can generally be broken down into four main areas: planning, organising, controlling and coordinating.

Planning

Data Analysis—Access to a full range of statistical and comparative data on schools, anytime, anywhere. Productivity tools should be available to enable the production of reports to upstream or downstream stakeholders.

Forecasting—Forecast future numbers for each school utilising historic and census data to ensure there is adequate school places provision both now and in the future. Use a range of historic and predictive data to forecast future finance and resource requirements.

Education Plan Monitoring (EPM)—Enables the management, recording and monitoring of Development Plans and their associated activities, tasks and targets. These can be allocated and owned by individuals or teams who can record their visits, observations, outcomes and associated costs for specific projects within the plan.

Organising

Timetable and Curriculum Organisation—This is about enabling the definition of a curriculum plan for individual students (preferably), or groups or students. At a basic level, this is about outputting lists of teachers, students, subjects and rooms i.e. a mapped timetable cycle for an academic year. A preferred scenario is where individual students receive individualised timetables on a frequent basis according to what their precise needs are at any specific moment. This function should also include features for the administration of absent teachers' classes plus organising and scheduling parents' evenings. It could include features to facilitate typical ranges of students' subject choices and modelling and construction tools to aid planning, analysis, costing and comparisons.

Governors/Council—This function is about managing the process of setting up governing bodies—monitoring governor appointments, committees, meeting planning, attendance, minutes, contact log and the generation of reports and letters.

Training Management—Managing the provision of courses and central bookings for courses or online learning.

Transport—Managing home to school transport for both mainstream and special needs students, and integrating with GIS to assess learner entitlement.

Children's Services—Support a casework approach for professionals working with children—provide linkages between education, police, social and health services, etc.

Grants & Benefits—Managing all state administered grants and benefits, such as free school meals.

Controlling

Personnel—Enabling the control of the many complex aspects of personnel management, supporting statutory returns, handling payment, development and HR functions, and minimising data entry by integration with relevant databases and applications.

Performance management—A Performance Management system should manage and administer the important functions of planning, monitoring, exchanging data, analysis and reporting. It could also support offline access to data for staff working in the field, such as inspectors.

Estate Management—Managing detailed information about schools or other establishments including all student capacity information, site contact details, and site locations. In conjunction with a GIS could calculate distances and mapping information.

Admissions & Transfers—Managing the co-ordinated allocation and transfer of students. Automating the allocation of places based on government defined criteria and resolves multiple offers down to a single offer. Enabling applicants to complete and submit an admissions application form online, saving time and resources.

Attendance—Support the import, display and analysis of detailed student attendance data from schools. Automate workflows associated with driving improved attendance. E-registration systems can enable the monitoring of students' complete record of attendance by:

- Recording and managing statutory school and lesson attendance
- Tracking learners' attendance throughout the school day
- Providing accurate information and simplifying the monitoring of every learner in every lesson
- Identifying post-registration truancy automatically
- Monitoring 'minutes late' to improve punctuality
- Supporting analysis and key decision-making with accurate data that is readily available.

Child Welfare—Monitoring and tracking children's welfare—e.g. if they are in care or employment—and automating workflows across multiple agencies to remediate problems.

Exclusions—Meeting the requirements of statutory legislation and managing all necessary analysis and returns.

Special Educational Needs—Managing the formal assessment and review processes.

Co-ordinating

Information Exchange

The regular and automatic scheduling of student data transfer can provide the "upstream" organisations with the very latest student information and the ability to monitor KPIs in real-time. Ideally, MIS would enable the seamless two-way transfer of data between the schools, local, regional, state and national ministries of education. When this happens well, it supports effective decision-making based on timely, accurate and consistent information.

The largest volume of information fed into an MIS is gathered at the individual school level. It's essential to have people equipped and trained to work with the system. The quality of information produced at school level is critical—if bad data goes in at this level, it renders useless most, if not all, data at national level.

Both regional and national services need to make sure that requests for information are timed optimally to avoid flooding schools with requests for ad-hock reports. A system that uses live dashboards is therefore much more efficient and effective.

At district and regional levels, the data coming "upstream" from schools needs to be verified before analysis, dissemination to regional services, and onwards transmission to the State or central Ministry of Education.

"Upstream" from the local/regional level is the central administration. At this level, information is aggregated and analysed. It is then mapped against information coming into other ministries which impact or are impacted by education— Trade and Industry, Health, Law and Order, etc. National trends are analysed and mapped against policy targets to ascertain progress and issues. Patterns and trends are communicated to relevant stakeholders and key findings are generally made public.

Systems Integration

"While planning, budgeting, and forecasting (collectively, the Plan capability) are essential business practices, it is un-nerving how few of us are able to do it effectively. The typical enterprise utilises 10 general ledger systems, 12 different

budgeting systems, 13 different reporting systems, and takes 6 months for planning, 5 months for budgeting, 2 weeks to develop a forecast. Such disparate information and slow execution make the basic practices of performance management a real challenge for most companies."

(Joey Fitts and Bruno Aziza, 2008)

Increasingly governments wish to have a "joined-up view" of information about children. Individual child or student level data can be imported for analysis from a variety of sources including police, health and social services. The idea is that when agencies have the right information, they are better able to co-ordinate their activities, and be more effective in the process.

Another benefit of integrating systems is not having to re-key-in core data, providing significant cost savings and enabling the sharing of quality information.

Schools/System Interoperability Framework—(SIF)

Schools/Systems Interoperability Framework (SIF) is a data sharing standard that enables diverse applications to interact and share data specification in schooling systems. The SIF specification is composed of two parts: one part for modelling educational data, the other for sharing data between institutions.

Essential Data

Whilst different countries have different mandatory requirements for essential data that they expect schools provide, UNESCO (UNESCO, 2003) has set out a recommended specification of essential data to collect at the national level from each education establishment.

Data on students:

- Distribution by grade, gender and age
- Distribution of repeaters by gender and grade
- Number of learners attending double-shift classes by grade.

Data on teachers and other categories of personnel:

- Distribution of teachers by level of qualification and certification, by grade and by gender
- Distribution of teachers by age and by gender
- Number of teachers working double shifts
- Number of teachers in multi-grade classes
- Number of non-teaching personnel by categories, age and gender.

Data on education establishments:

- Number of classrooms
- Places available in schools.

Education expenditures:

- The education budget in the overall State budget (budget voted and budget disbursed) broken down by level
- The expenditures at the local level, of private organizations by level.

What to Look for in a Management Information System

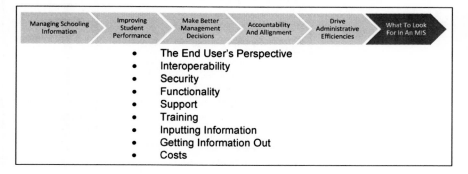

| Managing Schooling Information | Improving Student Performance | Make Better Management Decisions | Accountability And Allignment | Drive Administrative Efficiencies | What To Look For In An MIS |

- The End User's Perspective
- Interoperability
- Security
- Functionality
- Support
- Training
- Inputting Information
- Getting Information Out
- Costs

The End User's Perspective

According to UNESCO, national statistical services traditionally produce data from a "producer's" point of view. They do not often consider information needs and the uses and purposes that collected information could serve. They hardly ever approach other users' services and scarcely ever discuss the content of questionnaires and disseminated results (UNESCO, 2003).

Therefore, an MIS needs to be designed from the end-user—outwards. If we agree that the student is at the centre, MIS should also be designed from the student downwards. Below is an example of how this could work:

Level	Stakeholder	Required information	Data categories
School	Students	What do I need to learn now/next? What progress am I making? What do I need to do to improve? How does my progress compare to peers in this and other schools? What "extra-curricular" activities can I do?	Student Demographics • Admissions & Transfers • Exclusions • Child Welfare
	Parents	What does my child need to learn now/next? How is he/she progressing? What is my child's progress compared to peers?	
	Teachers	What are the best pedagogical strategies, content and assessment? How well do my students perform? Why are some students not performing well? Where has learning been successful? What are my students' learning profiles? How well do students attend my lessons? How satisfied are students and parents with my teaching?	Student Achievement • Attendance • Assessment • Academic, Vocational and 21st Century Skills • Special Educational Needs • Content & Equipment Effectiveness
	Senior Teachers	Subject by subject, group by group, student by student—how are they doing? Who's failing? Who's succeeding? What are the trends? What can we do about it? What teaching and assessment strategies	

		are we using?	
		How do these align with school, district, state and national plans?	**People**
		How might we change our teaching and assessment practices to achieve better results?	• Workforce Performance
			• Organisational Health
		What materials are teachers using in the classrooms?	• Stakeholder Satisfaction
		What learning opportunities do we and should we offer?	• Professional Development
	Headteacher/ Principal	How are we progressing against our plans?	
		How satisfied are students, parents and the wider community with the quality of our schooling?	
		How well are we connecting with parents?	
		Who are our students—how are they progressing?	**Operational Excellence**
		What are our strengths and weaknesses?	• Planning and budgeting
		What qualifications and talents do team staff members have?	• Financial Control
		What is the plan for developing staff?	
		How are different departments performing?	• Resourcing
			• Logistics
		How are different teachers performing?	• Physical Plant
		What's our budget and resourcing position?	• Estate Management
		What resources are being requested?	• Food
	Administrators	Who are our students?	• Transportation
		Who is/isn't attending?	
		What's our financial and resourcing position?	
		What's our staff pay status?	
		What's our "dinner money" and small expenditure status?	
		Which members of staff need to be covered today and who will cover them?	
		What is the usage and allocation of equipment?	

District/State	District/State Superintendent	Admissions and registration of students in each school in the region/district	
		What are our future workforce and resource requirements?	
		What are current/future student demographics?	
		What are the current resourcing requests?	
		Where and what are our strengths and weaknesses?	
		What areas should we target for improvement?	
		What are our priorities?	
		What local, regional, state, or national trends will affect schooling and the programmes offered?	
		How should we develop, revise, and align curricula?	
	CEO	Does the workforce understand the strategy?	
		Is the workforce executing on the goals?	
		Is the plan working?	
		What do we need to invest in?	
		Which parts of the operation are performing best and worst?	
	Operations Director	What are the costs of the system's operations?	
		What is the cost per student?	
		What specific cost reduction opportunities are there?	
		Where should we target specific investments for the high rates of return?	
		What incidents are occurring?	
		How are we performing against safety and security targets?	
	CFO	What is our current budgetary position?	
		What are our budgetary forecasts?	
		How can we make increasingly impactful allocations?	
		How can we better control costs?	
	CIO	How impactful are our ICT investments?	
		What do we need to do to develop the use of ICT?	
		Who is making the most and the least amount of use of ICT, and why?	

	HR	What is the workforce composition and qualifications?	
		What vacancies are filled/open?	
		How well do we retain our workforce?	
		How many people are leaving indicating dissatisfaction?	
		How do our clients rate our service?	
National Ministry of Education	National level and Planning Directorate at Ministry of Education	How effective is our education policy?	
		What are the disparities between the regions, and between different cohorts of students?	
		To what extent is our education system contributing to our national economic development plan?	
		What are the future workforce and resource requirements?	
		What are the future budgeting requirements?	
		How well are we narrowing the attainment gap?	
		What are the requests for resources from regional offices, and how do we prioritise?	
		Where is performance strongest and weakest?	

Table 25. End-user use of MIS.

There are a huge number of options open to those wishing to implement management information systems. Some systems are available "off the shelf", others need to be built and integrated with proprietary components on top of complex legacy systems. BECTA, when it was in existence, produced this guidance which can be used to help understand what to look for in an MIS:

Interoperability

The Interoperability Agreement (IA) is a self-accreditation scheme that enables suppliers to confirm that their product imports and exports in Common Basic Data Set (CBDS) format.

If a supplier has signed up to the IA, information on its system should be readable by other MIS systems.

Security

Because data sharing is a central aspect of many MIS software products, security is clearly an important factor. Different levels of security may be appropriate for different user groups. For example, school leaders, teachers and administrative staff may all require different levels of access to different areas of information. Students and parents may be given very limited access to appropriate information.

Functionality

Most schools will have an MIS that covers a number of functional areas. However, they may wish to increase the functionality by purchasing additional products that meet specific needs, for example, report writing or management of library books.

It is important to find out if information, such as learner names, can be extracted from the existing system, and if any information can be fed back into the main system.

Support

It is also important to establish the type of support provided (email, telephone, for example) and the quality of support the supplier is offering. This is crucial, because technical problems may be encountered, and it may be necessary to update or upgrade products.

Training

Some form of training is always advisable; the complexity of use of the software and the experience of the user will determine the depth of training required. Two other issues to consider are the cost and the method of training (face-to-face or remote).

Inputting information

A key goal of an MIS should be to allow someone to enter information once and use it many times. The method of input is an important concern so key questions are:

- Is data inputted by keyboard, internet, personal digital assistant (PDA), optical mark reader, swipe card, or imported from other systems?
- Is remote access possible, for example, from home?
- Can information be altered offline, and then be easily synchronised upon return to the school network?

Getting information out

Several important considerations are: how information can be accessed; how it can be viewed; who can access it; and is there multi-user access to data.

Costs

There is a plethora of pricing solutions: user licences; site licences; outright purchase and annual licence. Each has advantages and disadvantages. It is important that a school understands the type of purchase it is making and the associated restrictions.

Case Studies

Mexico

In 2007, the Federal Ministry of Education in Mexico embarked on a project entitled Habilidades Digiatles Para Todos—HDT, 'Digital Skills for All,' aimed at developing digital skills and the use of ICT in schools. HDT aims to use ICT to improve learning and the management of schools and reduce the number of students who do not reach the basic level of abilities.

Part of a five-year programme, HDT is implementing ICT across the entire schooling system in Mexico. Not only is it equipping and training teachers and giving students access to technology, HDT also has a sophisticated and extensive MIS enabling:

- Data-driven leadership for the school management, supervisors, regional directors
- Support for educational management—coordinating assessing, monitoring, advising and professional development
- IT supported coordination for State-led actions

Key pieces of information managed by HDT include:

- Goals—objective versus achieved
- Academic attainment by geography—national, region, state and municipal
- The taught curriculum
- Time spent learning
- School and teacher profiles.

Figure 38. HDT interface.

A student's experience with HDT starts with using a basic LMS. Assignments are set, digital content is given, the completed assignments and scores are aggregated for analysis at all levels in the system.

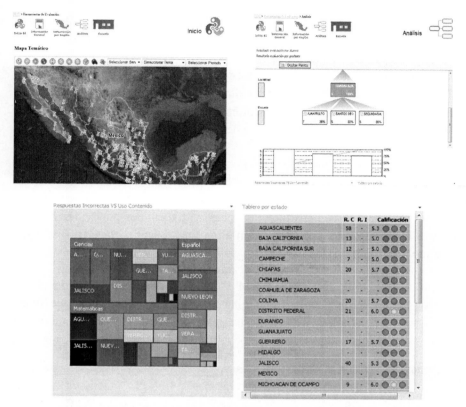

Figure 39. Heatmaps and assorted graphical devices are used to identify "hotspot" areas for remediation.

Gestar

In Brazil, Gestar—an independent software vendor—has built a student relationship management system (SRM). Built on top of a commercial customer relation management (CRM) software suite, SRM not only handles commercial relationships with the students and their parents in private schools—enrolment and fees, etc.—but academic aspects too.

The objective was to apply the concepts of "marketing one-to-one" to the complete relationship cycle with students—from the initial recruiting process to completion of school and beyond. By gathering and using the information generated in academic and e-learning management systems, such as attendance and individual assessments, it was possible for Gestar and the schools they serve to improve the quality and relevance of the educational services provided.

Gestar realised that it is practically impossible to personalise the relationship with thousands of students at the same time without technology. Only through technology can there be fuller alignment between educational services offered by the institution and the expectations of students.

In schools using the Gestar system dropout rates are reduced by cross-checking information on attendance and grades or evaluations. This makes it possible to identify students at risk of dropping out, and automatically trigger processes that will allow the appropriate department to speak with them personally, identify the causes of dissatisfaction, and once again align the student's objectives with the institution's learning services.

Through linking with the LMS, SRM is able to determine if students are accessing the e-Learning tools, completing assignments within given deadlines, and if they are satisfied with their learning activities. Through automated workflows, intelligent intervention can be used to address specific problems.

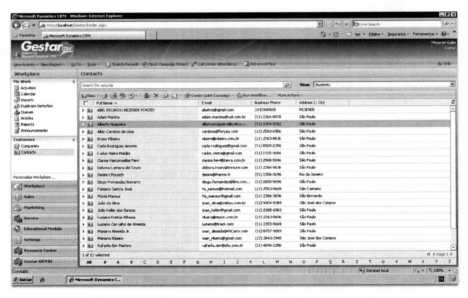

Figure 40. Gestar's SRM system lets schools manage students as customers.

Pre-defined workflows and escalations, in some cases completely automated, make it easier for a teacher to be more "granular" in how they address students' individual needs. The benefit for the teacher is that their administrative burden is reduced. The benefit to the student is that they get a more personalised service.

Ninestiles School, Birmingham

Ninestiles School in Birmingham, a large mixed comprehensive, has delivered both improved information for teachers and managers, and better services to parents and young people through integrating its information systems using the Systems Interoperability Framework (SIF). Student information, library and canteen systems, email and online services and teacher productivity tools such as parent reporting were integrated, enabling significant time saved in entering and processing of data. Upwards of 1000 staff hours per year have been saved, and this has had a direct financial benefit for the school. (The Department for Children Schools and Families, 2010)

7. DRIVING EFFECTIVENESS THROUGH TECHNOLOGY

There isn't a sphere of human endeavour that hasn't been transformed by technology—apart from education, and schooling in particular. Take Medicine for example. A Victorian surgeon would be lost in a modern day operating theatre, but a Victorian teacher would be at home in modern classroom.

David Bell, Former UK Chief Inspector of Schools

The purpose of this chapter is to give you an understanding of the following:

- Why is information and communication technology (ICT) so critical to effectiveness?
- How does ICT open up new possibilities for access to learning experiences?
- What areas of the curriculum can benefit from ICT?
- How can ICT be used to personalise learning?
- What are the key technological building blocks required in a schooling system?
- What's the best way to organise technology for maximum impact?
- What are the generally accepted ways of purchasing and implementing ICT and related services?

The key points made in this chapter are:

- ICT can be a catalyst for transformation, efficiency and effectiveness
- ICT can be used to accelerate learning by addressing different learning styles, multiple intelligences, and extending the boundaries of learning
- Merely adding an ICT "veneer" to industrialised schooling won't yield significant benefits
- For ICT to be exploited to maximum effect, careful and comprehensive planning and disciplined execution is essential
- Connected Learning Communities are key to increasing learning effectiveness
- Fully exploiting ICT in Management Information Systems can lead to significant efficiencies
- Cloud based approaches can help make significant cost savings and improve efficiency and effectiveness

I n the previous chapters we have laid out the key components and tasks involved in transforming schooling systems. It's now time to turn to ICT and how it can be used as a catalyst to modernise the schooling system to give us the kinds of outcomes we expect.

Why Invest in Technology?

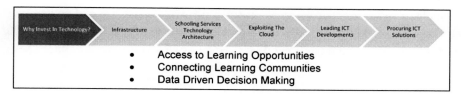

The goal of investing in ICT is to help drive effectiveness, whilst at the same time increasing learning and improving efficiencies.

Many respected organisations, including OECD, World Bank, and UNESCO advocate the use of ICT in schooling and the arguments against investment seem to be diminishing considerably over recent years. In 2008 The Swedish National Agency for School Improvement produced a report that summarised the main evidence collected about the impact of ICT in schooling. The report states that:

- ICT has a positive effect on learning (both measurable and perceived effects) and on performance in specific subjects
- The use of ICT increases student motivation and level of skills, levels of independence and development of collaboration
- There is a positive correlation between ICT and learning in all subjects included in the UK national curriculum; the correlation was most clear in English, Mathematics and Science.

ICT in schooling is hardly new. The first generation of computing in schools came with the arrival of the microcomputers. These were usually the domain of the maths or computer studies departments. A second generation was defined by the PC. The third generation was defined by the arrival of the local area network in schools. These let people share resources and some were set up to enable people to send electronic mail. With a much wider range of software, and the introduction of the graphical user interface, the whole school could now make use of computers. The fourth generation of schools computing is characterised by the Internet. This represented a paradigm shift—it changed the role of teachers and books as the key sources of knowledge.

Students everywhere are leading the push towards a more digital and more connected lifestyle. The profusion of mobile devices is making an impact; looking at numerous surveys of students from both developed and developing worlds it's plain to see significant use of technology outside school. For example, a survey conducted by Microsoft showed 84% use a social networking service on a weekly basis, 30% use a mobile device to access the Internet, 94% send text messages, and they spend an average of 16.3 hours/week online. These numbers may well represent current upper limits, and clearly they will be different in different parts of the world, but the point is that whether schools like it or not, students everywhere are living increasingly digital lifestyles.

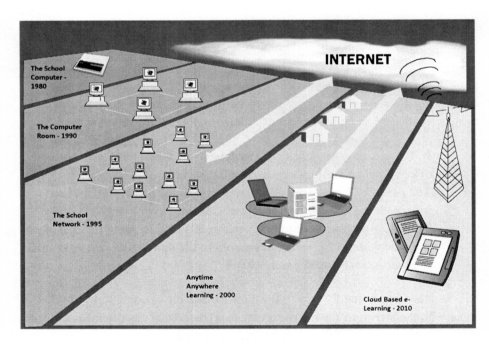

Figure 41. The evolution of technology in schooling.

The worldwide education technology industry is worth around $64bn a year according to Gartner. But could the billions of dollars spent on technology in schooling over the years have more impact? Surely, the answer is "yes". Most other sectors of the economy have been completely transformed—in terms of productivity, effectiveness and profitability—through the introduction of new technology.

Technology on its own is neither good nor bad—it's what you do with it that counts. Simply grafting a layer of technology onto a factory schooling system is no different to adding a layer of veneer on a piece of furniture—nothing changes functionally, so you can't really expect the results to change significantly.

Schooling is an ecosystem—change one thing and everything else changes too. So, for technology to be effective, the introduction of ICT has to be a part of a much bigger transformational agenda. In fact, the introduction of ICT in many cases drives a transformational agenda.

Access to Learning Opportunities

The top reason for investing in technology in schooling should be to improve learning.

Students usually learn more in less time when working with computers because ICT is a powerful tool for helping understand difficult concepts. It is also a vital tool for personalisation—giving the opportunity to tailor tasks to learners without hours of extra work for teachers. ICT also delivers the potential to do things like mark and analyse work automatically, monitor learners' progress, pick out areas where a particular child has not understood, or where the whole class has missed the point and needs more explanation.

"Computers are everyday tools for us all, seen or unseen, but their value in learning is as tools for creativity and learning rather than as machines to deliver the curriculum. These tools, in our children's hands, are forever pushing the envelope of expertise that previous technologies excluded them from: they compose, quantise and perform music before acquiring any ability to play an instrument, they shoot, edit and stream digital video before any support from media courses, they produce architectural fly-throughs of incredible buildings without any drafting or 2D skills, they make stop frame animations with their plasticine models, they edit and finesse their poetry, they explore surfaces on their visual calculators, swap ideas with scientists on-line about volcanic activity, follow webcam images of Ospreys hatching, track weather by live satellite images, control the robots they have built and generally push rapidly at the boundaries of what might be possible, indeed what was formerly possible, at any age. Little of this was easily achieved in the school classroom ten years ago..." (Stephen Heppell)

There are five interrelated areas where ICT can be used to develop learning:

- Acquisition of qualifications and skills
- Feedback and assessment
- Intelligent Intervention
- Personalising Learning
- Accessibility

Acquisition of Qualifications and Skills

ICT skills developed through schooling serve two purposes—preparation for the world of work, and acquisition of qualifications.

According to the former UK Government's Education ICT Agency, BECTA, the use of ICT has a direct link to the acquisition of qualifications:

- In GCSE Science, the average gain from ICT use is 0.56 of a grade
- Where technology is integrated across the curriculum there are lower absence rates and higher scores in Maths tests and examinations
- Schools with broadband show a statistically significant improvement in the percentage of learners gaining five or more A* - Cs at GCSE in the year after broadband introduction
- There is a significant positive association between learners' home use of ICT for educational purposes and improved attainment in national tests for Maths and English GCSE
- In national tests in English, Maths and Science, schools with interactive whiteboards perform better than schools without interactive whiteboards.

(BECTA, 2009)

Computer-based learning can give instant feedback to students and explain correct answers. Moreover, a computer is patient and non-judgemental, which can give the student motivation to continue learning. ICT supports the acquisition of qualifications in the following ways:

- It is a tool for independent learning—students can research, summarise and present their findings using the Internet and productivity tools
- It is convenient for students to edit their written work on word processors, which can, in turn, improve the quality of their writing

- Efficient production of coursework
- Helps students present their work clearly
- Helps speed up the feedback process
- Multimedia allows many different "ways in" for learners and allows them to learn in ways that best suit their individual learning styles
- Addresses different intelligences, enabling concepts to be understood in different ways
- ICT can be used to simulate costly experiments and provide rich explanations.

According to the OECD, "every young person will need to use ICT in many different ways in their adult lives, in order to participate fully in a modern society" (OECD, 2005).

The kinds of skills that will help both in adult life and in school are:

- Finding things out—obtaining appropriate information by selecting appropriate sources; and questioning the plausibility and value of information found
- Developing ideas and making things happen—using ICT to measure, record, respond to and control events
- Exchanging and sharing information—using ICT to share and exchange information, such as web publishing and video conferencing
- Reviewing, modifying and evaluating work as it progresses—reflecting critically on own and others' use of ICT
- Editing and media production—using ICT to clearly and powerfully express thoughts
- Creativity and innovation—using ICT to generate and model ideas
- Critical thinking, problem solving and decision-making.

Curriculum Area Examples

The following examples are based on the UK's ICT entitlement for primary and secondary students (BECTA):

English

- Exploring and investigating
  - o The complete works of Shakespeare are available online as are thousands of out-of-copyright books. Scripts from TV comedies and dramas, reviews of films, books and plays are all freely available and instantly accessible
  - o Enabling a library of texts to be readily stored, accessed, displayed, shared and explored by whole classes, groups or individuals.
- Responding and interpreting
  - o Providing powerful tools for analysis, disassembling and reconstructing a text to explore an author's use of language in terms of vocabulary and grammar.
- Reflecting and evaluating
  - o An enormous spectrum of writing styles can be seen on the World Wide Web. For example, most newspapers now have a website, and the style of writing used differs greatly in entertainment, academic and technical sites providing a rich source of material for analysis.
- Composing and transforming
  - o Writing "scaffolding" can be used to help students start the creative writing process
  - o Sending e-mail heightens the awareness of audience and causes learners to pay more attention to clarity, accuracy and good grammar and spelling. When return messages are received they have to be interpreted and summarised
  - o Students can use ICT to build a narrated story from pictures.
- Presenting and performing
  - o Using podcasting to improve close analysis of language in poetry
  - o Students can set up their own programmes—e.g. the news—for broadcast on the internet/intranet.
- Communicating and collaborating
  - o ICT can go way beyond word processing, and has created another genre where texts are layered and not scrolled, and can

contain internet hyperlinks and moving images, sound and video

- o The nature of ICT, particularly the internet, enables learners to interact with peers and other communities, to access and research information and to publish to a real audience worldwide
- o ICT has the potential to offer students opportunities to work in role, and engage with 'real time' situations which promote team work, citizenship, thinking skills, and the choice of genre to address purpose and audience.

Mathematics

- Learning from feedback
  - o Students can use floor robots to measure (lengths and angles) as they attempt to guide them around a prepared floor plan. Students take it in turns to programme the robot, estimating the distance and angle of turn required to reach their target
  - o The same principle can be applied onscreen—using the Logo software programme to draw patterns, students quickly learn the importance of expressing their commands unambiguously and in the correct order
  - o Word processing software now enables students to "word process" Maths to clearly show complex formulae, along with 2-D and 3-D graphs, making it easier to communicate their thinking and get feedback on it.
- Observing patterns
  - o Using a handheld device, students can enter data, plot graphs and match functions for a given quadratic number sequence based on a growing pattern made from square tiles
  - o Dynamic geometry software can allow students to explore a circle theorem by constructing an appropriate dynamic figure and use geometrical reasoning to make conclusions and report them to others.
- Seeing connections
  - o The computer enables formulae, tables of numbers and graphs to be linked readily

- o   A software Graphing Calculator can be a great tool for teaching Maths when used with a data projector for whole class teaching, or better still when given to students to use. A lesson can be built up and stored, then each stage "replayed"
- o   Software can be used to manipulate 3-D images of cuboids to enable them to solve Pythagoras problems in 3-D by unwrapping nets and constructing the 2-D shapes.
- Developing visual imagery
  - o   Various software packages can be used to create a motif and then copy and translate it on the screen to design a tiling pattern
  - o   Software is available which allows children to draw grids of numbers and shade multiples quickly and easily.
- Exploring data
  - o   Students can enter the heights of their peers and teachers into a spreadsheet to learn about averages. They can also measure their hands to find out if there are correlations.

Science

- Providing information
  - o   There are vast resources on the web providing interactive learning on subjects spanning the whole of the science curriculum.
- Supporting fieldwork
  - o   Use a web cam to watch a bird's nest
  - o   Measure conductivity at different points in the river and present data using mapping software
- Assisting observation
  - o   A digital microscope can be used to take snapshots of mini beasts, explore materials, and light and shadow.
  - o   Electronic telescopes enable learners to collect images from different locations on Earth and at different times of the day. Telescope sites also provide learning resources and galleries of images.
- Recording and measuring
  - o   Sensors and data loggers can be used in the classroom to record results, plot graphs and analyse data.

- Sharing and interpreting data with others
  - o Use of analytical tools, such as spreadsheets and graphing functions.
- Providing models or demonstrations
  - o Simulating experiments can enable students to experiment with phenomena that may be too slow, too fast, too dangerous or too expensive to experience in school
  - o Electronics circuit software provides on-screen tools which allow learners to select basic pieces of virtual electrical equipment and connect these together in a circuit.

Geography

- Mapping
  - o ICT has created new ways of exploring the world through maps and satellite images. These can now be interactive, of variable scale, and supported by multimedia. They are easily accessible and can be integrated into a variety of media.
- Connection with the wider world
  - o Multimedia software can help learners to investigate geographical topics that would be too remote, too dangerous, or involve too long a timescale, to be studied without ICT.
  - o The Internet and email enable learners to interact with peers and other communities, to access and research information and exchange details of weather, environment and culture. This brings otherwise inaccessible localities into the classroom, and can help to develop global citizenship and awareness of the sameness, differences and diversity in the cultures of the world.
- Fieldwork
  - o Using environmental measuring equipment, accurate basic weather data can be collected and entered into a spreadsheet for analysis. This type of activity could, for example, produce a graph that shows clearly how wind strength varies considerably between the foot and the summit of a hill.

Art and design

- Access to art
    - o Some of the world's finest art galleries have substantial presences on the Internet. Access to these opens up a world of possibilities for learning.
- Presenting to a wide audience
    - o The Internet is also becoming widely used as a medium for students to publish their work
    - o Students can present information in a range of ways, for example by creating a slideshow of work to display at a parents' evening or school assembly, or by creating an online gallery.
- Collaboration
    - o Collaboration on projects with students in other schools, or with working artists or designers, becomes a real possibility with electronic communication.
- Manipulating images
    - o ICT can improve efficiency, for example work in progress can be retrieved and modified
    - o Students can scan photos and other digital images; select sections with interesting textures, colours, shapes etc.; then resize, rotate and combine them to create a montage.
- New creative opportunities
    - o ICT enables learners to take risks and demonstrate creativity, for example by combining sensory experiences, through the use of digital video or animation techniques incorporating sound effects
    - o Creating interactive games and stop-frame-animations offers significant opportunity for visual creativity
    - o 3-D modelling software opens opportunities for virtual sculpture.

The full set of examples is available from:
http://www.teachernet.gov.uk/teachingandlearning/subjects/ict/bectadocs/

Feedback and Assessment

Teachers invariably understand the value of giving immediate feedback. The longer a learner thinks that a wrong answer is right, the harder it is to correct. Put another way, the longer a learner waits for their work to be marked, the less effective the learning. Therefore a key goal for providing feedback is to give it as close to immediately as possible. In today's classroom, and with all the distractions that teachers face, just how attainable is this goal? ICT can be used to automatically mark work as well as constantly track the performance of learners, and then present the data in a form that makes it easy for teachers to analyse and assess specific competencies.

Assessment systems can also be linked to reporting systems, so that reports can be automatically generated for each student—and at increasingly granular levels of detail. As a result, assessment and reporting become less of a chore and more of an opportunity for helping teachers to help their students.

At Broadclyst Primary School in Devon, UK, for example, teachers can assess a student's performance and achievements against each aspect of the core curriculum using systems that link directly to planning.

Achievement Tracking

Achievement tracking enables on-going and automatic analysis of student attainment by correlating each individual student against benchmark results and curriculum-defined competency templates. It provides students with details on individual attainments and, via Intelligent Intervention, recommended actions for improvement. It provides teachers with class, year and school-wide reporting enabling identification of trends such as individuals or groups that require additional assistance. Key uses of achievement tracking include:

- Automatic identification of students requiring additional assistance, combined with a "resources route" that recommends support and learning resources
- Automatic identification of peer reviewers, subject matter experts, and tutors
- Automatic aggregation of results to provide per-class, per-subject, per-teacher and per-school attainment reporting

- Flexible ad hoc reporting to measure specific initiatives
- Identification of changes in attainment pattern (e.g. pace and motivation) and recommendation of appropriate support resources
- Parental advice based on analysis of cross-curricular activities
- Create opportunities for collaborative skill development by matching students from different locations against attainment profile.

Using ICT to Personalise Learning

The first principle behind personalising learning with ICT is to use technology to more deeply engage learners and students through a range of learning experiences.

No matter how talented a teacher is, he or she will find it difficult to set the pace and style of learning so that it suits all the students in a classroom. Students have different abilities, interests, aptitudes, experiences and learning preferences.

People who think predominantly in images and have a natural affinity for pictures and graphics are **Visual Learners.** ICT can be used to stimulate visual learning with the use of digital images, graphics, animations, simulations and paint programmes. Interactive whiteboards and PowerPoint presentations allow teachers to present various concepts in a highly visual way. Other practical examples include:

- Using Tablet PC's (which use a pen and 'digital ink') for design projects
- Use video software to create animated movies. This develops a multitude of skills and intelligences including storytelling and Design and Technology
- Setting up daily news report "channels" on school networks.

Auditory Learners prefer to learn via spoken or written word, sound or music. For these learners, oral presentations, class discussions and debates offer the best ways of learning. Multimedia computers offer sound, music and speech recording, recognition, playback and reading on-screen text. Once recorded, speech or sounds can be embedded into slides or documents. Some practical examples of auditory learning through ICT:

- Use speech technologies to read onscreen text and input speech or commands.
- Embedded the sound that bats make to catch their prey into a PowerPoint presentation
- Compose songs or sound tracks using music composition software.

People who prefer active forms of learning are **Kinaesthetic Learners**. They tend to be "hands-on" people who enjoy sports, activities that involve hand-eye co-ordination. Computers can be operated by a variety of devices that involve touch—mice, keyboards, joysticks, switches and pen tablets, for example. Devices like the Tablet PC—which allows users to write, sketch or draw on a computer in the same way as using pen and paper—are especially stimulating for this group of learners. These learners also like making models, playing games, moving objects and doing practical experiments. They are also stimulated by the use of games controllers and flight simulators, both of which involve much physical activity. Some examples of Kinaesthetic/Tactile Learning:

- Build and programme robots
- Use of flight simulation software to teach Geography topics such as latitude and longitude
- Use a pen to control software—this combines visual, auditory and kinaesthetic learning in one task.

Another useful way to exploit ICT is to use it to address multiple intelligences, e.g.:

- Logical-mathematical—use of Maths software and spreadsheets
- Spatial—3-D Computer Aided Design (CAD) and modelling software for design and technology subjects
- Bodily-kinaesthetic—use of video to enhance movement in sports and dance
- Musical—composition software
- Interpersonal—Instant Messaging and video conferencing
- Intrapersonal—E-folios for reflection on achievements
- Naturalist—analytical tools for uncovering patterns in nature.

Accessibility

For students with some disabilities, technology can open up new windows of learning opportunity. For example:

For people with **vision** difficulties, Refreshable Braille displays provide tactile output of information represented on the computer screen. The user reads the Braille letters with his or her fingers, and then, after a line is read, refreshes the display to read the next line. For those with less severe difficulties, areas of the screen can be enlarged using a (software) magnifier. A screen reader can be used to "speak" everything on the screen. Speech recognition allows people to give commands and enter data using their voices.

Those suffering from **motor (co-ordination)** impairments, typing aids, such as word prediction utilities and spelling checkers, are available. These products reduce the required number of keystrokes. Keyboard filters enable users to quickly access the letters they need and to avoid inadvertently selecting keys they don't want. Touch screens are devices placed on the computer monitor (or built into it) that allow direct selection or activation of the computer by touching the screen. Alternative input devices (including alternative keyboards, electronic pointing devices, sip-and-puff systems, wands and sticks, joysticks and trackballs) allow individuals to control their computers through means other than a standard keyboard or pointing device.

For people with **hearing** difficulties, it's possible for computer systems to visualize sound messages—e.g. sounds that would normally be played when an e-mail arrives, can be displayed as a flashing caption. For those with lower levels of hearing disability, using headphones can help block out background noise.

People with **learning, language** and **communication** difficulties can use word prediction programmes which help users increase written productivity and accuracy, and increase vocabulary skills through word prompting. Reading comprehension programmes focus on establishing or improving reading skills through ready-made activities, stories, exercises, or games. These programmes can help users practice letter sound recognition and can increase the understanding of words by adding graphics, sound, and animation.

Access to Learning—Functional Architecture

Being able to offer a comprehensive range of applications and tools makes hardware and infrastructure investments worthwhile. The wider the choice of applications, the bigger the payback can become.

Hardware

Both proponents and opponents of educational technology agree that the full effects of technology in schools cannot be fully realized until the technology is no longer a shared resource (Damian Bebell & Rachel Kay, 2010).

Portable computing devices such as laptop PC's, and Tablet PC's mean that ICT can be used for teaching and learning anywhere and anytime. Wireless networking makes ICT even more flexible. Add to this the proliferation of online digital content and "input" technologies—such as cameras, pen and voice, and "output" technologies—such as whiteboards or video. It's easy to see why so many teachers are embedding ICT into the curriculum.

Worldwide, there has been explosion of national level project for the wide-scale introduction of personal learning devices. Many of these wrongly focus on a blanket approach of providing huge numbers of cheap portable PC's. Unfortunately most of these projects have been driven by getting the most computers for the lowest price, rather than focusing on getting the right device for the learning that needs to be done.

A more sensible approach is to have a range of devices available to students of different stages in their learning.

Sophistication of learning tasks ↓	Shared Applications	At the most basic level, multiple students (up to 25) can use their own mouse, to simultaneously engage with an application.	Mobile Phones and Personal Digital Assistants (PDAs) and slates now offer a range of applications and productivity tools for learning Portable media players offer a range of possibilities for consuming content such as audio or video lessons
	Shared Computers	Multiple monitors, keyboards and mice can be attached to a single PC enabling a group of students of up to 10 students to share a single PC.	
	Dedicated PC	Computers in labs can provide individual access. When connected to a Local Area Network, these computers can share resources, internet connection and printing & scanning capabilities.	
	Ultra low cost devices	Low cost, low power laptops, tablet and netbook options are now widely available and provide students with learning opportunities—anytime, anywhere.	
	1–to-1	The best level of 1-to-1 access is where full powered portable PC's are used to access a full spectrum of high quality learning experiences.	

Table 26. Appropriate devices at different levels of learning sophistication.

Of course, computers aren't the only hardware devices used in the classroom. Digital cameras; video cameras; voting devices; interactive whiteboard tools; robotic kits; digital microscopes; and projectors all have a role to play in the learning process.

Appropriate Facilities

Once the issue of power is addressed, the next step is to provide dry, accessible accommodation with adequate benching and power sockets. Decisions need to be made about whether to have a "laboratory" or to spread computers throughout the school.   In a laboratory, decisions need to be made about arranging worktables. For example, U or L shapes to allow group interaction. An "island" arrangement with two PC's on each side of a table works well and encourages students to share information.

Learning Software

Productivity software is used to produce documents, spreadsheets, presentations and databases. Integrated notes software can be used to combine a range of media—text, sound, video etc, on an individual or group basis.

Social Networking—the significant uptake of popular Internet social networking sites, Instant Messaging, Wikis and Blogs can be capitalised on.

Drill and Practice—provides students with practice in areas such as learning a new language, or mathematical operations.

Problem Solving—many simulations and games have some problem solving aspects.

Tutorials—present a new concept where text illustrations, description, and simulations are provided to teach a specific task, skill or application.

Graphics and **digital image** processing enable the creation and manipulation of still images, often built up in multiple layers. Vector drawing packages enable the precise manipulation of lines, and can be used to produce technical drawings.

Reference—many encyclopaedias, medical and educational research journals, as well as geographic references are now available for reasonable costs.

Multimedia—combining sound, pictures, graphics, video, text, and hypertext is often used to produce learning content by students, for students.

Simulation—can be used to simulate scientific experiments, mathematical problem solving, engineering designs, environmental scenarios, movement of planets.

GroupWare—software is designed to be used for groups of students, generally to collaborate on a project and make decisions about an issue or topic.

Connecting Learning Communities

There may be elements of learning that require independent work, but learning is very much a social experience. Learning only really acquires meaning in a social context, and the most immediate and direct social context for schooling is the local community.

ICT in a Connected Learning Community can be used to connect together all those who can make a contribution to students' and teachers' learning—e.g.

local business, community resources (e.g. museums/libraries), parents and 3rd party learning services. It can connect students to inspiring individuals and inspirational speakers; promote debate and engagement between collaborators in face-to-face or virtual groupings; and provide mentoring opportunities. Connecting stakeholders together in a Connected Learning Community has enormous benefits such as engaging parents more deeply in the learning process, speeding up processes and improving students' connections with the outside world.

A Connected Learning Community can change the paradigm in line with 21st Century needs, the key to which is putting the student at the centre of a range of electronically mediated services.

In this model, students learn within a web of supportive connections.

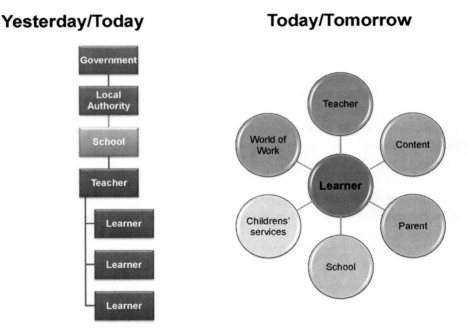

Figure 42. Students at the centre of electronically mediated services.

The concept of a Connected Learning Community is as applicable in the developing world as it is in the developed world. As mentioned in chapter 4, some schools in Uganda are used as community access points. Traders from different villages use school based ICT resources to communicate with each other over email to find out what supplies are required before departing, thus ensuring that the demand and supply is in equilibrium.

A starting point for building a Connected Learning Community is to make the computers available to students also available to the wider community when not being used by students. The benefit is that a local pool of skills, knowledge and interest in ICT can be developed. In some situations, small charges for training can be made, helping to meet costs. To deliver this service to the community institutions need to provide secure access and software that resets computers after shared use.

Beyond providing community access to the school's computers, technology can help build learning communities in many different ways, including:

- Integrating parents into the schooling process
- Providing virtual schooling
- Enabling new models of content generation and consumption

Parent Connection

Research demonstrates that active parental involvement in educational activities delivers a positive impact on attainment. Technology can be used to connect parents with a rich seam of information regarding the educational progress of their child, and a range of supplemental activities in which the parent can support the learning process.

The usual way in which schools communicate directly with parents is via "parent evenings"—many parents end up seeing a teacher once or twice a year for five minutes—hardly enough time to say "hello" and "goodbye". The advantage with using technology, then, is to:

- Enable parents and teachers to communicate more frequently with each other
- Identify problems and issues at an early stage and involve parents in rectifying them
- Give parents the tools to support learning activities at home
- Provide parents with immediate news about the school and its activities.

Examples of what ICT can contribute include:

- Web-based collaboration
- Discussion groups, shared calendars, document and meeting workspaces, picture libraries
- Online dashboard indicating student attainment, enabling drill-down to subject and class
- Digital learning resources to assist the student with coursework
- Educational resources for parents, such as behavioural management guidance
- Subscription mechanism for alerting on critical issues such as lack of attendance, dropping attainment levels, behavioural issues, etc.
- School and community news and information.

Virtual Schooling

The *New York Times*, quoting a US Department of Education commissioned report, stated that "On average, students in online learning conditions performed better than those receiving face-to-face instruction" (Lohr, 2009).

Until fairly recently, online education amounted to little more than electronic versions of traditional methods of teaching. That has really changed with the arrival of Web-based video, instant messaging and collaboration tools. Now, online learning has an impact both inside and outside school. It can enable schools to offer advanced or specialist courses that would be impossible to do otherwise, given their size or location. Live lessons can be accessed over the internet from home, or archived lessons can be accessed at a time which is convenient to the learner. Learners can post questions at times when they are working, for others (peers, teachers, other experts or collaborators), to engage with synchronously or asynchronously.

Computer-based learning scales with ease and as it scales, costs are falling. Over time, computer-based learning can become more personalised, and software developers can customise learning by setting out different learning paths for different students.

Virtual schooling is core to driving personalised learning by enabling schooling systems to offer a curriculum that is broader, deeper, more flexible, more adaptive and more responsive to the needs of the individual student. In subjects where there is a shortage of specialist teachers (such as Mathematics), students can participate in virtual lessons by linking up to other schools or classes via video conferencing or desktop conferencing systems to share a specialist teacher. Many of these systems—such as Instant Messenger—offer much interactivity, with students able to share resources, exchange ideas, pose questions and use a virtual whiteboard through a simple interface.

A connected learning community can give students access to people who are relevant to their interests. This sort of specialisation could not and should not be expected to be delivered by a single institution. In fact, to rely wholly on teachers as educators ignores the benefits and resources that individuals in a range of different settings can bring to learning. Access to other adults could be introduced through experts coming into schools via ICT to run workshops or courses. Face-to-face contact is expensive, so digital technologies in a connected learning community offer the opportunity for collaboration and teaching and learning at a distance through video-conferencing, e-mail and online communities.

Learning Content

In traditional systems content production and consumption has been a top-down process. ICT turns this on its head by allowing users themselves to create learning modules. With the full spectrum of productivity and creativity tools available, students can be given the task of producing learning content.

With cheap webcams; basic video editing software; drawing, graphics, and productivity software; and web development tools, students can produce high quality learning resources for distribution via a portal across the connected learning community. People throughout the community should be able to use and rate this content just as they rate books on Amazon.com or movies on Netflix.

In an ideal world a student, parent or teacher struggling with learning or teaching a certain concept, should be able to log into the connected learning community to find content that another student, parent, or teacher developed for that specific challenge.

There will always be a role for professionally produced content, however. But the world of publishing needs to evolve from providing digital versions of books, to fully embracing the idea that students and teachers will want to build their own learning resources from individual learning objects, in much the same way as building models using Lego®.

The role of the connected learning community here is to provide the content management facilities that enable the community development of learning resources.

Connected Learning Community—Functional Architecture

Portal

The core of a connected learning community is a portal that can be accessed from anywhere. For it to be effective it needs to be "role based", i.e. present users with information and tools relevant to their role and to them as individuals. In other words a teacher in the community sees the information relevant to all teachers, their fellow subject specialists, but also information specific to their particular group of students, their particular HR information, and their particular teaching content, tasks, calendar, e-mail, etc.

A connected learning community portal gives students, parents, managers, teachers, their own "spaces" and delivers to them the resources that are important individually to them through a single web page portal. It aggregates information from diverse systems into one interface with a single sign-on ID—and organisation-wide search capabilities so that users can access relevant information quickly. Teaching and administration staff can use the portal to distribute information to students based on their enrolment, classes, security group or other membership criteria, while enabling them to personalise the portal content and customise the layout to suit their needs.

Function	Purpose
Single sign-on	Provide access to all portal functionality.
My Email	Provide access for users to email through the portal.
My News	Consolidate user's news from multiple sources onto a single page in the portal for ease of access.
My Schedules	Provide access for users to their calendars through the portal.
My Calendar	Provide access for users to their personal calendar through the portal.
My Planner	Provide a view of all appointments relevant to the user from all relevant calendars.
My Communities	Provide collaboration sites for portal users.
Team Site Navigation	Provides a list of team sites the user has access to.
Site Templates	Provide consistent look and feel for team sites which are created for specific purposes.
Search	Provide user the ability to search establishment and central portals.
My Site	Provide a customised view of the portal functionality.
My Profile	Provide a location for users to maintain their public profile information.
Staff Home	Provide a common portal screen for staff to access.
Personal view	Allow users to modify portal pages to meet their specific requirements.
My Communication	Provide access to list of contacts that the user is entitled to contact, by email, phone, or Instant Messaging.
Learning Resources	Provide a list of approved learning resources to staff, both at an establishment level and at central level.
Learning Resource Search	Restrict search of learning resources to approved resources in the establishment and central level.
Managed Learning	Provide learning management functionality.
SCORM Creation Utility	To create SCORM content from learning resources created locally by members of Staff (using Learning Essentials).
Student Home	Provide a common portal screen for students to access.
My Assignments	Provide access for students to their assignments from within the portal.
Sync Team Sites	Create team sites so students can collaborate on assignments and in classes.
My Classes	Allow students to see which classes they are a member of.
Parent Home	Provide a common portal screen for parents to access.
Public Home	Provide a common portal screen for public (anonymous) users to access.
Tasks	Allocate, update and manage tasks at an individual and group level.
Instant Messaging	Real-time desktop video conferencing, file sharing, VoIP and chat services.
Presence	Ability to identify the connectivity 'status' of an individual
Blogs	Allow students to maintain a running dialogue, like a journal, of thoughts, ideas.

Wikis	An online library of shared community knowledge—can be built up as a single site for the collected knowledge of the community.
Application Sharing	Sharing access to a live application enabling remote working on a single project.
Whiteboard Sharing	Ability to view and control whiteboard allowing free-form collaboration and teaching to remote parties.
Discussion	Provision of discussion forum services, providing an asynchronous means of collaborating on topics of common interests.
Workspaces	Virtual working environments.
Document management	Ability to develop documentation collaboratively and to organise document in a way that leads to maximum efficiencies.
Workflow	Provision for creation of workflow elements allowing connection of collaborative tools within an application.
Polling & Voting	Ability to create surveys.
Voice & Video	Provision of Voice over IP (VoIP) service and video streaming to be integrated in collaborative applications.
Access	The portal should be accessible through desktop computers; laptops; netbooks; PDAs; Smartphones; Game Consoles; browser based access (e.g. internet café, kiosk, etc.).
E-folio	The role of an e-folio is to enable students to build a profile and bank of evidence of their achievements, experiences, courses, reviews, and assessments. The e-folio should contain a range of files that can be cross-referenced to specific criteria or assessment grades.

Table 27. Essential functions of a schooling portal.

Enabling many of the functions in the portal are several sub-systems including:

Content Management Systems (CMS)

When ICT is fully implemented, vast amounts of content gets created. In order to get maximum efficiencies from ICT, this content needs to be organised and managed in a way that means that people don't replicate one another's work.

A content management system in a connected learning community helps education institutions organise and facilitate the collaborative creation of documents and other content. They enable the full life cycle of content—from initial creation to delivery to end users. CMS comprise document and records management, web content management, forms, search, library systems, curriculum frameworks, curriculum systems, curriculum exemplars and resource assemblers.

Unified Communications & Collaboration (UC)

Today it is typical that people will have multiple contact addresses—direct line phone number; mobile phone number; e-mail; Instant Messenger; home number; personal mobile number; home e-mail, etc. Unified Communications (UC) takes identity and presence and then has all of these other ways of interacting simply connect up to that.

A single integrated identity can simplify how you find and communicate with others. One integrated desktop application can provide easy access to all the ways users are likely to want to communicate. Another key advantage to UC is that in using Voice over IP (VOIP) for telephone calls, it has the potential to significantly reduce communication costs.

UC enables students, teachers, parents and other stakeholders to confer and consult in the way that suits their work style by switching seamlessly between videoconferencing, telephone, email and instant messaging.

Also within UC are task and calendaring functions.

Data Driven Decision-Making

In chapter 6 we looked in detail at the functions associated with data driven decision-making. Here we turn to the technology building blocks that make data driven decision-making happen.

In a schooling system, data driven decision-making is supported by a huge number of information systems. Any process that involves the creation and transmission of information can be considered an information system—even informal discussions.

The collective term for the information systems in schooling is Management Information Systems (MIS).

Functions Supported by an MIS

Returning to the functions we explored in Chapter 6, the functions that a Management Information System need to support are:

Improving Student Performance	Progression Management
Learning Management	Intelligent Intervention
Engaging Parents in Learning Process	Better Teaching Decisions
Make Better Management Decisions	Monitor, Analyse and Plan
Tactical Decision Making	Data Visualisation
Manage Resources More Effectively	Planning and budgeting
Financial Control	Asset Control
Reporting	Accountability and Alignment
Performance and Assessment Data	KPIs, Scorecards, Dashboards and Reports
Key Performance Indicators (KPIs)	Drive Administrative Efficiencies
Planning	Organising
Controlling	Co-ordinating

Table 28. Functions that a Management Information System (MIS) needs to support.

Management Information Systems—Functional Architecture

In this context, an information system really means an organised hierarchy of information sub-systems. Management Information System (MIS) is a term used as a container for all of the electronic information systems within a schooling system. These systems vary in size, scope and capability, from packages that are implemented in relatively small organisations to cover student records alone, to enterprise-wide solutions that aim to cover most aspects of running large multi-site organisations.

MIS includes the following sub-systems:

- Decision Support Systems (DSS)
    - Finance
    - Performance Management
    - HR
    - Student Relationship Management (SRM)
    - Enterprise Resource Planning (ERP)
    - Analytics and Business Intelligence (BI)
    - Timetabling
- Student Information Systems (SIS)
    - Record keeping
    - Electronic grade book
    - Attendance management

- Learning Platform
  - o Learning Management Systems (LMS)
    - ▪ Computer Based Learning (CBL)
    - ▪ Communication and collaboration
    - ▪ Testing
  - o Managed Learning Environment (MLE)
    - ▪ Learning workflows
  - o Virtual Learning Environments (VLE)
    - ▪ Wikis and blogs
    - ▪ File stores
  - o Content Management Systems (CMS)

Decision Support Systems (DSS)

Finance

Financial metrics; management; forecasting; and accounting. Automated e-procurement of goods and services.

Performance Management

Systems for managing every aspect of employee performance—from target setting to professional development. Linked to HR systems.

HR

Employee information; payroll direct deposit; integrate to general ledger; project management; bank reconciliation; compliance with government reporting requirements

Student Relationship Management (SRM)

Based on Customer Relationship Management (CRM), SRM manages the students' schooling experience as if they were customers. Automated workflows around interventions make SRM a core component in a schooling technology platform. (See Gestar Case study in Chapter 6.)

Enterprise Resource Planning (ERP)

Manage internal and external resources including tangible assets, financial resources, materials, and human resources. ERP allows organisations to connect their subsidiaries, divisions, branches, to a central headquarters to control and plan resourcing across the entire enterprise.

Analytics and Business Intelligence (BI)

BI can reveal patterns and trends in operations so that organisations can plan, predict and deploy resources with greater accuracy and cost-efficiency. BI helps visualise complex information and make better decisions regarding learning trends, staffing levels and resourcing, for example. Business Intelligence technologies extract, correlate, analyse and interpret information from a range of sources across the entire management information system (MIS).

Timetabling

Whilst static timetabling software is commonly used in schools today, a bigger challenge is how to make timetabling dynamic so students are given a timetable that constantly evolves to meet their needs, not something that is fixed once a year.

Learning Management Systems (LMS)

An LMS generally covers the following functions—learning content delivery; workflows; grading and feedback; and reporting. An LMS can contain several subsystems including:

> **Computer Based Learning (CBL)**—the original model of CBL (or e-learning) was based on the transmission of knowledge principle, and involved students comprehending a piece of learning and then being tested on it. More modern approaches assume that knowledge is socially constructed, so involves using collaborative learning tools.

> **Virtual Learning Environments (VLE)**—a collection of tools and content to support learning. Can include wikis and blogs; file stores; assessment tools; RSS feeds; communication and collaboration tools; peer assessment; and surveys.

Managed Learning Environment (MLE)—can contain all the functions of CBL and VLE but adds workflow management for learning tasks—i.e. assigning, tracking, grading, feeding-back, and returning learning assignments

Student Information Systems (SIS)

An SIS will allow users to track progress and attendance, build schedules, and manage other student-related data.

Record keeping

Student records should include:

- Personal—name; address; photo; family contacts
- Performance—actual and predicted grades; teachers' comments
- Attendance—by day, by lesson, over time
- Risk profile—learning, social, medical and demographic
- Intervention history
- Timetable.

It should be possible to take data in from the LMS and make data securely accessible to the SRM and other related systems.

Electronic grade book

An electronic grade book is used to record grades, attendance and other data in the classroom. This data is then sent to the centralised record system.

Attendance management

When a student is marked absent in the electronic grade book, attendance management triggers an automated workflow to make relevant people, especially parents, aware. It is also there to track, discover and escalate longer term attendance issues.

Automated workflows

Central to using ICT to drive efficiencies, is the use of automated workflows. Many administrative tasks can be broken down into component parts that can then be linked together to form workflows. This drives out the cost of people doing the work, and speeds up processes; examples include:

- Policy document production
- Automatic notification of teacher illness, with associated toolset to arrange class coverage
- Online resourcing of supply (substitute) staff
- Alerts and escalations, for example, learner non-attendance, dropping attainment level, bullying, behavioural issues, etc.
- RFID (Radio Frequency Identification) smartcards to enable automatic presence detection
- Electronic procurement provides facilities for teachers, staff and learners (subject to consent) to purchase goods and services from a predefined online catalogue of approved vendors
- Cashless vending enables students to purchase items such as food or learning resources without the need to carry cash. Payment would be made electronically and provides an additional stream of data regarding purchasing habits.

E-Forms

Significant numbers of administrative processes and schools are driven by forms, so it makes sense to make these processes electronic where possible. It's also inefficient to ask students or staff to repeatedly re-enter data that is already in the system onto forms. The other advantage of e-forms is that if the data they require is already in the system, this will be pre-loaded onto the forms.

Types of forms that can be turned into e-forms with relative ease are:

Medical form on joining	Parental approval form	Trip request form
Medical questionnaire for trips	Routine outing form	Parental approval for routine outing
Accident report form	Accident investigation form	Activities request form
Out-of-school activities	Catering request	Staff leave of absence
Cover request	Support ticket—ICT	Support ticket—maintenance
Expense claims	Purchase requests	

Table 29. E-forms.

Infrastructure Foundation

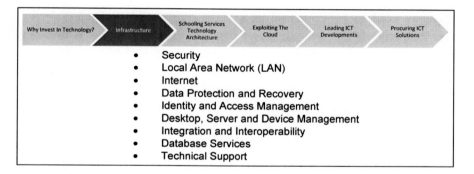

The foundation on which the entire schooling solution architecture is built is an "optimised infrastructure". This provides a scalable, secure platform which can be built on to provide a spectrum of solutions.

Increasingly, organisations are pushing more and more Infrastructure Foundation capabilities and services to the "cloud"—i.e. centrally hosted services that can scale according to demand, and significantly reduce cost.

Key capabilities of an optimised infrastructure are:

Security

The key component without which none of this will work is stringent security and networking protocols. This is needed to protect students and employees from unauthorised users, viruses and unsuitable content. Security systems should automatically identify and respond to threats.

PC's have high value, so physical security is critical. Communities that benefit from the value of computer labs are more likely to buy into the ICT facilities, which can help to reduce crime and vandalism. However, physical security is also usually required, for example, "Kensington® Locks", burglar bars on windows, padlocked doors, biometrics, access controlled areas, storage units for laptops and other mobile technologies. There are also disablement and recovery securities, including automatic PC disablement and encrypted hard-drives.

Local Area Network (LAN)

Computers need to be connected to a LAN—wired and/or wireless—with a server that controls the network, stores files and enables printing. A classroom might have just a few computers that all the students take turns using, so it's important that an educational computer be configured just the way the teacher wants. The teacher shouldn't have to waste valuable teaching time troubleshooting. Each PC in a LAN needs to be "locked down" and reset easily.

Internet

There are now a range of ways of delivering internet access to remote locations, including Satellite and WiMax. With Internet access, PC security becomes an even more important issue.

Data Protection and Recovery

As ICT becomes increasingly "mission critical", it's important to manage data so it can be rapidly recovered. When infrastructure is fully optimised, recovering information should be as simple as browsing the network.

Identity and Access management

Identity and Access Management can help organisations centrally manage user information and access rights. It allows administrators to manage each student, teacher, administrator individually by setting their role, access and functional level. This enables individual users to have information and software tools that are specific to their individual requirements—a personalised IT service. A directory service holds each user account and its access functions and allows the user to access various systems using the same set of credentials. Authentication can be by various mechanisms such as smartcards, logon credentials, and biometrics.

Desktop, Server and Device management

In an optimised infrastructure, IT professionals have the tools and knowledge to help manage their IT infrastructure; easing operations; reducing troubleshooting time; controlling quota; password re-setting; provisioning users; improving planning capabilities; and managing mobile devices. Virtualisation technology enables applications to be easily deployed, workloads to be dynamically shifted and power consumption to be reduced.

Integration and Interoperability

Many schooling systems lack integration of the various systems responsible for managing learning and operational data. These systems are often treated as "silos" offering very little in the way of interoperability. A tremendous amount of time and money gets wasted on manually processing critical information, often just to meet externally imposed requirements. An optimised infrastructure enables users to see many integrated perspectives of data, by making "silos" such as Student Information Systems, Financial Ledgers and Learning Management Systems, interoperate.

Database Services

Databases are the "engines" of information management. They are used to capture, store, analyse and interpret a wide variety of information, and deliver this information to a range of different applications and devices including servers, desktops and mobile systems. Data includes text, numbers, pictures, video streams, audio content, and geo-spatial information. Not only do databases store data but they interpret, index and enable it to be searched. Detailed auditing should be available to enable compliance with relevant regulatory requirements.

Technical Support

Schooling system networks need to be reliable to encourage user confidence and to support learning and teaching, as well as school management and administration. This requires access to technical support, which can come from technicians within the school, or from another provider, or sometimes from students themselves. In an optimised infrastructure, schooling systems need to move away from a reactive system in which incidents are dealt with only as they arise. Instead they need to create a more pro-active system where technical support prevents problems occurring and ensures that individual ICT systems are robust and reliable and available when required.

Schooling Technology Architecture

- Four Levels of Optimisation
- Schooling Enterprise Services Architecture

In building design, form follows function—and the same can be said of ICT system design too.

However, an ICT system is different to a building inasmuch as it dynamically moves through levels of maturity, and constantly evolves.

In building schooling technology architectures, we need to optimise systems through four phases:

Four Levels of Optimisation

Level 1—Basic

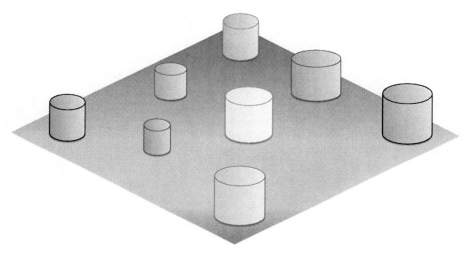

Figure 43. Basic architecture—no real overall structure.

The Basic IT infrastructure is characterized by silos of data and applications; manual, localized processes; minimal central control; non-existent or un-enforced IT policies and standards regarding security, backup, image management and deployment, compliance, and other common IT standards. Schooling systems with basic infrastructure find their environments extremely hard to control, have very high computer management costs, and are generally very reactive to security threats.

Level 2—Standardised

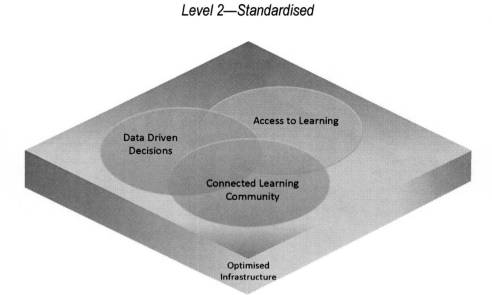

Figure 44. Standardised architecture.

In the Standardised phase, technology functions are organised into 4 main categories:

- Access to Learning
- Connected Learning Community
- Data Driven Decision-Making
- Infrastructure Foundation

The Standardized infrastructure introduces controls through the use of standards and policies to manage computers, resources, and access. Security measures are improved and policies are in operation.

Level 3—Rationalised

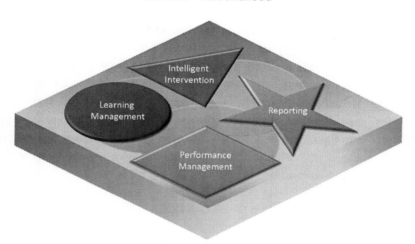

Figure 45. Rationalised architecture.

In the Rationalised phase, processes (learning and administrative) are broken down and re-assembled into standardised modules.   The Rationalized infrastructure is where the costs involved in managing computers are at their lowest and processes and policies have matured. ICT is now beginning to play a large role in supporting and developing the schooling system. Security is very pro-active and responding to threats and challenges is rapid and controlled.

Level 4—Dynamic

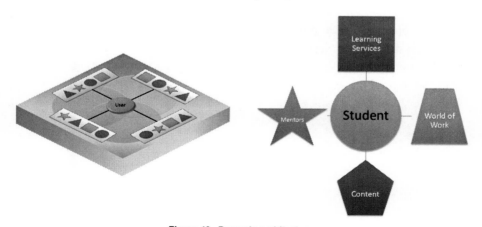

Figure 46. Dynamic architecture.

In the Dynamic phase, standardised process modules are organised into "sub-assemblies" and delivered to users. Each user has a personalised interface to the system that ensures that services are tailored to their specific needs. ICT in schooling systems with a dynamic infrastructure represents a strategic value to their organisation. Costs are fully controlled; there is good integration between users and data, desktops and servers; collaboration between users and departments is pervasive; mobile users have high levels of service and capabilities regardless of location. Processes are fully automated—often incorporated into the technology itself—allowing IT to be aligned and managed according to the organisation's needs. Additional investments in technology yield specific, rapid, measurable benefits for the business.

Schooling Enterprise Services Architecture

The way networks are built needs to follow the function of networked enterprises as set out in Chapter 4.

Operational Unit Perspective

The main operational units in a schooling enterprise are:

- Schools—public and private
- "Strategic cores"—Ministries of Education and Local Government Education Departments
- Internal and external suppliers

Each unit operates on a provision-of-service basis so ICT needs to allow appropriate data to be accessed and analysed by anyone anywhere in the network. Enterprise Resource Planning (ERP) systems connect suppliers both within and beyond the organisational boundary.

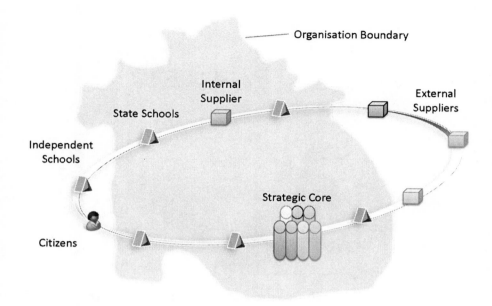

Figure 47. Enterprise networks connect organisational units and suppliers to a strategic core.

The critical point is that there is no "one size fits all" approach to organisational design so there can't be a "one size fits all" for the technology architecture either. At the same time, and in order to drive maximum efficiencies, the entire system needs to conform to a set of standards. Therefore, governments need to set frameworks within which a variety of network configurations can evolve according to local needs. The rapid evolution of cloud-based services—including communication and collaboration; database; financial; CRM; HR and an array of functions—is making this increasingly easy.

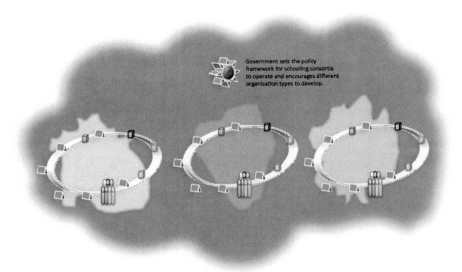

Government sets the policy framework for schooling consortia to operate and encourages different organisation types to develop.

Figure 48. Different organisational structures can emerge within a standards-based enterprise network framework.

Functional Summary

Student

For students to learn effectively with and through ICT, the main functional building blocks they need are:

- Access to learning opportunities
    - o Hardware
    - o Learning Software
- Access to the Connected Learning Community Portal
- Feedback and assessment, achievement tracking
- ICT for personalised learning experience
    - o Intelligent Intervention
- Data driven decision-making
    - o Learning Management Systems

Teacher

For teachers to function effectively with ICT, the main functional building blocks they need are:

- Hardware
- Learning Software
- Training
- Access to the Connected Learning Community Portal
- Feedback and assessment, achievement tracking
- Management Information System, including:
  - SRM
  - BI
  - LMS
  - SIS

Learning Space

- The learning spaces that teachers and students work in need to be supported by the following ICT:
  - Hardware—e.g. projectors, IWBs, scanners, printers, digital cameras
  - Accessibility—specialist hardware and software for students with disabilities
  - Connectivity—to the LAN and the Internet
  - Technical support
  - Network infrastructure—cabling, hubs and routers, electrical points
  - Appropriate facilities—furniture and benching, air conditioning, seating arrangements, storage and organisational flexibility.

School

At school level the primary functions are:

- Access to Learning Opportunities
  - Curriculum Feedback and Assessment

- Data Driven Decision-Making
  - All MIS functions and sub-systems
  - Automated workflows
  - E-forms
- Connected Learning Community
  - Portal and sub-systems

Local Government Education Department and Ministry of Education

At the "strategic core" level, the functional building blocks are based mainly around Data Driven Decisions. However, communication and collaboration systems sitting on top of an optimised infrastructure need to be in place to enable alignment, and information and resource flow throughout the system.

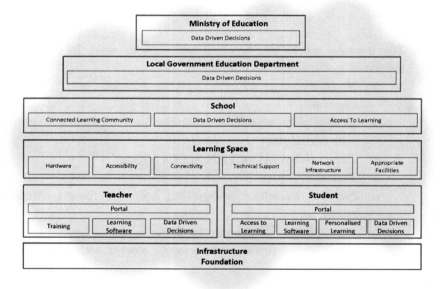

Figure 49. Schooling System Functional Architecture.

Exploiting the Cloud

In many countries, state and local authority education departments solve very similar information management and technology problems in isolation, which is expensive and wasteful. It's quite possible to aggregate the kinds of functions needed at various organisational levels and sell these as hosted services, enabling individual organisational units to make savings on energy, hardware and platform maintenance costs. The principle idea behind cloud-based services is to centralise data centre functions, then to let individual customers choose the services they want from a menu.

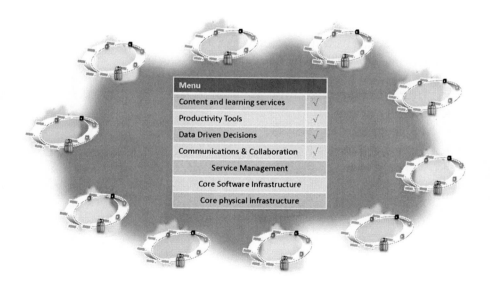

Figure 50. Menu driven cloud based services example.

Leading ICT Development

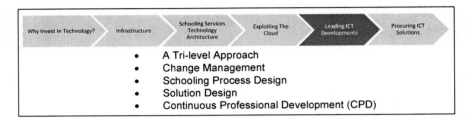

- A Tri-level Approach
- Change Management
- Schooling Process Design
- Solution Design
- Continuous Professional Development (CPD)

A Tri-Level Approach

ICT policy is often effective when it's synchronised between state or local government education department level, and school level, all with a policy and guidance framework set by national government. This brings consistency and economies of scale.

At a practical level, a typical approach is to have a team at the local government level comprising of the following functions:

- Board/steering group
- Project manager
- Pedagogy team and Manager
- Technical team and Manager
- Administrator

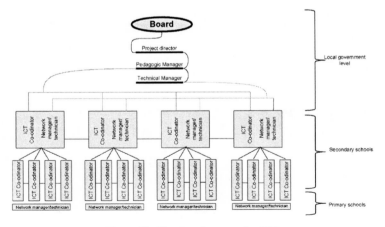

Figure 51. Structure for managing ICT.

At the school level, it's expected that all staff will have an involvement in ICT, lead and supported by the senior management. Secondary schools can be expected to have a co-ordinator whose focus is to ensure that ICT is embedded into all curriculum activities, and a technician to ensure continuity of ICT service. At Primary school level, often the technician role is shared between schools and delivered remotely.

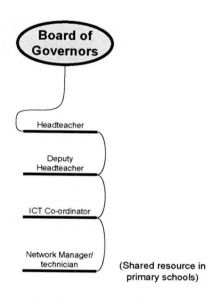

Figure 52. ICT management structure at school level.

Change Management

Introducing technology is inevitably going to bring about some change, and this change needs to be managed to ensure a smooth transition from old to new practices.

A change management process, at any level in the schooling organisation, typically involves five steps:

1. **Analysis of current practice**—To fully understand the impact of any change on a schooling system, it is important to identify and document the current practices

2. **Stakeholder agreement on future practice**—this is about agreeing a vision for the use of technology to achieve the outcomes that are being sought (Chapter 2)
3. **Gap analysis**—each schooling system, and subsystem within, will be at a different starting point and will want different outcomes, so conducting a gap analysis identifies and prioritises the changes that need to happen
4. **Readiness assessment**—in each case, the ability of the organisation to undertake required changes will be different and needs assessing and managing
5. **Change implementation plan**—this is a comprehensive project plan detailing clearly measureable targets, milestones and named responsibilities.

Schooling Process Design

Learning and administrative processes must be re-designed to take advantage of technology. Some processes may already be based on legacy ICT systems, possibly within a "silo" type environment. The job of schooling process design is to work out the most efficient and effective way to get learning and administrative tasks completed. Often the goal is to significantly reduce paperwork and the steps taken to complete a process. Types of processes can include:

- Learning processes
- Learning performance management
- Examination processes
- Reporting
- Planning and policy formation
- Staff performance management
- HR management
- Electronic Information exchange with other institutions
- Governance
- Data provision to other institutions

Advances in technology, changes in funding body rules, new buildings and the pressure to communicate with stakeholders more effectively all mean that processes need to continually evolve and be redesigned to meet these needs. Key stages in schooling process design include:

- Clarifying objectives
- Reviewing usability
- Assessing technology
- Defining information needs
- Recognising and defining interactions
- Mapping decision points
- Defining logistics
- Risk management

Solution Design and Implementation

Driving effectiveness through technology is highly complex. As with schooling as a whole, the ICT infrastructure is an ecosystem—touch one part, and all other parts are affected.

It's critical, therefore, to use specialist, qualified and experienced experts to design the technology systems and that these people work to tried and tested standards when developing ICT solutions. One such standard is MSF.

MSF

MSF—Microsoft Solution Framework—is a tried and tested model for developing large scale technical solutions.

MSF Process Model consists of five phases:

1. Envisioning
2. Planning
3. Developing
4. Stabilizing
5. Deploying

Envisioning Phase

Create a broad description of the goals and constraints of the project. In this phase, you identify the team and what the team must accomplish for the customer. The purpose of the envisioning phase is to build a shared vision of the project among all the key stakeholders of the project.

This phase culminates in a vision/scope document, agreed and approved by all key stakeholders. The document sets out what the project aims to achieve, what is in and out of scope, the project structure and a risk assessment. The document is built during an envisioning process that includes the following steps:

- Defining the business goals
- Defining the project structure
- Setting up the team
- Assessing the current situation
- Creating a vision statement
- Identification of the scope of the project
- Defining requirements and user profiles
- Developing a solution concept
- Assessing risk

The Planning Phase

Deliverables of the planning phase are:

- Analysis
    o Business requirements
    o User requirements
    o Operational requirements
    o System requirements
- Use scenarios and use cases
    o The team then creates usage scenarios for all user profiles. After creating usage scenarios, the team creates use cases. A use case specifies the sequence of steps that a user will perform in a usage scenario.

- Functional specification—including design and architecture
  - o The functional specification describes the behaviour and appearance of each feature of the solution. It also describes the architecture and the design for all features.
  - o Architecture; conceptual design (perspective of the users); logical design (services); physical design (technologies and interfaces)
- Master project plan and master project schedule
  - o Cost estimates
  - o Creating project schedules
  - o Risk management plan
- Environments
  - o Development, testing, and staging environments

The main outcome of the planning phase is an approved project plan—due dates are realistic, project roles and responsibilities are well defined, everyone agrees to the deliverables for the project.

The Developing Phase

In this phase, the team develops the infrastructure for the solution. This involves the source code and executable files, installation scripts and settings, and support elements.

The development process includes creating a prototype application; developing the solution components; completion of all features; and delivery of code and documentation.

Stages of the developing phase are:

- Proof-of-concept application
- All features complete and have gone through unit testing
- Product ready for external testing and stabilisation
- Customers, users, operations and support personnel, and key project stakeholders can evaluate the product and identify any issues that must be addressed before the solution is shipped

The Stabilizing Phase

At the end of this phase the solution will meet the defined quality levels. The stabilisation process involves running the solution in a staging area with actual users and real usage scenarios, including an extensive and comprehensive range of tests.

The stabilizing phase goes through the following stages:

- Zero-bug release
- Release candidates
- Golden release—zero-defect and meeting success criteria metrics

At the final release, the responsibility for managing and supporting the solution is officially transferred from the project team to the operations and support teams.

The Deploying Phase

During this phase, the team deploys the solution technology and site components, stabilizes the deployment, transfers the project to operations and support, and obtains final customer approval of the project.

Deliverables of the deploying phase

- Operation and support information systems
- Documentation repository for all versions of documents and code developed during the project
- A training plan
- Project completion report

The milestones of the deploying phase are:

- Core components deployed
- Site deployments complete
- Deployment stable
- Deployment complete
- Customer approval

Continuous Professional Development (CPD)

Professional development plays a key part in ensuring the integration of any new ICT implementation. As with all other aspects of ICT implantation, professional development requires careful planning and implementation.

Often, just giving product training is considered enough. It isn't. CPD is about developing skills, knowledge, competencies, and above all else, an appetite for exploiting ICT.

The key elements of professional development that need to be understood and managed are as follows:

- **Strategic planning**—the elements of an ICT training and development plan are outlined, along with who should be involved, and how to bring your plan 'to life'
- **Leading (CPD)** — CPD works best when it fits into existing performance management structures
- **School technology innovation centres**—physical spaces with exemplar and cutting edge learning solutions to inspire leaders, trigger ideas and help teachers develop competencies
- **CPD needs**—gap analysis and prioritisation of competencies
- **CPD and training programmes**—managers need to have a good understanding of the availability and value of a wide range of training courses across a spectrum of delivery methods
- **Monitoring and evaluation**—including evaluation frameworks, monitoring the effect of CPD, and recording the impact of training and continuing professional development

Professional development falls into four main categories, each with different sets of requirements:

Leadership

Effective leadership is a prerequisite for delivering any form of institutional change, and embedding technology as a tool for whole-school improvement is no different. School leaders and governors need to understand the potential of technology and be able to harness it, so that it is used effectively. All schooling leaders need to be ICT literate. They need to be aware of the potential of ICT, how to plan and manage ICT, and should be able to develop effective ICT and professional development strategies. Principals have a particular role to play in encouraging the use of ICT—they need to be aware of the benefits of ICT across the school, in all contexts, and should set an example using ICT themselves.

Teaching Staff

Teacher training and development opportunities should focus on how to exploit a range of ICT resources to achieve the best learning outcomes.

Training and development opportunities must be flexible by allowing choice and guidance for teachers who are at different stages of ICT literacy, different age ranges and subjects, and different stages in their career progression.

A set of ICT competency standards for teachers has been designed by UNESCO and its partners, the main points of which are that teachers should:

- Be aware of policies and be able to specify how classroom practices correspond to and support policy
- Have a firm knowledge of the curriculum standards for their subject, as well as knowledge of standard assessment procedures. In addition, teachers must be able to integrate the use of technology and technology standards for students into the curriculum
- Know when (as well as when not), and how to use technology for classroom activities and presentations
- Know basic hardware and software operations, as well as productivity applications software, a web browser, communications software, presentation software, and management applications
- Be able to use technology with the whole class, small groups, and individual activities and assure equitable access
- Have the technological skill and knowledge of Web resources necessary to use technology to acquire additional subject matter and pedagogical knowledge in support of teachers' own professional development.

(UNESCO, 2008)

ICT Co-ordinators

An ICT co-ordinator's job is to ensure that ICT is embedded into the curriculum—across all main subject areas. Main duties and responsibilities include:

- Overall leadership of all ICT innovations
- Full member of the school leadership team
- Evaluate the impact of ICT on learning
- Develop cross-curricular learning via ICT
- Monitor ICT accreditation for all students
- Oversee the development of the school intranet and the wider connected learning community
- Bid for new projects
- Teach IT
- Administer all ICT budgets
- Procure new equipment
- Ensure top-quality ICT experience for students
- Ensure disciplined use of ICT by students
- Contribute to the strategy for and delivery of ICT training

Skills needed by ICT Co-ordinators should cover the following:

- Leadership
- Use of ICT in teaching and learning
- Good understanding of technology, products and solutions and their applicability in schooling

ICT Technicians

It's critical that teachers are not burdened with the job of technical support and ICT system development. This, ideally, would be dealt with by dedicated resources at school level, or shared sources at school consortium level.

ICT technicians are responsible for general maintenance of computer equipment and for the resolution of technical problems, in addition to promoting the use of ICT across the curriculum. Day-to-day tasks could include:

- Administrative tasks (such as logging assets, labelling and security marking, keeping track of repairs and service failures, maintaining stocks of consumables such as toner and paper)
- Basic maintenance and replacement of consumables (e.g. replacing toner, cleaning screens)
- Day-to-day set-up of computers, audio-visual equipment and specialist peripherals
- Regular or pre-emptive checking of computers, network components and connections
- Checking and testing of software and hardware for compatibility prior to installation
- Installation of new equipment and software
- Manage network security
- Installation of software updates
- Configuration of hardware and software
- Regular back-up of data and ensuring recovery capability
- Network management, such as allocating resources, and setting up access rights and user profiles.

Skills needed by technical staff should be certificated by vendors and reputable technical organisations, and should cover the following:

- System Engineering
- Networking, infrastructure, and hardware products
- Software products—especially server software

Procuring ICT Solutions

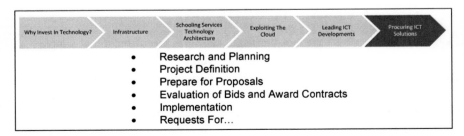

Whilst each country has their own laws for procurement, schooling system ICT solution procurement usually falls under public sector procurement regulations.

For countries within the European Union, there are EU wide laws governing contracts above €125,000, and it's to this category that we will now turn.

The procurement process spans the whole life cycle, from the identification of the need to purchase, through supplier selection and contracting, to the delivery of the required solution to service closure.

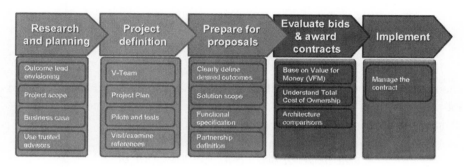

Figure 53. Procurement process timeline.

Research and Planning

Pre-procurement planning should include consultation with stakeholders about what is needed, what the evaluation criteria should be, and the budget that is available to fulfil the need—this should be documented as a business case.

There should be engagement with the market to understand the solutions that may be available and to get feedback on how the requirement may be best met. Expert advisers should be appointed early in the process.

Project Definition

At this phase a detailed project plan should be written and the v-team for executing on that plan appointed. Pilots and tests, visits to reference sites should take place. Effective governance needs to be set up.

Prepare for Proposals

With a full understanding of what outcomes are required, and a sense of what it will take to realise these outcomes, the market can be invited to bid for specific contracts. These are often broken down into the following categories:

- Services
- Software and content
- Hardware
- Infrastructure

The market needs to be given sufficient detail in outcome-based specifications, and enough time to respond to requirements. Specifying accepted industry standards in a technical solution is good practice.

Evaluation of Bids and Award Contracts

The goal of the tendering process is value for money through fair and open competition. In addition, tendering processes need to comply with relevant legal obligations and principles. The principles governing tendering and contract awards in the European Union include:

- Equal treatment
- Non-discrimination
- Mutual recognition
- Proportionality
- Transparency

For particularly complex projects, shortlisted suppliers are invited to participate in dialogue, to "clarify, specify and fine-tune" their final bids before a preferred bidder is chosen.

Bids are assessed against the criteria set out in the tender documentation. The assessment should follow the pre-defined evaluation criteria. Weightings may be applied to the criteria to allow price and non-price factors to be scored to reflect their importance to the project and to arrive at a final value for money judgement—the final selection being based on the bid which offers best overall value for money.

Implementation

Implementation is about contract and supplier management for successful service delivery. Activities in this phase can be grouped into three areas:

- Service delivery management—ensuring services are being delivered as agreed, to the required level of performance and quality
- Relationship management—resolving problems early
- Contract administration & change management—the formal governance of, and changes to, the contract

A good introductory guide can be found in *An Introduction to Public Procurement* published by the UK's Office of Government Commerce (http://www.ogc.gov.uk/policy_and_standards_framework_introduction_to_publ ic_procurement.asp).

Requests For...

During the procurement process, there are four commonly used requests:

RFI: Request for Information—an open enquiry to obtain broad data and understanding.

RFT: Request for Tender—potential suppliers to submit an offer to supply goods or services against a detailed tender.

RFP: Request for Proposal—a requirements-based request for specific solutions

RFQ: Request for Quotation—an opportunity for potential suppliers to competitively cost a final chosen solution.

Case Studies

Latvia

In the late 1990s, the Latvian Ministry of Education (MoE) began an IT programme to get a clearer picture of school and learner performance across the country. As well as collecting information about schools, teachers, and students, it began building a library of electronic learning resources to help teachers plan and deliver lessons more effectively.

All the information collected by the MoE was stored in a number of different databases, which were difficult to search and access. It was time consuming for ministry employees to report on schools' performance, there was poor data quality, and very few useful online teaching resources. The system offered no support for electronic learning, and teachers had to print out assignments and distribute them to students by hand. Teachers also graded students' work and recorded results manually, which was extremely inefficient and time consuming.

As an additional challenge, each school was responsible for building and supporting its own Website and e-mail system, resulting in high infrastructure and support costs. There were also compatibility issues between disparate e-mail systems, making it difficult for the ministry to communicate with schools electronically.

The MoE needed a new information and communications technology (ICT) solution to help report on performance nationally and communicate effectively with schools and stakeholders, deliver e-learning opportunities for students, and reduce the time teachers spend on routine administration and grading.

To increase communications between schools, save time for teachers, and enhance online learning opportunities, the MoE decided to deploy a new learning management system in 2006.

The solution provides a range of features that help teachers save time and work more effectively. These include a portal that helps teachers create and deploy e-learning content, grade assignments and tests automatically, and feed results into centralised systems with no manual intervention. Teachers have reduced the time they spend on grading and recording results by 30%. Because teachers spend far less time on manual administration, they can increase focus on value-added activities.

Users can log on to the system to access information that is relevant to them and collaborate on joint projects. Teachers can easily view important school communications and teaching materials online. At the same time, students can view their assignments and test results, and parents can follow the progress of their children from any Internet-connected computer.

Miami Dade

When Miami-Dade County Public Schools (M-DCPS) needed to communicate with its 1.5 million students, parents, teachers and administrators, the district found it lacked a consistent way to deliver information. Whether they needed educational resources or critical instructions in case of emergencies, users were forced to hunt for necessary information. The use of different software applications throughout hundreds of schools kept this large, urban and culturally diverse school district from effectively using the communications and educational resources it had at its disposal.

So, the school district arrived at a new "Learning Gateway" solution using an integrated portal-based platform that delivers collaboration, management of online content and increased productivity by eliminating the need for paper and changing the way people work and learn.

By optimising their infrastructure they were able to design a portal strategy across the district that incorporates all application and data sources, and serve these to individuals according to their role and specific needs. The district is now able to push the right data to the right stakeholders rather than forcing users to navigate a maze of resources to find the information they need.

In 2007, Gartner undertook a case study on Miami-Dade School District in the United States and concluded that:

- Students are now monitoring their own progress and are using the portal to take additional classes
- M-DCPS has seen an improvement in attendance since the portal came online
- Parents are taking a more active role in the educational process. Information is available to them on a 24/7 basis; they are no longer dependent on scheduling conferences with teachers if they want to keep up with their children's educational progress and activities
- Teachers have immediate access to student information and curriculum resources for planning instruction

- All employees have easy access to payroll information and professional development information
- There has been a general improvement in the communication between school district departments
- M-DCPS also reported improved community involvement and more visibility of innovative district programmes and other news.

Glow, Scotland

Glow is the world's first national intranet for education and is transforming the way education is delivered in Scotland. Glow, like Miami Dade's Learning Gateway, is a portal-based solution. It provides:

- An area to create personalised programmes of work and share curricular resources
- A variety of online tools to enhance learning experiences
- Virtual learning to share information and take part in lessons
- Communication and collaboration tools

The system covers 3,000 schools, 50,000 teachers and over 1 million individual users. It contains:

- A virtual learning environment (VLE) including tools to share, organise and search for digital resources and courses, monitor student progress and provide learners with content
- An index of all the users of Glow throughout Scotland
- An area that connects people and ideas using discussion boards, chat rooms, document stores, image galleries and web conferencing.

Guatemala

The Ministry of Education (MOE) in Guatemala aims to equip every student with a PC by 2012. The MOE rightly recognised that teachers must be equipped and trained first so they created a public-private partnership that equipped more than 58,000 teachers (2/3 of its teacher workforce) with technology and resources, in a programme directly linked to economic development plans.

With more than 80,000 teachers in 12,000 schools spread across the country, the MOE was working with a cumbersome system of training and preparation that required teachers to travel to Guatemala City from one to three times a year. The journey to and from the capital city, along with the training, took as long as four days—causing disruption, expense, and other complications for the teachers, their families, and the MOE.

The solution was to provide teachers with online training enabled by teachers having their own PCs. The teachers pay for the PCs themselves through a Private Public Partnership. A government subsidy covers between 30–75% of the cost and teachers pay the balance through monthly instalments deducted directly from their salaries. As more teachers acquire PCs, more Professional Development and Training can be delivered online, which greatly increases efficiencies.

Uganda

The Uganda Ministry for Education wanted to prepare its students for a knowledge-based economy. They knew that the best way to do this was through incorporating ICT in the classroom, but insufficient computers and less than 2% of its population online presented a significant challenge. Furthermore, existing course content was not relevant to students, and there was a lack of teachers trained in ICT education. The government set up a Public Private Partnership to support a pilot programme in eight schools, from 2004 to 2005. It comprised three main strands: building infrastructure, training teachers, and developing content. As capacity building was the priority, the partnership used a donated PC's programme to provide refurbished computers, and then established two centres to train educators in ICT basics, and provide on-going technical support systems for teachers and students.

Relevant content is crucial to a successful ICT education programme, so in an innovative move Uganda linked the partnership with its National Curriculum Development Centre. The pilot was a success, with over 60% of participants gaining significantly higher exam results than the norm. A key milestone was reached with development of content for four subjects, with the aim of expanding to eight subjects. The Ugandan partnership is now rolling out new ICT-based learning to schools across the country.

8. SCHOOLING AT THE SPEED OF THOUGHT

"Where do you want to go tomorrow?" Bill Gates

- The purpose of this chapter is to portray a set of scenarios that define and describe an idealised schooling system, using approaches and technologies that exist today.

- This chapter explores a day in the life of a schooling system five years from now, and illustrates the kinds of experiences that the key stakeholders can expect when all of the kinds of changes covered in this book have been implemented.

- There is no single right model for modernised schooling, but this vision represents key pieces of "DNA" which one would expect to see in schooling systems that have been transformed for the better.

- This chapter also covers the key components and organisational principles that enable these scenarios to happen, and explores the challenges that would be faced in moving towards this vision.

- Finally, this chapter challenges you to think about how you can make a difference and play a part in the greatest challenge we collectively face today.

We started this book with a description of one model of schooling at the speed of thought—one-to-one learning at the Akademia in Athens.

We traced the industrialisation of schooling and showed how it has reached the limits of its current paradigm and become massively ineffective compared to what it could be. Schooling has become slow and cumbersome, where thought generally travels as fast as pieces of paper through bureaucratic bottlenecks.

To conclude, we imagine a schooling system in the future—a future where high quality learning takes place continuously at the speed of thought, where excellent decisions are made quickly, and schooling is deeply integrated into the fabric of the community which its serves. In this vision, thinking flows freely and instantly across vast networks of connections, enabling every function of schooling to operate infinitely more effectively than at present.

Whilst there are very few places worldwide that currently exemplify this vision fully, the future that we imagine below is actually achievable right now.

Thanks are due to Dan Buckley, Naser Ziadeh and Chris Poole, who imagined this future, and whose work the following section is based on.

A Day in the Life of a Schooling System, June 28th 2015

The Cast

Julia
Julia is a keen student, aged 12. She has a real passion for art and design-related study, an above-average level of achievement and is heavily involved in the cultural life of her school. She dislikes sport and physical activity.

Mark
Mark (15) has recently joined a new school. He arrived at school having been asked to leave another school due to behaviour problems. He completed a re-direction programme with the support of an inclusion team associated with the school. Keen to make a new start, he has developed a positive working relationship with Dave who works in the inclusion team.

Dave
Dave is a part-time inclusion team worker and mentor, but spends most of his working time as a member of staff in a Sports Centre. Dave became Mark's main caseworker when Mark was identified as a candidate to join the school. From the start he has made home visits and established a positive working relationship with Mark. He is supporting increased participation and directed work for Mark, which have been issues in the past. Dave is well aware of Mark's strong interest in a possible career in either the leisure or hospitality industry.

Janice
Janice is Julia's mentor and an Art and Technology teacher, teaching a popular Packaging Design course. She is concerned that Julia is dodging sport-related activity.

Alan
Alan is Julia's father.

Michelle
Michelle is a 'lifelong learner'. She is 19-years-old, and is taking part in a work-based learning programme.

The Day

Early Morning

Before starting work in the Sports Centre, Dave logs in to check to see if Mark has been on campus over recent days. He is keen to see whether Mark has begun to spend more time studying onsite and less time working alone, as agreed with his parents. Although arrival on-site first thing in the morning is still poor, Dave is pleased to see that in every other respect Mark is doing very well indeed. Dave could have chosen to be alerted if Mark's presence met a particular pattern, but he prefers to check for himself.

Julia quickly reviews part of her previous Packaging Design unit online from home, using the family computer system. Having made a few last minute changes, she hands in her assignment electronically and heads off for her first class.

Janice notes that there are now 42 students scheduled to attend today's class on Packaging, four more than she expected. She is informed by the scheduling system that a larger seminar room is available, near her usual venue. Janice approves the recommendation, relieved she can concentrate on supporting a larger group in a room that can comfortably accommodate them.

Michelle has arrived early at the office and checks the campus information system for any updates before starting her job. Today is the deadline for presenting evidence of information-handling skills. She agreed with her tutor to submit a report based on her administrative duties at work, and makes a reminder to put this together today. Her other message reminds her that a language session is taking place later in the evening to substitute the regular one she could not attend last week.

Michelle indicates interest in attending the session, but later realises it clashes with a drama group meeting at her old school, which she is still involved with. She also makes a note to check with her line manager that the material she wanted to submit as learning evidence is not confidential.

Mid-Morning

Mark is working on an assignment—arranging part of a forthcoming award presentation. He is taking part in a meeting to confirm the running order of the ceremony with the teachers involved and two younger students.

After the meeting, the three students go to a nearby study area, which Mark found earlier and booked online. The group produces a draft of the documents they plan to make and distribute for the event. He shares his knowledge of how to use a software tool with the younger students.

During the session, Mark identifies some content which the team can use to improve the document. His tutor will be pleased to hear about this contribution, so Mark asks his colleagues to countersign a record of the help he has given. He can add this to his e-portfolio. Mark peer-assesses an aspect of their work in return. He makes a note in his profile to explain how he believes this demonstrates evidence of his progress, and what he thinks the next steps are. He is enjoying acting as a tutor for the younger students.

Julia attends Janice's Packaging Design course session. It is popular with students, who work in groups to compare different types of packaging and discuss their responses. The course combines a high degree of learner participation with thought-provoking questions.

In today's session, students are focusing on materials used for packaging and comparing cost implications. Julia reports her group's findings to the whole class. Her friend records the presentation on a handheld device and gives Julia a copy for her e-portfolio, plus the slides and visuals they prepared. Julia's main target for the session was not to develop her presentation skills, but it was too good an opportunity to miss—she rarely has the confidence to speak in front of a big audience.

As she leaves the session, Julia deletes her appointment for her scheduled volleyball session and calls into the art workshop instead. Janice is alerted to the change in agreed schedule. The art workshop is Julia's favourite space on campus: here, she works on tasks from all parts of the curriculum. She finds it a really positive and comfortable space. Julia makes some final touches to her self-portrait work. The teacher marks a piece with her and suggests she produces a report that reflects on and explains some of her techniques, rather than further develop the piece. They agree to add the report to her work plan. Julia refers to her handheld device to check what work and evidence she needs to complete for this area of study. While she is using it she receives a suggestion to attend another volleyball session that evening or tomorrow.

Julia takes the opportunity to use a desktop computer with a larger screen and review some examples from last year's art class, which were selected as examples of good practice. She receives a message from a friend who has just finished a swimming lesson. They chat for a while and invite a third friend, who is offline at present, to join them at lunchtime to eat and then go with them to a drama event.

Mark buys a sandwich on the way to his mentoring meeting. His smart card is recognised at the food counter and the price of his sandwich is deducted from his card account balance by the payment system.

Mark has booked a room for his meeting, so that he can conference with his tutor in private. He arrives before his interview and browses a wall screen for campus news. He is the only person in the immediate area, so a highly personalised set of news feeds that he has subscribed to is displayed. Mark's preferences include a profiled set of aims and interests corresponding to his student profile, and he has some authority to filter out some channels he dislikes. The feeds include notices, events, blog entries, and media galleries produced by and for members of the school community.

Michelle wonders if she can use any of her work from last year's creative writing course for her evidence submission. She did not complete the course before leaving school but thinks some of it might be relevant to her current work. She accesses her e-portfolio, which archives her work, and selects the creative writing course. Michelle only has access to material which she was involved with, and does not have access to the work of others. Michelle reviews the material and decides to go back to her original plan of using work-based evidence.

Lunchtime

Alan returns from lunch and sees Julia's self-portrait on his desktop computer screensaver. He has subscribed to a feed of work that Julia feels is her best, and that she wants to share with others. He receives notification that her credit for school expenses has dropped below the agreed level, and authorises a top-up payment.

Mark has an online review meeting with Dave, who is at work today. Dave is pleased with Mark's improved attendance and behaviour. They review some evidence of progress that Mark wanted to share. He has been working on developing his skills to pursue a career in the leisure industry, but is concerned the evidence he has recorded does not adequately reflect his achievements. Dave suggests they meet on campus next week to explore this together. They can identify differences between his current profile and typical progress of students who have taken leisure-related courses.

The meeting goes well, and they spend so much time chatting informally that they over-run. Mark realises he won't make it to a lecture at the catering department of the local college. Disappointed, he arranges to view a streamed version live. A digital agent acts on his behalf, negotiating access and updating relevant schedules and profiles. Mark realises he will also miss a meeting with two friends who are at the lecture, so he sends them instant messages to suggest meeting later in the evening.

Julia joins her two friends for lunch in the cafeteria. Her handheld device alerts her that an item she has chosen may contain traces of nuts: this information is held an RFID tag in the packaging. She has a nut allergy, but has agreed with her parents she can make her own food choices.

After lunch, the three go to support their friends who are in a theatre group. As they arrive at the drama studio, their handheld devices automatically make a small micro-payment for admission. This is credited to the school council, to help cover production costs. Many of the 20 people involved take part as a leisure activity. For others, this is one of their learning activities; the planned outcomes vary between individuals. Two students ask Julia to give some feedback at the end of the show, which they will record to use later for their report. During the conversation Julia is invited to attend a meeting that night, where she can audition for a part, or help in another way.

Janice's lunch is interrupted, because of an incident on campus involving a student she supports. She uses her handheld device to indicate she is busy and cannot be disturbed, interviews the student to take a statement, then reviews CCTV and the student's location information. Janice has been sent a notification of a change in Julia's schedule that should have been agreed, but her 'busy' status means this has been given a lower priority for now.

Michelle's manager has confirmed she can use data from her workplace as evidence for her portfolio. She submits three pieces of evidence to complete a large missing block of her skills profile, and requests a meeting with her school-based tutor and workplace mentor to plan her next steps.

Mid-Afternoon

Julia uses a scheduled break to prepare for her mentoring meeting at a desk in a 'quiet study' room. She reviews her profile on a large display screen, using a summary to quickly view action points from the last meeting and identify what she needs to do before her next meeting in two weeks.

Julia now prefers to approach her meetings with a clear idea of what she would like to achieve. That way, she has a greater influence on her work programme. This has helped her look for opportunities where she can take on enjoyable tasks and work towards agreed objectives.

Although she does not like to admit it, Julia has become aware of a pattern showing she is avoiding sport activities; more of these have appeared in her suggested programme. Numeracy-related activities have also been added and marked as a high priority, which comes as a surprise to her.

Janice begins her daily mentoring work and catches up with her messages. She notices Julia missed another PE activity this morning, so adds this to her preparation for their scheduled mentoring session. She also reviews the latest timetable suggested for Julia. Janice can review Julia's e-portfolio in several ways; she can view progress within each area of learning or choose a specific skill, and look across Julia's entire academic career. Julia's e-portfolio is more than a record of her learning; it also contains the objectives planned over several years, and her progress towards them. These different views help Janice to identify some areas to consider, but do not constrain her decisions.

After completing her mentoring work, Janice has time to review her own professional development; she is interested in offering a new course at a local primary school. A local online resource for primary teaching, containing lesson plans and resources related to the course she intends to offer, helps Janice refine her ideas. She posts a question to a related online community, which she has found to be responsive and helpful. In turn, she replies to a query from a colleague in another school.

Mark joins the live-streamed catering lecture and demonstration, using the campus connection to connect and register, using his smart card. He is inspired by the superb demonstration, and the fine-detailed transmission can be reviewed later from different angles. He can take part in the question and answer session, and access the assignment set at the end of the lecture.

Mark highlights the session as one he would like to review again, and sees another partner college has a similar demonstration already available, which has been highly rated by other students with a profile similar to his.

Julia arrives early for a statistics lesson. The wall displays deliver content best matching the learning preferences of learners in the immediate area. She takes part in a structured teacher-led session, and leaves with several small assignments to complete in the next few days.

Several students, like Julia, attend the course regularly, as it matches their learning plan. Others join the group occasionally, booking sessions to meet specific goals. The teacher is aware that the majority of today's class need to develop their ability to interpret pie charts and bar charts, so focuses on this using worked examples and student participation.

Late Afternoon

Janice and Julia meet for a mentoring session in an interview room near the main foyer. They review progress and quickly agree on Julia's learning programme for the next few weeks; this includes specific learning targets, deadlines, and activity choices. Janice is concerned that Julia is clearly avoiding sport and discovers she is reluctant to take part without her group of close friends, preferring to work with them in the art area.

Julia agrees to attend a Saturday afternoon volleyball event at a local sports centre, plus some on-campus sessions. She accepts responsibility for making last-minute switches to avoid sports classes, so temporarily loses the facility to reschedule her own timetable.

They review Julia's last assignment for Janice, along with feedback from other work since their last meeting and changes in her skills profile during the past three months. This helps to identify priorities for learning. They agree that Julia seems to show greater gains when she takes part in group-based activities, although her stated preference is to work alone, and discuss this at length. In common with her recently submitted packaging task, Julia accepts and understands that she clearly needs to revisit some Maths work that is actually at a lower level than expected—a combination of workshop and online work is agreed from the suggested programme and booked in.

Alan has expressed willingness to do some coaching to support Julia in this area in the past and it has proved successful, so that's added to the plan. Despite losing the rights to reschedule her timetable for now, Julia feels well able to influence her final programme and is pleased with the outcome.

Alan sees that he has a message waiting from Janice and Julia, but he is about to go into a meeting so leaves it for later.

Janice checks her messages as she is about to leave and sees a message from her manager in the school leadership team. It is agreeing to her request to offer more practical-based activities for her design work as take up for the current one—which is based largely on discussion and theoretical work—has continued to increase. The results of a pilot smaller practical workshop last week show a greater impact for all those involved, compared to other sessions in their school and others. She replies, agreeing to replace one of her seminars each week with two workshops instead. As she doesn't have any more appointments that require her presence on campus today, and indeed most of tomorrow morning, she will be able to work off-site. As she heads to the gym to unwind, she marks herself as unavailable on the messaging system.

Evening

As he is about to leave work to head for home, Alan skims the message with the result of Julia's mentoring session. Although he agrees to the proposed support he is to give, he decides to wait until he has spoken to her tonight before responding. He is able to access a short summary of her e-portfolio, filtered to show key areas for improvement and the most recent pieces of evidence highlighted by Julia. He is in a hurry because he has a class of his own tonight. He is learning Spanish and was notified this afternoon that a place was available with his tutor for a conversation class, due to a cancellation from another student. First, he eats with the family at home and then gives Julia a lift back onto campus again for the drama audition. They arrive at a campus that is only slightly less busy than the one Julia walked into this morning. There are classes, meetings, interviews and recreational events happening everywhere. Julia heads off to the drama area; Alan, checking his personal device, finds out where his conversation class is taking place.

Mark, having met his friends, is catching up with work from home. He knows that letting assignments pile up was one factor in his problems at his previous school. He is also aware that Dave regularly monitors his progress, so he has set aside 90 minutes of quality time to get on top of everything. Initially he looks at his work plan and anything marked as overdue, finding several half-finished and relatively simple things that simply need a few minutes to complete, submit, and request assessment. He then begins a longer piece that he has been putting off for some time, and finds it difficult.

He checks for the presence of any of his peer group who might be able to help online. Mark posts a couple of queries, and also requests access from his tutor to examples of similar work from other students. Mark found that these groups of students with similar learning goals and profiles across the region were a tremendously useful resource whilst he was excluded from his previous school. He continues to use it as a preferred place to sound out ideas. Whilst there, he helps another student with his work by sharing a link to a resource he found helpful himself six months ago. Again, by choice, Mark is able to add that record of an online conversation to his evidence of progress in working collaboratively with others. A little frustrated that he didn't quite finish everything, Mark leaves a message for Dave before taking some time to wind down.

Alan is with his usual Spanish tutor, but with two different students as he has switched to a different group. They are also joined by Michelle. Together they watch a news programme from today and complete some discussion exercises that reinforce their learning. Parts of the session are recorded for later use by the tutor for assessment and by the students for review. The group heads down to the community lounge at the end of the lesson, where Alan waits for Julia to return from her drama session. Even now people are still coming onto the campus, which will be in use well into the night.

Dave is at home giving some thought to a request to host a session at his workplace for some students from school, in part to look at health and safety, and in part as a careers guidance programme. He'd like to be involved, and having enjoyed mentoring, is beginning to consider enrolling with the school on its trainee teacher development programme. He's a little nervous, but finally agrees. He already has clearance to work with young people alone or in groups and some evidence of teaching skills in his e-portfolio. Dave gives some thought to how this new opportunity might help him to have more useful experience. Although he does not consider himself to be a teacher as such, Dave is already an effective coach and mentor. He has substantial knowledge in his vocational subject area. Indeed, one of his sources of income is responding to questions and giving support on a pay-to-use expert tutor service.

Julia is late because her audition/rehearsal goes really well. She is meeting with the usual group of young people and adults involved in the school production. Tonight they have access to the drama studio for a read through and rehearsal for two scenes that Julia might be in. With a friend she records a short sequence that is eventually used on the show's promotional blog. Through the school news-feed system, the blog will be seen by more than 2,000 people tomorrow. Some other students are looking at the results of a survey last week in which the student body was asked several questions about their preference for the organisation of the show. Only 64 people responded, but this is still going to be useful for the people who have chosen to use this work for their e-portfolio.

On their way home Alan talks to Julia about the day and points out to her that, although she has signed up for the drama production purely for fun, she has shown some of the skills she is supposed to be working on this evening. They agree a time when they'll get together to look at some of the areas that she is finding hard in Maths.

Night

Michelle does not have an early start at work tomorrow and has been enthused by her language session. She stays on site in a private study area before heading home to practice and perfect some of her work, finding this the perfect time of day to do this kind of work. Fewer people are around now. Many parts of the campus are closed for servicing, but she feels safe working there and gets more done than she would have done at home.

Even after the last regular class is finished and the community lounge is emptying, there is still activity on campus. As well as security, cleaning and maintenance, there are people taking advantage of the low cost, off-peak access to services. These include the recording studio and gym. There is also some activity in the medical area, where the out-of-hours health response service for the area is based. Digital resources related to the school, both on-site and at various other locations, are busy late into the night and from early morning. People communicate, access feeds and content, and publish resources and work without pause. Batch processes such as converting media for publication, database updates and automated scheduling make use of the processing power of the school's systems and access to Cloud services in the quietest part of the day.

The Vision Behind this Schooling System

The schooling system to which Julia, Alan, Mark, Dave, Janice, and Michelle belong has a range of approaches, structures, capabilities and features that have taken many years to build including:

- Peer learning and peer assessment
- Multi-site learning
- Working from home
- Co-ordinated working with different organisations, schools and other learning places
- Workplace learning
- Multi-age communities
- Multi-pace working
- Competencies-based assessment
- Extensive mentorship models

It seeks to empower learners to become more actively engaged in their own and others' learning. It encourages them to take an active role in the operation of their school. 1:1 computer access helps teachers move away from whole-class, single-age, and single-stage teaching.

Learning and Teaching

The school day contains extended periods of time for more in-depth work. Students are set extended problems that give them the opportunity to manage their time and plan complex working patterns. Some students will manage such blocks of time better than others. A system of continuous and progressive assessment of ability enables the teacher to create appropriate limits and opportunities for students.

Subjects are usually grouped to develop wider themes, topic areas, or perspectives and to make time within the curriculum for extended project work. Many students lack the skills to direct their own learning and that of others. To address this, the personalised school will provide progressive training and assessment in these skills.   Such programmes will take different forms in different schools, but will usually involve students:

- Working in a range of teams, taking responsibility for what their classmates achieve
- Managing services, projects, and budgets that have a direct impact on others
- Being consulted and engaged through meetings of their own and, in some cases, in their own office areas
- Working on extended problems using a range of facilities, from multimedia and expressive arts, to the more traditional breakout and library areas.

IT systems

A Virtual Learning Environment (VLE) will:

- Enable students to create their own web pages, using web parts of their choice
- Offer teachers many easy ways to view tasks and work that their students have both completed and not completed
- Contain version control that helps students to keep a complete set of draft copies along with the final copy

The timetabling and school management software must be flexible enough to:

- Support real-time, dynamic changes to individual's timetables in accordance with their precise needs
- Support variable learning session lengths
- Automatically register learners working in other centres which have been endorsed by the school

Every student's e-portfolio must:

- Store evidence of progress both from school and home
- Contain filters that help mentors focus on specific aspects of the learner's work

- Have 'show and tell' public access so that learners can choose which bits of their work they would like other people to see, without necessarily revealing their own identity.

Facility access and registration is controlled by RFID. This helps learners to move freely within the areas where they are permitted. Portal access is via single sign-on and also ensures that students can always contribute to their portfolio—whether they are learning at school, at home or in another location.

Although the model encourages responsibility and trust in students, security and incident tracking must be supported. Access logs, CCTV and print management solutions can be combined to create an effective monitoring solution. Additional solutions can help teachers to view all of their students' computer screens at the same time—and ideally, school-based students' actual location.

Wireless PDA/slate devices or laptops for teachers help them to record data on-the-spot. This is essential if they are to capture evidence to support learner progression. Having a paper-free policy encourages all staff to use the school's portal to store, modify and share work.

Extended Provision

A more effective schooling system has more open and varied facilities, supporting extended provision—especially adult learning.

Larger periods of learning time help involve the community in several new areas, presenting greater scope for mentoring. Mentors can include people from the local community, business community and parents. Mentoring sessions at weekly or fortnightly intervals offer the greatest impact on learning. Many people in the local community are willing to offer this kind of commitment and have talent and knowledge that adds real value.

This approach to learning helps create more links between students and local businesses. For example, students seeking support for a marketing project often approach local companies to identify real-life situations they can work on. Experienced external speakers can be used for important lectures and experts can address group sessions.

Longer project timescales frequently lead to higher quality and more in-depth outcomes from the students. Such outcomes may benefit from being shared with a wider audience, either through the web or face-to-face through presentations and performance. For example, putting on a film festival at the end of each term, showing videos and exhibitions of the best work achieved in all subjects.

Of course, examinations still have a role, but have shifted to be much more computer-based and do not require student attendance on such a large scale. Much of the curriculum is delivered across extended periods of time, so work areas within schools must be multi-functional to support this. There are several solutions, including:

'Department clustering': by placing breakout and resource areas at the heart of department areas, students can use specialist facilities more flexibly. Consider, for example, a learner using music resources to support part of an English project. By pooling resources across departments, learners have far more choice and opportunities in their work. This will help further creativity and support the many different ways in which a learner prefers to learn. Facilities clustered around a central work area provide this required flexibility. Many of the best technology departments already work this way. For example, if students need to design and build an electronic device that has wood and metal elements, they will need access to resistant materials and electronics facilities, plus CAD, CAM and possibly graphic design resources.

Specialist small group facilities: students wishing to create production-quality media as part of their projects will need specialist facilities which are not yet common in schools. These include digital video studio facilities, sound recording facilities in quiet areas and areas for staging, group meetings, presentation practice and role-play. An example activity would be getting learners to investigate Newton's third law of motion through active engagement. A group of students may need access to video equipment, overlay editing software, large areas suitable for shooting an experiment, workbenches, and small rooms for chroma ('blue-screen') video production equipment. This is where schooling systems need to be entrepreneurial—is it better to rent this kind of external facility, or invest in facilities with the aim of deriving an income?

Conference facilities: schools require areas for guest lectures from inspirational speakers, delivered in larger areas or halls and complemented by nearby 'breakout' and private study areas. Professional conferences typically use this model, where large groups break off into smaller working groups. This model supports the idea that students have different learning styles and work best in environments that suit their individual needs.

'Corporate identity': students need to identify and connect with the environments in which they are working. Extended projects requiring self-motivation from students will not work otherwise. This can be achieved through uniting staff and student facilities and reducing 'staff-only' areas. Such an environment can also be enhanced through a corporate identity approach to colours, signs and plasma displays, all helping identify school-owned facilities. Providing students with areas to manage themselves is another good way to develop values and skills. These may include student-led radio and TV facilities, student-managed bulletin boards and interactive whiteboard 'scribble walls'. The balance of trust and opportunity must reflect the school ethos as must the physical structure of the school reflect its learning ethos and educational vision.

Challenges

To achieve the kind of vision described above obviously involves major challenges. To get schooling to run at the speed of thought is about enabling much faster learning through formal schooling systems. Faster learning is a result of the entire ecosystem of schooling being significantly more effective.

No one reform is likely to survive unless it is connected up with other parts of a new system that will support it. Change just one thing, and the rest of the system will pull that reform back into the old equilibrium, as many reformers have discovered. Try to change one aspect—the lengths of lessons, for example—and you have to change other parts of the system too. It's not just about the introduction of ICT—if only things were that simple! It's about ensuring that the schooling system is able to exploit technology.

The massive re-engineering of schooling is the equivalent of rebuilding a ship whilst sailing it. Imagine a three-masted wooden sailing ship racing to a destination through high seas, whilst at the same time changing the hull from wood to steel; the propulsion from sails to an engine; the navigation and instrumentation from sextant and magnetic compass to GPS and radar—all from within the ship!

But it *is* possible to do. Pioneers, such as Richard De Lorenzo, have proved this.

We have dealt with the challenges in detail throughout the book, and proposed a practical methodology. However, it's worth summarising some of the biggest challenges ahead:

- The first challenge is having the right kind of vision. Having a vision is relatively easy. Having a vision that is holistic and comprehensive with a good chance of working is another matter.
- The second challenge is getting strong, diffused leadership which balances innovation with governance.
- The third challenge is alignment. This is about aligning schooling with broader social and economic goals, and then ensuring that every single stakeholder in the system is a "cathedral builder", not a "bricklayer".

This last point is the most important of all. To change anything at scale, everyone must feel part of the change process. Ultimately, success will come from what individual people choose to do.

But I'm Just a Small Cog in a Big Machine!

I will conclude this book on a personal note. I'm personally driven by a deep desire to do something about what I consider to be an extreme waste—the wasted opportunity and potential of schooling systems across the world.

Imagine standing on a desert island. Picture the white sand, the clear blue sea. Feel the heat from the sun. Now look to the middle of the island and note a huge pile of money in used dollar bills. A hill made of paper money. Now picture someone standing on the top of the pile of money and pouring petrol over it— gallons and gallons of petrol. They go on doing this until the money hill is saturated. Then they get a burning rag and set fire to the hill. It burns for days and nights until only ash is left. After the wind blows the ash away, a small core of unburned money remains. Imagine now what the wasted money could have been used for. How do you feel about this appalling waste? Is this acceptable?

Well, yes, it is actually—it's what we are allowing to happen in our schooling systems all around the world, year after year.

I taught in the UK secondary school system for ten years. If I'm honest, I loved working with the children, but I was a pretty average teacher. I really disliked being boxed-in and having come from a mix of engineering and arts background I found teaching stifling. I don't want to deride the millions of excellent teachers battling against the odds—but I will be honest—compared to the business world where I have been fortunate enough to flourish—teaching was awful. To me, personally, I found the main difference between teaching and the world of business was attitude. In teaching it was too easy to slip into a commonly held "why bother" attitude. Many years on, one incident that sums up that attitude, sticks in my mind.

When I started teaching I was already hooked on computers. Yes, as sad as it seems, I even turned down the opportunity to take a holiday in Greece so I could buy a Commodore 64 and learn how to programme. Later, having burned gallons of "midnight oil", I finally got the World Wide Web working on my personal PC at home in the very early days of the Internet. I discovered the World Wide Web for the first time just as the first browsers became available, and for me, this was a breakthrough moment—a flicker of some obscure geographical data website in a Mosaic browser via a 1200bd modem set me alight. I stayed awake all night scrutinising two websites (I only had two URLs!). The following morning I burst into school and told a bemused senior management team that I had to have them assembled during lunch break for something that would blow their minds. In the only office with a direct outside telephone line socket I managed to show the Bodleian Library's website before my precarious TCP/IP stack fell over and brought my PC down with it. The response was moderately enthusiastic—my headmaster said, "Marvellous—do show it to me again when you can get the cricket scores"! Shortly after that I received my first e-mail—a wondrous event that filled me with glee and joy!

Six months later after pursuing a parallel strategy of ranting and charm I managed to persuade a local hockey club (don't ask!) to provide some cash for an ISDN line—the first in the area—so we could get the Internet on a small network. This is when I really encountered "why bother". The librarian refused to have the ISDN router and a small cluster of PC's internet hosted in the library.

Not being one to readily take "no" for an answer I got the ISDN line installed on a Saturday, much to the fury of the librarian the following Monday morning. After more ranting than charm, the internet installation was eventually a great success and my school became one of the best equipped in the country. We even went on to have the first browser based intranet in a school in the UK.

So why am I telling you this story? Transforming schooling is the single most important challenge on the planet, but transformation at scale is predicated on billions of micro-decisions on a day-to-day basis. Decisions such as "Shall I allow the internet into my area?"; "Shall I start treating students as customers?"; "Shall I personally take hold of a sledgehammer and knock down some walls to create a better space?"; "Shall I persistently demand changes to out-dated rules?"; or "Shall I just not bother, accept that I'm a small cog in a big machine, and hope my union can negotiate a marginal improvement in my pay and working conditions?"

On a typical day there are 55m teachers teaching and 1.2bn students learning. The effectiveness of this massive human endeavour—compared to what it could be—is pitiful. Students and teachers the world over achieve way below their full potential because of the way that schooling is organised. As a teacher, parent and someone who visits schools across the world, I hate to see students being processed like batch production farm animals. These conditions exist only because we have got used to them. I'm inspired by the levels of energy and ingenuity shown by a small few to change the system, but at the same time deeply saddened by deep resistances from the "why bother" brigade, self-serving unions, and traditionalists from the top to the bottom of the decision-making process.

There are many reasons why complacency outweighs change action—the absence of a major and visible crisis; organisational structures that focus on narrow functional goals; "low confrontation" cultures; human nature with its capacity for denial, especially if people are already busy or stressed.

So what can *you* do to break the "why bother" cycle?

Firstly, we have to realise that we *all* have some power—social power. Gladwell, in his seminal book *Tipping Point*, says that "what really matters is the little things". We make micro decisions about the little things on a minute-by-minute basis, and these become significant when taken collectively.

Secondly, we need to use the power of controlling micro decisions to become leaders of transformation. It's within everyone's gift to take a leadership position—but it's the kind of leadership that counts. Returning to our section on leadership in Chapter 5, you will remember that we discussed Transformational Leadership. In the same review as we discussed in Chapter 5, the Exeter authors show how Stephen Covey contrasts leadership models:

Transactional Leadership	Transformational Leadership
• Builds on man's need to get a job done and make a living • Is preoccupied with power and position, politics and perks • Is mired in daily affairs • Is short-term • Focuses on tactical issues • Relies on human relations to lubricate human interactions • Follows and fulfils role expectations by striving to work effectively within current systems • Supports structures and systems that reinforce the bottom line, maximise efficiency, and guarantee short-term profits	• Builds on a man's need for meaning • Is preoccupied with purposes, values, morals, and ethics • Transcends daily affairs • Is orientated toward long-term goals without compromising human values and principles • Focuses more on missions and strategies • Releases human potential—identifying and developing new talent • Designs and redesigns jobs to make them meaningful and challenging • Aligns internal structures and systems to reinforce overall objectives.

Table 30. Comparison of Transactional and Transformational Leadership.

(Covey, 1992)

Clearly, to achieve transformation at scale, transformational leadership is needed.

Thirdly, we need to commit to change. This is the hardest bit. Every transformational project—some would argue every relationship too!—goes through phases where there is disillusionment and despondency. It takes tenacity and bravery to continue pursuing a vision—especially when all around are taking the path of least resistance. A true leader is someone who has strong enough vision and conviction to ride the waves of emotion and energy.

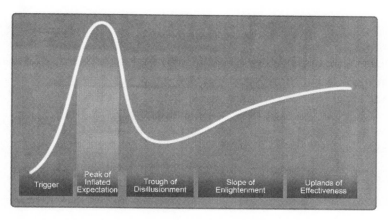

Figure 54. Waves of emotion and energy that leaders need to ride.

Captain James Cook—the last of the great explorers—is a hero of mine. His ambition was to go not only further than any other man had been before, but "as far as I think it possible for man to go". Cook charted many areas and recorded several islands and coastlines on European maps for the first time. "His achievements can be attributed to a combination of seamanship, superior surveying and cartographic skills, courage in exploring dangerous locations to confirm the facts (for example dipping into the Antarctic circle repeatedly and exploring around the Great Barrier Reef), an ability to lead men in adverse conditions, and boldness both with regard to the extent of his explorations, and his willingness to exceed the instructions given to him by the Admiralty" (Collingridge, 2003).

This last point is crucial. Cook went beyond the instructions that were given to him, and he gave us a brilliant insight into a required attitude for leadership and success—"Do just once what others say you can't do and you will never pay attention to their limitations again."

Cook's attitude ensured that his foremost limitations were the speed and direction of the wind. With the tools and resources available to us today, our limitations are defined only by where we choose to direct our thoughts.

What Next?

To implement the methodology set out in *Schooling at the Speed of Thought* in a practical way in your institution, contact the author at mikestevelloyd@msn.com to find out about workshops, seminars and courses that are available.

For web-links, updates and additional material go to
http://www.facebook.com/SchoolingAtTheSpeedOfThought

Follow Schooling at the Speed of Thought on Twitter -
http://twitter.com/#!/schspeedthought

BIBLIOGRAPHY

Abadzi, H. (2003). *The Economics of Classroom Time: How to Measure Classroom Time on Task?* World Bank.

Acana, S. (2006). Reporting Results of National Assessment: Uganda Experience. *32nd Annual Conference of the International Association for Educational Assessment.* Singapore.

Alistair Smith, N. C. (1999). *The ALPS approach, Accelerated Learning in Primary Schools.* Network Educational Press Ltd.

Associated Press. (2009, Sept 27). *MSNBC.* Retrieved from Obama Would Curtail Summer Vacation: http://www.msnbc.msn.com/id/33044676/

ATC21s.Org. (2010). *Assessment & Teaching of 21st Century Skillls.* Retrieved from Assessment & Teaching of 21st Century Skillls: http://www.ATC21s.Org

Barber, M. &. (2007). *How the world's best-performing school systems come out on top.* McKinsey and Company.

Bass and Avolio. (1994).

Basu, R. (2009). *Implement Six Sigma and Lean.* Oxford: Elsevier.

BBC. (2009, April 14). *Bad behaviour 'wastes five weeks'.* Retrieved from Education News: http://news.bbc.co.uk/1/hi/education/7998728.stm

BBC. (n.d.). *The River Journey.* Retrieved from BBC News: http://www.bbc.co.uk/devon/content/articles/2008/06/16/river_journey_otterton_video_feature.shtml

Beare, H. (2001). *Creating the Future School.* Routledge.

Beare, H. (2007, Summer). How to Pay Teachers in the 21st Century. *Principal Matters.*

BECTA. (2005). *ICT and whole-school improvement.* BECTA.

BECTA. (2006). *Functional Requirements for Information Management Systems* . BECTA.

BECTA. (2009). *Enabling Next Generation Learning, Enhancing Learning Through Technology* . BECTA.

BECTA. (n.d.). *ICT Curriculum Entitlement Documents.* Retrieved from http://www.teachernet.gov.uk/teachingandlearning/subjects/ict/bectadocs/

Bolden, R., Gosling, J., Marturano, A. and Dennison, P. (2003, June). *A Review of Leadership Theory and Competency Frameworks.* Retrieved from Exeter University Leadership Studies: http://www.leadership-studies.com/documents/mgmt_standards.pdf

Boyle, H. (2006). *Opening Minds: A competency-based curriculum for the twenty first century.* National Teacher Research Panel.

Branson, R. (n.d.). *Why Schools Can't Improve.* Retrieved from http://www.cpt.fsu.edu/pdf/upperlimithypothesis.pdf

Bray, M. (2008). *Double-shift schooling; design and operation for cost-effectiveness.* UNESCO International Institutie for Educational Planning.

Buckley, D. (n.d.). *Personalisation by Pieces.* Cambridge Education Associates.

Carr, H. &. (1996). *How to Use Standards in the Classroom.* ASCD.

Clayton M. Christensen and Michael B. Horn. (2008, August). *Disrupting Class: Student-Centric Education Is the Future.* McGraw Hill.

Collingridge, V. (2003). *Captain Cook: The Life, Death and Legacy of History's Greatest Explorer.* Ebury Press.

Collins, J. (2001). *Good to Great.* Random House .

Covey, S. (1992).

Cross, C. (2005). *It's Time to Rethink the Hours America Spends Educating.* Retrieved from Edutopia—what works in public education: http://www.edutopia.org/school-daily-yearly-schedule

Damian Bebell & Rachel Kay. (2010). *One to One Computing .* The Journal of Technology, Learning, and Assessment.

David Cameron MP. (2010). *David Cameron: Good government costs less with the Conservatives.* Retrieved from The Conservatives: http://www.conservatives.com/News/Speeches/2010/03/David_Cameron_Good_government_costs_less_with_the_Conservatives.aspx

DeLorenzo, Battino, Schreiber, & Carrio. (2009). *Delivering on the Promise.* Solution Tree.

Demos. (2009). *A Stitch in Time: Tackling educational disengagement.* London: Demos.

Department for Children Schools and Families. (2009, April). *FMSiS Purpose, Key Benefits, and Summary of the Standard.* Retrieved from http://www.fmsis.info

Designshare.com. (n.d.). *Projects.* Retrieved from Designshare.com: http://www.designshare.com/index.php/case-studies

Earl, L. (2006). *Leading Schools In A Data Rich World.* Corwin Press.

Fisher, D. K. (2005). *Linking Pedagogy and Space.* Rubida Research Pty Ltd.

FON. (n.d.). Retrieved from Foghlaim Ón Nuatheicneolaíocht or Learning through New Technologies: http://foghlaim.edublogs.org/

Fullan, M. (2004). *Learning to Lead Change.* Changeforces.

Fullan, M. (2007). *The New Meaning of Educational Change.* Routlidge.

Futurelab. (2005, November). *Personalisation and Digital Technologies.* Retrieved from www.futurelab.org.uk/resources/documents/opening_education/Personal isation_report.pdf

Futurelab. (2006, November). *Timetable for change.* Retrieved from Futurelab: http://www.futurelab.org.uk/resources/publications-reports-articles/web-articles/Web-Article466

Gladwell, M. (2009). *Outliers: The Story of Success.* Penguin.

Green, H. (2006). *Personalisation and Digital Technologies.* Bristol: FutureLab.

Haigh, G. (n.d.). *Innovation takes a new line with learning plazas.* Retrieved from NCSL: http://future.ncsl.org.uk/PrintNews.aspx?ID=190

Hanushek, J. W. (2008, Spring). *Education and Economic Growth.* Retrieved from EducationNext: http://educationnext.org/education-and-economic-growth/

Heppell, S. (2004). *Building Learning Futures.* Ultralab.

Heppell, S. (n.d.). *Professional Doctorate for All Teachers.* Retrieved from Heppell.net: http://www.heppell.net/doctoral/

Hinds, D. (2010). *Plenty of space to play with.* Retrieved from The Guardian: http://www.guardian.co.uk/bsf/space-play

House of Commons Education and Skills Committee. (2006-07). *Sustainable schools: Are We Building Schools for the Future.* London: The Stationery Office Ltd.

Jed Emerson, Jay Wachowicz, Suzi Chun . (2001). *Social Return on Investment (SROI): Exploring Aspects of Value Creation.* Retrieved from Harvard Business School, Working Knowledge: http://hbswk.hbs.edu/archive/1957.html#graph

Joey Fitts and Bruno Aziza. (2008). *Drive Business Performance.* Wiley.

John Seely-Brown. (2004). Retrieved from http://www.johnseelybrown.com/

Johnson, G. (1988). Rethinking Incrementalism. *Strategic Management Journal Vol 9,* 75-91.

Kelley, P. (2008). *Making Minds.* Routlage.

Kotter, J. (1996). *Leading Change.* Harvard University Business School Press.

Leadbeater, C. (2005). *The Shape of Things to Come.* Retrieved from www.standards.dfes.gov.uk/sie/documents/shape.pdf

Lindstrom, M. (2005). *"Brand Child"* . Martin Lindstrom.

Lohr, S. (2009, August 19). *Study Finds That Online Education Beats the Classroom.* Retrieved from New York Times: http://bits.blogs.nytimes.com/2009/08/19/study-finds-that-online-education-beats-the-classroom/

Marano, H. E. (2006, May). Retrieved from Psychology Today: http://www.psychologytoday.com/articles/200604/education-class-dismissed

McKinsey & Company. (2005). *Building Effective Public-Private Partnerships.* McKinsey & Company.

McKinsey & Company. (2009). *The Economic Impact of the Achievement Gap in America's Schools.* McKinsey & Company.

Murnane, L. a. (2004). *The New Division of Labor: How Computers Are Creating the Next Job Market* . Princeton University Press.

Nair & Feilding. (2005). *The Language of School Design.*

National College for School Leadership. (2004). *Shaping up to the Future.* National College for School Leadership.

National College for School Leadership. (2006). *Everyone A Leader.* National College for School Leadership.

National Conference on State Legislatures. (2010). Retrieved from National Conference on State Legislatures: http://www.ncsl.org/IssuesResearch/HumanServices/NewResearchEarlyEducationasEconomicInvestme/tabid/16436/Default.aspx

New Tech High School. (n.d.). *New Tech High School.* Retrieved from New Tech High School: http://www.newtechhigh.org

OECD. (2001). *Schooling for Tomorrow report "What Schools for the Future?".* OECD.

OECD. (2003, October). *OECD Report Highlights Problems of Student Disaffection in Schools.* Retrieved from OECD: http://www.oecd.org/document/13/0,2340,en_2649_201185_16407181_1_1_1_1,00.html

OECD. (2005). *Are Students Ready for a Technology-Rich World?* OECD.

OECD. (2005). *School Factors Related To Quality And Equity.* OECD.

OECD. (2006). *Education in the Information Age: Scenarios, Equity and Equality*. OECD.

OECD. (2006). *Schooling for Tomorrow, Personalising Education*. OECD.

OECD. (2006). *Think Scenarios. Rethinking Education*. OECD.

OECD. (2008). *Education at a Glance*. OECD.

OECD. (2008). *Improving School Leadership*. OECD.

OECD. (2009, 06 16). *Teacher effectiveness hampered by lack of incentives and bad behaviour in classrooms*. Retrieved from http://www.oecd.org/document/35/0,3343,en_2649_33723_43018915_1_1_1_1,00.html

OECD UNESCO. (2002). *Financing Education—Investment and Returns*. OECD UNESCO.

Ontario Ministry of Education. (n.d.). *Involving Parents in the School: Tips for School Councils*. Retrieved from http://www.edu.gov.on.ca/eng/parents/involvement/

Orazio Attanasio, e. a. (2005). *How effective are conditional cash transfers? Evidence from Columbia*. London: Institute for Fiscal Studies.

Prakash Nair, R. F. (2009). *The Language of School Design*. Designshare.com.

Qualifications and Curriculum Authority. (n.d.). *National Curriculum*. Retrieved from English National Curriculum: http://curriculum.qcda.gov.uk/key-stages-1-and-2/Values-aims-and-purposes/index.aspx

QCDA. (2005, Feb 14). Retrieved from NAA. Report into the cost of the examination system: http://www.qcda.gov.uk/9955.aspx

Reuters India. (2009). *PLUGGEDIN—Homework help site flourishes in hard times*. Retrieved from Reuters India, Technology: http://in.reuters.com/article/technologyNews/idINIndia-39769920090520

RSA. (2008). *Opening Minds: Impact update*. London: RSA.

Schleicher, P. A. (2009). Benchmarking the Performance of Education Internationally. *Learning and Technology World Forum 2009*. London: OECD Directorate for Education.

Senge, P. (2000). *Schools that Learn*. New York: Doubleday.

Simon Willis (Editor). (2005). *Connected Cities*. Cisco.

Sir Ken Robinson. (2006, June 27). *TEDBlog*. Retrieved from TED: http://blog.ted.com/2006/06/sir_ken_robinso.php

Souza, E. (2009, Sept). *E-assesment in the Lumiar Project in Brazil.* Retrieved from New Millennium Learner: http://www.nml-conference.be/wp-content/uploads/2009/09/Estela-souza.pdf

Stanford, N. (1996). *Organisation Design.* Economist.

Stephen Heppell. (2007). *Learnometer.* Retrieved from Learnometer: http://www.learnometer.net/heppell/doctoral/default.html

Stephen Heppell. (n.d.). *Stephen Heppell's Weblog.* Retrieved from heppell.net: http://www.heppell.net/weblog/stephen/

Steven Hastings. (2003, September 12). *Times Education Supplement.*

Teaching in the UK. (n.d.). *Teaching in the UK.* Retrieved from to http://www.teachingintheuk.com/go/uk-teaching-info/school-system/

The Department for Children Schools and Families. (2010). *Using Our Resources Well.* The Department for Children Schools and Families.

The Economist. (2008, June 6th). Our Friends in the North. *The Economist.*

The Economist. (2009, June 4th). *Still A Lot To Learn.* Retrieved from The Economist: http://www.economist.com/world/americas/displaystory.cfm?story_id= E1_TPSRNVSD

The Economist. (2010, Feb). *Classes apart.* Retrieved from The Economist: http://www5.economist.com/research/articlesBySubject/displaystory.cf m?subjectid=526356&story_id=15469407

The World Economic Forum. (n.d.). *Jordan Education Initiative (JEI).* Retrieved from The World Economic Forum: http://www.weforum.org/en/initiatives/gei/Jordan%20Education%20Init iative/index.htm

Treadwell, M. (2008). *School 2.0.* Hawker Brownlow.

Tyack and Cuban. (1995). *Tinkering Towards Utopia.* Harvard University Press.

U.S. Department of Education, National Center for Education Statistics. (2009, January). *1.5 Million Homeschooled Students in the United States in 2007.* Retrieved from http://nces.ed.gov/pubs2009/2009030.pdf

UK Government. (n.d.). *Which Way Now.* Retrieved from Connexions-direct: http://www.connexions-direct.com/whichwaynow/

UNESCO. (2003). *Information tools for the preparation and monitoring of education plans.* Paris: UNESCO.

UNESCO. (2005). *Education Trends in Perspective.* UNESCO.

UNESCO. (2005). *EFA Global Monitoring Report.* UNESCO.

UNESCO. (2006). *Education for All Global Monitoring Report.* Retrieved from www.unesco.org/education/GMR2006/full/chapt2_eng.pdf

UNESCO. (2006). *Money Counts: Projecting Expenditures in Latin America and the Caribbean to the Year 2015.* UNESCO.

UNESCO. (2008). *Education for All by 2015—Will We Make It?* UNESCO.

UNESCO. (2008). *Education for All by 2015, Will we make it?* UNESCO.

UNESCO. (2008). *ICT Competency Standards for Teachers.* Retrieved from http://portal.unesco.org/ci/en/ev.php-URL_ID=25740&URL_DO=DO_TOPIC&URL_SECTION=201.html

UNESCO. (n.d.). *Education For All Goals.* Retrieved from Education For All Goals Global Monitoring Report: http://portal.unesco.org/education/en/ev.php-URL_ID=43811&URL_DO=DO_TOPIC&URL_SECTION=201.html

UNESCO Institute for Statistics. (2007). Global education spending concentrated in a handful of countries. *Global Education Digest 2007.*

UNESCO Institute of Statistics. (2002). *Financing Education—Investments and Returns.* UNESCO.

UNESCO Institute of Statistics. (n.d.). *2008 Education Data.* Retrieved from UNESCO Institute of Statistics 2008 education data: http://www.uis.unesco.org/ev.php?ID=7825_201&ID2=DO_TOPIC

UNESCO-UIS/OECD. (2002). *Financing Education—Investments and Returns.* UNESCO-UIS/OECD.

Veja. (2008, February 13). *Reward for merit.* Retrieved from Braudel: http://www.braudel.org.br/en/noticias/midia/pdf/veja_20080213.pdf

W. Chan Kim, Renée Mauborgne. (n.d.). *Blue Ocean Strategy.* Retrieved from Blue Ocean Strategy: http://www.blueoceanstrategy.com/

Warner, D. (2006). *Schooling For The Knoweldge Era.* ACER Press.

Wikipedia. (2009). Retrieved from Wikipedia: http://en.wikipedia.org

World Bank. (n.d.). Retrieved from Learning Outcomes: http://web.worldbank.org/WBSITE/EXTERNAL/TOPICS/EXTEDUCATION/0,,contentMDK:21911176~menuPK:5495844~pagePK:148956~piPK:216618~theSitePK:282386,00.html

World Bank . (2009). *Decentralized Decision Making in Schools, The Theory and Evidence on School-Based Management.* The International Bank for Reconstruction and Development / The World Bank.

Lightning Source UK Ltd.
Milton Keynes UK

177974UK00003B/2/P